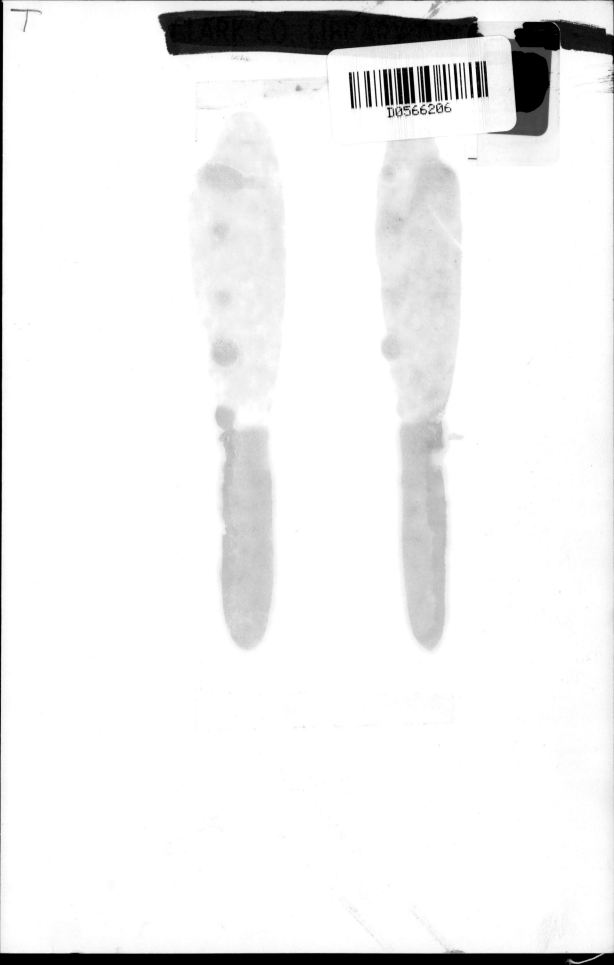

A. Lincoln:
The
Crucible
of
Congress

A. Lincoln: The Crucible of Congress

by
Paul Findley

CROWN PUBLISHERS, INC., NEW YORK

Printed in the United States of America

Published simultaneously in Canada by General Publishing Company Limited

Library of Congress Cataloging in Publication Data

Findley, Paul, 1921–
    A. Lincoln, the crucible of Congress.

    Bibliography: p.
    Includes index.
    1. Lincoln, Abraham, Pres. U.S., 1809–1865—Political
career before 1861. 2. United States—Politics and
government—1845–1861. 3. Presidents—United States—
Biography. 4. Legislators—United States—Biography.
5. United States. Congress. House—Biography.
I. Title
E457.4.F5 1979   973.7'092'4 [B]   79-4256
ISBN 0-517-53463-3

Foreword
by Congressman Paul Simon

Abraham Lincoln's life and views have received as much attention from historians as almost anyone, but until now his formative years on the national scene have remained inadequately covered.

Significantly, the person who enriches the Lincoln literature in this area is someone who serves Sangamon County, Illinois, in the U.S. House of Representatives more than a century after that area's most famous citizen filled the same office.

There are differences and similarities between the two Congressmen.

Lincoln was six feet four inches tall, Paul Findley is five feet nine inches in height.

Lincoln was extremely thin, Findley less so.

Lincoln had dark hair and grew a beard. Findley has gray white hair and is clean-shaven.

Lincoln experienced some awkwardness in social situations while Findley does not.

Lincoln from the start opposed our war with Mexico; Findley more slowly (like this writer) reached the point of serious questioning of the war in Vietnam.

But there are similarities also.

Both came from small-town America.

There is a striking combination of pragmatism and compassion in the records of both.

Lincoln and Findley share an interest in history.

Lincoln and Findley have a simple, direct speaking style devoid of pretension.

And perhaps as significant as anything, both came from limited backgrounds that would not suggest a sensitivity to the larger issues facing humanity, yet both somehow broke from the provincial mold to view things from a broader perspective.

The Lincoln congressional term did not have any great significance for what he contributed in that period to the nation. But it had great significance for what it contributed to Lincoln.

For those who seek drama, intrigue, and sex, the Findley book will be a disappointment, though probably few who select this book will be anticipating that.

But those who seek a greater understanding of the most revered of this nation's Presidents will find it here.

A somewhat rough-hewn young lawyer of Whig persuasion came to Washington after eight years in the Illinois General Assembly. In Illinois he had surprised himself by finding that he could hold his own among those who were the leaders of the Prairie State. It gave him a sense of self-confidence.

The same thing happened at the national level. Without the one term in Congress it is doubtful that Lincoln would have spoken up after the controversial, slavery-related Nebraska Bill passed in 1854, leading to his Senate candidacy in 1858, and ultimately to the Presidency.

That important one term in Congress is detailed in this volume by a man who understands the House of Representatives.

Acknowledgments

If this book enriches your appreciation of an important part of Abraham Lincoln's career, as I trust it will, the credit must go to many people.

More than most books, it is the product of a team effort. Several who made major contributions are Lincoln scholars. Others with lesser backgrounds in Lincoln and his times, certainly myself, gained new understanding of this remarkable man. It would be difficult to list everyone who helped bring the book to fruition, but some cannot escape identification.

First and foremost is Charles F. Cooney, without question a Lincoln scholar of the first order. He labored over the text with me for all the five years of its preparation; indeed, he was there when the book was an idea still germinating. He assisted mightily in the research, and more than once turned up the hidden or obscure bit of information that would play a central part in a chapter. Mr. Cooney is a former editor of *Civil War Times Illustrated* magazine and, as one might expect, an authority on the Civil War as well as Lincoln. He is also a master of black history, the Harlem Renaissance, and a seemingly nonending stream of diverse subjects that constantly embellish his conversation. The years ahead, I forecast, will find the literature of our nation's history increasingly interpreted by Charles Cooney. For now, I freely acknowledge that without his assistance it would have taken another five years to write this book.

I am also deeply grateful to several other Lincoln scholars for reading the manuscript and giving me their criticism. Dr. Roy P. Basler, editor of the *Collected Works of Abraham Lincoln*, gave the text a careful working over, as did Gabor S. Boritt, whose new book, *Lincoln and the Economics of the American Dream*, is a landmark in the Lincoln literature. It was Dr. Boritt's scholarly article in the *Journal* of the Illinois State Historical Society that started me on this book. In it, he challenged William H. Herndon's theory that Lincoln committed "political suicide" by opposing the Mexican War. Mark E. Neely, Jr., Director of the Louis A. Warren Lincoln Library and Museum in Fort Wayne, Indiana, also consented to critique the book, and so did James T. Hickey, Curator of the Abraham Lincoln Collection in the Illinois State Historical Library. Former Congressman Fred Schwengel, President of the U.S. Capitol Historical Society, and George Cashman, for many years the Curator of the Lincoln Tomb in Springfield, made valuable suggestions.

I am deeply indebted to an Illinois colleague and longtime friend, Congressman Paul Simon, who, like myself, had a career in country journalism before coming to Capitol Hill. Mr. Simon is himself a recognized Lincoln scholar as the author of the splendid study of Lincoln's career in the Illinois legislature, *Lincoln's Preparation for Greatness*. He accepted my manuscript as bedtime reading, examining in great detail a chapter or two a night over a period of two weeks. His recommendations on style, content, and organization led to a complete redrafting of the entire book (for which the reader can be grateful). His criticism was especially valuable, because it came from a person uniquely qualified to assess my interpretation of Lincoln's impact on Capitol Hill and vice versa. He also agreed to write the book's foreword. All this I acknowledge with gratitude, because I know from personal experience that endless time-consuming demands come to a Congressman.

The book has been enormously enriched because of the resources available at the Library of Congress. I am particularly indebted to Dr. Oliver Orr, John McDonough, Mrs. Carolyn Sung, Mrs. Marilyn Parr, and Ms. Mary Wolfskill, all of the Manuscript Division. In the Loan Division, Mrs. Kay Blair greatly facilitated interlibrary loan requests. Jerry Kearns and George Hobart of the Prints and Photographs Division were invaluable in locating illustrative material. The Stack and Reader Division furnished research facilities and the Photoduplication Service expeditiously processed my numerous requests for copies of photographs. The Congressional Research Service, especially Rhoda Newman, Vanessa A. Cieslak, and Anne Harley also assisted mightily.

Many others deserve recognition. Dr. George White, Architect of the Capitol, and Mrs. Florian Thayn cheerfully responded to my many requests for information on the Capitol Building. The staffs of the House and Senate libraries provided similar services. Clement Conger, Curator of the White House, supplied several items from the White House collection, as did the Department of State. James Goode, Curator of the Smithsonian Institution Building, lent his expertise on Washington's early buildings and architecture, which was of inestimable value in several chapters.

Others at the Smithsonian also helped locate information I had no reason to suppose still existed. And August Kiplinger made available to me his superb collection of lithographs and paintings of Washington as it appeared in Lincoln's day. The curator of the Kiplinger Collection, Mrs. Frances D. Turgeon, was especially helpful in making copies of the items I needed.

In Illinois, William K. Alderfer and James Hickey threw open the doors of the Illinois State Historical Library. Dr. Archie Motley of the Chicago Historical Society made it possible for me to examine the John J. Hardin Papers. Albert W. Banton, Superintendent of the Lincoln Home National Historical Site in Springfield, supplied both information and photographs. John A. Patterson, Superintendent of the Historic Sites Division of the Department of Conservation, supplied photographs of New Salem, and Milo Pearson, Jr., Pleasant Hill, Illinois, provided valuable references. Special notice should be taken of Charles C. Patton's *Glory to God and the Sucker Democracy*, a unique collection of materials bearing on early Illinois history. The author had these printed at his own expense, and they are an important contribution to scholarly research of the history of Illinois.

Two others who assisted in this project are Sarah Fuller of the Ohio Historical Society and Frank J. Williams, President of the Lincoln Group of Boston. Miss Fuller made available to me the papers of Joshua R. Giddings and Mr. Williams critiqued the section of the book dealing with Lincoln's travels to New England.

Sig Moglen, senior editor at Crown Publishers, has nurtured this project for some time with rare patience. Unforeseen circumstances, the intervention of official duties, and a campaign for reelection often made it impossible for me to meet the timetable he prescribed, but he accepted delays with good humor. He always got revenge, however, by mercilessly editing with his red pencil. (He and Congressman Simon have much in common.) In the process I have made a lasting friendship and hopefully improved my writing style.

Those most continuously confronted with the preparation of this book, of course, were my wife, Lucille, and members of my congressional staff. During the five years since its inception scarcely a day at the office or at home escaped the intrusion of Mr. Lincoln. It was always pending business, pending conversation—and for me it became a pending obsession.

To my staff it became known as "the thing." Each member of this patient, able, and helpful crew—joined heartily by Lucille—must have heaved history's deepest sigh of relief when the book, at long last, ceased to be pending.

While a project of many combined efforts, the text of course is mine, and I assume responsibility for everything here, for good or ill. And although those who assisted me may not agree with every word or thought written, I hope all have found—as I have—something in the experience of preparing a book on this extraordinary man to inspire them and renew their spirit for the challenges ahead.

Introduction

Abraham Lincoln served a single two-year term in the United States House of Representatives.

The experience was momentous. Before going to Congress he was little known beyond central Illinois. He had never campaigned against slavery. He had not spoken out against the Mexican War. He usually skirted controversial issues.

In Congress he quickly achieved national prominence—as a war critic, as an opponent of the extension of slavery, and as a leader of the Whig party. The time he spent on Capitol Hill helped clarify his thinking about the burning political issues of the day and prepared him for the Presidency. Surprisingly, these two years have been either neglected or wrongly interpreted by almost all his biographers.

Lincoln is the subject of more literature than any other personality in history except Jesus Christ. More than eight thousand major works have been written concerning his life. Only one of these is devoted to his service in Congress. And this lonely volume—like almost all other references in the last seventy years—perpetuates the myth that Lincoln was a failure in Congress. Under this erroneous but widely believed evaluation, Lincoln's stand against the Mexican War and an apparently excessively partisan record alienated his Illinois constituency and amounted to political ruin.

The near-unanimity with which Lincoln's biographers have embraced this myth is startling in view of the intensive and sound examination they have made of every other phase of his life. They accepted without careful examination the "political suicide" judgment pronounced by Lincoln's law partner, William H. Herndon.

They simply closed their eyes to the facts. By the end of his term Lincoln had become one of the two leading Whigs in the entire state of Illinois. His role as a national campaigner for the Whig presidential ticket had spread his reputation far beyond the borders of Illinois. His critical views on the Mexican War were echoed by virtually every major figure in his party, and the war had become the most unpopular one in America's history up to that time. His was the voice of moderation and practicality on the divisive issue of slavery. His congressional service was a prelude to his election once again to the Illinois General Assembly, his candidacy (twice) for the United States Senate, his nomination and broad support for the Republican vice-presidential nomination in 1856, and, of course, his two terms as President.

The purpose of this volume is to set the record straight and promote a better understanding of Lincoln the Congressman. For sixteen years I have been a Member of the House of Representatives, representing in large part the same area that Lincoln did, and I am constantly amazed at the number of my colleagues who are unaware that Lincoln served as a Congressman.

The public, of course, is even less informed. Each year millions of visitors are escorted through Statuary Hall in the Capitol, the room used as the House chamber when Lincoln served. They are all told that Congressman John Quincy Adams had a fatal stroke in that room, and tour guides always point to the metal disk marking the spot where he fell; but they fail to mention that from a few feet away Congressman Abraham Lincoln anxiously watched as his stricken colleague was carried from the room. The location of Congressman Lincoln's desk is identified by an unobtrusive bronze plate that reads "Abraham Lincoln, Representative from Illinois, 1846–1848," but it is rarely noted by visitors or pointed out to them by guides.

Lincoln's home, Springfield, Illinois, has been in my constituency for fourteen years. Every local resident considers himself an authority of sorts on the Civil War President, but even there Lincoln's congressional career is little known. Postmaster, surveyor, storekeeper, rail splitter, storyteller, lawyer, state legislator, candidate for the U.S. Senate, martyred President—in all these capacities Lincoln is well known. But Lincoln the Congressman? A gap exists that is both curious and unfortunate.

Lincoln's service in Congress has not yet become part of the Lincoln legend, but it deserves to be a major part. His experiences in the House of Representatives, leavened by the ebb and flow of national events, tinged every subsequent experience and action of his political life.

I have always considered myself a student of Lincoln, but until my election to Congress I was only dimly aware of his service in the House. I had always accepted without question the Herndon evaluation. My work and associations as representative of the "Lincoln District," however, caused me to dig deeper.

Although he actually served only one two-year term, Lincoln was intimately connected with the politics of the congressional district for two previous terms, and he did not take office until sixteen months after his election. All told, Lincoln's congressional experience, from his first fleeting thoughts of seeking the office until the expiration of his term, encompassed seven years, a substantial part of his adult life.

And it was in Congress that Lincoln first moved outside the parochial politics of the Illinois prairie. Since childhood Lincoln had followed national events, but not until his arrival in Washington did he play a role in them. On Capitol Hill he was a colleague of the movers and shakers of the era—Alexander H. Stephens, Horace Mann, Caleb Smith, Joshua R. Giddings, Daniel Webster, Horace Greeley, Robert Toombs, and John Quincy Adams. This was the first great step along the national road that took Lincoln to the Presidency, and eventually made it possible for him to chart a course for the future of the nation. The effect of his congressional term on Lincoln's personal development was profound.

Assuredly, I am not a historian. I am a country newspaperman turned Congressman. I have carried out this project with a reporter's determination to get the facts and report them straight. Perhaps my experience in Congress has helped. There, intangible forces are always at work that may escape the nonpolitician. Service in Congress provides an awareness of factors that influence legislators and sway votes. To be sure, the House of Representatives has changed a great deal in the past 125 years. The membership is twice as large, the chamber bigger, committee facilities and staff have expanded tremendously—and so has the legislative work load.

But the extent to which the 30th Congress resembles the Congresses in which I have served is striking. The basic legislative process has emerged with remarkably few changes. The main elements are still at work, differing only in personality and degree.

To me, however, this book has a deeper meaning. The character of Abraham Lincoln exerts a powerful and enduring force over millions of people. Simply by being an Illinoisan one is touched, however lightly, by the Lincoln mystique. In my own case, the force has been great. Since boyhood, Lincoln has been an important part of my life. One of my earliest and most prized possessions was Carl Sandburg's *Abraham Lincoln: The Prairie Years,* and in high school I began committing to memory some of Lincoln's best known speeches.

Soon after World War II service I became a part owner and manager of the Pike County *Republican,* a county seat weekly newspaper in Pittsfield, Illinois; the paper has since been renamed the *Pike Press.* One of the most appealing aspects of the move to Pittsfield was the Lincoln saga associated with both my newspaper and the community. As a circuit riding lawyer, Lincoln had visited Pittsfield, and some of the homes where he stayed or was entertained still stand. In the 1858 senatorial campaign, Lincoln delivered a major speech in Pittsfield, although it was not one of his famous debates with Stephen A. Douglas.

Earlier in 1855, riding the judicial circuit to Pittsfield, Lincoln made the acquaintance of John G. Nicolay, an immigrant youth who was associated with the Pike County *Free Press,* ancestor of the Pike County *Republican.* At first a printer's devil, Nicolay later became an editor, and finally editor-owner of the newspaper. In 1856 Nicolay moved to Springfield as an employee of Ozias M. Hatch of Griggsville, a Pike County political leader whom Nicolay successfully helped to elect as Illinois Secretary of State. In Springfield, Lincoln renewed his acquaintance with Nicolay, who became Lincoln's only paid staff employee in the presidential election of 1860, his private secretary during the White House years, and one of Lincoln's principal biographers in collaboration with John Hay.

A famous photograph of President Lincoln and his secretaries, John G. Nicolay and John Hay . . . *(Library of Congress)*

. . . became a painting with figures slightly altered and cabinet-room background added. *(Author's collection)*

When I arrived in Pittsfield in 1947, the editor of the Pike County *Republican* was a fascinating, colorful journalist and local historian named Jess M. Thompson. From him I heard the local folklore about Lincoln and his Pike County associations, local incidents that influenced national history. The associations between Lincoln and Nicolay and between Nicolay and the *Pike Press* created a natural interest in any news relating to Nicolay. Thus, in 1954, when Nicolay's only child, Helen, died, the news was thoroughly covered in the Pike County *Republican*. I learned that Miss Nicolay had left her personal property to her housekeeper, Fay Elizabeth Beij. Mrs. Beij died a few months later and her daughter, Mrs. Barbara Benoit, inherited the property.

I chronicle these events here because one piece of personal property that Mrs. Benoit inherited had a profound influence on my own life: a unique photograph-portrait of Lincoln and his two secretaries, Nicolay and Hay. It began as a simple black and white photograph taken in Washington by Alexander Gardner on November 9, 1863, a few days before the Gettysburg Address. Only six prints were known to have been made from the negative. One of them became the prized possession of John Nicolay, who commissioned a prominent artist to convert the photograph into a watercolor painting. The artist tinted the figures, altered the position of Nicolay's left leg, and replaced the plain background with a full-color reproduction of the room in the White House used for Cabinet meetings. For years the framed picture hung in the Washington residence of the Nicolays.

I had never seen the picture, but had heard of it from a distant relative of the Nicolay family who still lived in Pittsfield. When word arrived of Mrs. Beij's death, I made a mental note to look up her heir, Mrs. Benoit, at the earliest opportunity. I wanted that picture for my office wall.

The opportunity came in June 1956, when our family visited relatives in Boston. Two months earlier I had waged an unsuccessful effort to be the Republican nominee for State Senator. While in New England, I took an overnight trip to Center Harbor, New Hampshire, met the Benoits, visited the rustic summer studio-residence the Nicolays had used for years, and inquired about the picture.

It was still there, tucked away in the attic, but Mrs. Benoit hadn't thought of selling it. I explained the intimate connections of Lincoln, Nicolay, and Hay with Pittsfield and the Pike County *Republican*. Mrs. Benoit said she might consider selling. The question of the picture's worth came up, and since neither of us had any idea, I suggested we refer the question to Frederick Hill Meserve, a noted Lincoln collector then living in New York. Fortunately, he answered my phone call. We agreed on a price and early the next morning I put the picture into my borrowed car and headed for Boston.

The picture hung in my newspaper office, a great source of both pride and conversation. Subsequently, I advised John Hay Whitney, then U.S. Ambassador to Great Britain, of my purchase. I did so because correspondence I had seen earlier indicated that his family at one time had been interested in the picture. Mr. Whitney responded with thanks, and added: "If the Pike County *Republican* ever wants to part with this photo-painting I would certainly appreciate your letting me know." Little did I then realize the impact this sentence was to have on my future.

My interest in politics persisted, but my interest in legislative office was necessarily tempered by the realization that all positions in western Illinois were held by veterans who would likely remain in office for many more years. I concentrated, therefore, on the development of the newspaper enterprise and my own interest in it. I began my newspaper career heavily in debt for a one-third interest. In 1958 an opportunity to purchase full ownership arose. At the time I was still in debt for my part interest and a substantial house mortgage as well. I looked around for ways to make the opportunity manageable. I decided to part with my prized picture, provided I could get a good price.

I wrote John Hay Whitney in March 1958. For several months letters flowed among Mr. Whitney, myself, and Brown University. It became clear that if he purchased the picture, Mr. Whitney wanted to present it to an appropriate repository. Brown University, already replete with John Hay connections, seemed a logical place. In July the university acquired the picture from me.

The proceeds from the sale of the picture enabled me to purchase the shares of the remaining stockholders. At the time I had no idea what an advantage to my own political prospects this would prove to be; I soon learned.

On the eve of the election in 1958, veteran Republican Congressman Sid Simpson died suddenly after giving a speech in Pittsfield. I had introduced him to the audience. Later that day I made up my mind I would do my best to succeed him in Congress. I felt it would be the chance of a lifetime. Once elected, Congressmen tend to stay in office. If I didn't make it this time, the chance might never come again.

The Republican leadership persuaded Simpson's widow to run in his place. She won, but quickly announced she would serve only one term. I needed no further invitation. Beginning in December 1958, I devoted every possible moment in the next eighteen months to establishing an acquaintance throughout the district. I sought and filled hundreds of speaking engagements and called on hundreds of precinct chairmen. I used three "set" speeches, the most popular on Lincoln and his Pittsfield connections. I delivered the Lincoln speech more than a hundred times during the next eighteen months—once over district-wide television.

This schedule kept me from newspaper management much of the time. My staff carried the load for me. Had it not been for their diligence and the timely and profitable sale of the Lincoln picture I would not have had the freedom to neglect my business responsibilities and hit the demanding campaign trail. Had it not been for the popularity of my Lincoln speech, I might never have been elected. After I had won the general election in November, Arthur Higgins, editor of the Quincy *Herald-Whig,* told me in jest: "I hope you did not neglect to send a letter of appreciation to Abraham Lincoln." His quip was appropriate.

My debt to Lincoln, however, extends beyond the lift he gave to me in my campaign for Congress. In my first term my district included Menard County with its rich Lincoln lore in New Salem village, Petersburg, and Athens. Beginning with my second term, my district has always included Sangamon County with Lincoln's home, tomb, law office, the Old State Capitol, and a host of scholars who focus on the Lincoln tradition.

These associations have quickened and kept intense a kinship with Lincoln that was already substantial. Never a day passes with him totally out of sight or mind.

More than any other personality he has been my guide and inspiration. Lincoln once said he never had a political impulse that was not inspired by the Declaration of Independence. I never seem to have one that is not nurtured in some way by Lincoln.

His commitment to freedom has been a special inspiration to me. He contended that to keep our own freedom, we must give freedom to others. Ours can be assured only if we keep striving to extend it to more and more citizens. If we falter in this quest our own liberty is in jeopardy. Our greatest moments as a nation have been those occasions when we have worked the hardest to extend freedom. He put it succinctly: "In giving freedom to the slave, we assure freedom to ourselves."

This principle has guided me all through my congressional years. Ever since 1961, when I first took office, issues of human freedom—civil rights—have been before the Congress in one form or another. The searing controversies of these years have been desegregation of schools, voting rights, open housing, and public accommodations. I did my best to see that members of the party of Lincoln were on the affirmative side. Although they did not always respond, enough Republicans voted "yes" each time to provide the crucial margin of victory.

The vote on open housing was a particularly contentious one. To me the issue was clear: blacks would never have the chance to buy or rent homes where they wished unless the federal government put its force behind that right. But I knew that many of my Republican colleagues viewed open housing as an unwarranted invasion of property rights. To help turn the tide, I sent each of them a letter urging a yes vote in the name of Lincoln. Whether it changed votes or not, enough Republicans voted yes to pass the bill.

The new Republican leader of the House, Gerald R. Ford, held a different view. Positive on most civil rights issues, he nevertheless opposed this one. To Ford, a person should have the right to sell or rent his house to anyone he wished and to refuse to do so on the basis of race.

Two years later I stopped at his office to ask a favor, and before granting it Ford chided me for not always cooperating with him. To make his point he pulled from his desk drawer my letter appealing for Republican votes in support of open housing.

I saw in the open housing bill, as well as in many others, the same basic principle of human rights: equal justice. To me, in all issues in which the extension of a basic human right is at stake, all other interests must be subordinated.

When the constitutional amendment concerning equal rights for women came before the House, I voted yes without hesitation. Here again, Lincoln served as an inspiration. Eighty-four years before the 19th Amendment to the Constitution was ratified, in a statement he gave as a candidate for the Illinois General Assembly in 1836, he supported women's suffrage. I knew that women were not given equal opportunities, especially in employment practices, and I felt certain that the constitutional amendment would be useful in diminishing discrimination based on sex.

I am sure too that Lincoln would have supported my efforts to end employment practices that discriminate arbitrarily on the basis of age.

Lincoln had a profound influence on my actions and votes concerning our involvement in Vietnam. I became an early war protestor and took comfort in the fact that Congressman Lincoln had been a war critic too. In many of my speeches calling for an end to our Vietnam involvement, I cited Lincoln's position against the Mexican War.

The Vietnam experience led me to draft several measures aimed at restricting the war powers of the President. Here too Congressman Lincoln was a motivating force. In arguing for the War Powers Resolution (P.L. 93–148), which I helped to draft and maneuver to enactment over a presidential veto, I quoted often this statement by Congressman Lincoln:

> The provision of the Constitution giving the warmaking power to Congress was dictated, as I understand it, by the following reason: Kings had always been involving and impoverishing their peoples in wars, pretending generally, if not always, that the good of the people was the object. This our convention understood to be the most oppressive of all kingly oppressions and they resolved to so frame the Constitution that no one man should hold the power of bringing this oppression upon us. But [President Polk's] view destroys the whole matter, and places our President where kings have always stood.

It is noteworthy that the Congress in which Lincoln served was dominated by exactly the same fundamental issues—civil rights and presidential war—as the Congresses in which I served more than a century later. Then, as now, Congress searched for the path to fulfillment of the idealism expressed in the Declaration of Independence.

A century after Lincoln, much remains to be done. Injustice still exists. But over the years progress has been substantial, and much of the progress must be credited to Abraham Lincoln and the ever-increasing influence of his life's work. I hope this book will help provide an understanding of the profound impact the congressional years had on his life and character. They were a turning point.

With the greatest of our national heroes, he set worthy goals for our society and then helped take heroic strides toward them. His example has inspired many others in each generation, and the strength of his example becomes greater with the passage of time.

Time and again, history has shown that men and women nurtured in the Lincoln heritage can mold reality from the dreams of our founding fathers.

1

"He made a very considerable impression . . ."

He WAS TALL, UNGAINLY, and—some said—a bit ugly. The inhabitants of New Salem could scarcely have seen in him a prospective United States Congressman. It was the spring of 1831. The sun warmed the flowing water of the Sangamon River. The woods and prairie grass of the countryside offered hope, both to the New Salem villagers and to the awkward stranger.

Denton Offut, a neighbor of the Lincoln family in Macon County, had hired Abraham Lincoln, John Johnston, and Lincoln's stepbrother, John Hanks, to help him take a flatboat from Illinois to New Orleans. Yearning for a career in commerce, Offut had his crew load at Sangamotown, near Springfield, a cargo of live hogs, barrel pork, and corn. In April the four shoved off. They hadn't gone far—to New Salem—when their flatboat became stuck on the Rutledge Mill dam and began to ship water. A small crowd of villagers watched their predicament with a mixture of amusement and concern, and had their first glimpse of their future Congressman.

Clumsy looking as he may have been, Lincoln had the ingenuity that got the boat off the dam. At his suggestion the trio moved part of their cargo to another boat and shoved the remaining barrels aft. With a borrowed auger, Lincoln bored a hole in the part of the boat that stuck out over the dam. The water ran out, the boat rose slightly in the water and slipped over the dam. The hole plugged, the crew was ready to resume its journey to New Orleans.

Yet they remained awhile. Offut sized up the community as a prospective site for a store while Lincoln joined a crowd of men near the mill. He listened as the villagers talked. It seems the flatboat incident worried the men more than they had first let on. Their hopes for the future of New Salem were tied to the navigability of the river.

Skeptics wondered—if a flatboat couldn't pass through, what could? Others proclaimed that they had only to wait. Prosperity was just a matter of time. Washington would provide the answer. Joseph Duncan of Jacksonville, the lone Congressman from Illinois in Washington, exercised his lungs regularly on Capitol Hill urging the government to use the proceeds from the sale of public lands to finance internal improvements. When that happened, the optimists said, the Sangamon River would be dredged, and New Salem would develop into an important transportation center.

Talk turned to another topic. Was the new Bank of the United States a menace or a blessing? Was President Andy Jackson right in demanding hard

Lincoln had the ingenuity that got the boat off the dam. *(Library of Congress)*

money? What relationship did the states have to the federal government? Could states nullify a federal law they didn't like?

Capitol Hill, the center of the political storms, was eight hundred miles due east, so far away in that horseback era as to be almost in another country. In New Salem hardy pioneers fought for economic survival, but political contests were intriguing—especially for young Lincoln.

For the moment, a flatboat held first allegiance. During the long journey, Offut made up his mind. New Salem seemed a promising place, and he decided to open a store there. He would need a clerk. His thoughts turned to Lincoln. He had been impressed by his initiative and resourcefulness. Would Lincoln like the job? The young man, already fond of New Salem, readily agreed.

Lincoln's return to New Salem from the flatboat episode was the first time he settled down away from his parents. He took a room at John Camron's house. While waiting for Offut to arrive and open his store, Lincoln cast his first vote in an election on August 1. And the same day he served in his first political office. Bowling Green, clerk for the election, needed help in recording the votes. When he learned that Lincoln knew how to read and write, he made him assistant clerk. As such, Lincoln recorded votes as they were voiced by the voter. The secret ballot didn't exist. Each man announced his choices for the various offices and the clerk or assistant clerk marked them down. Fortunately for frontier democracy, literacy tests weren't administered.

Lincoln also entertained the voters with the droll humor that became his trademark. In an account published in 1865, Rowan Herndon recalled the 1831 elections:

> In the afternoon, as things were dragging a little, Lincoln, the new man, began to spin out a stock of yarns. One that amused me more than any other he called the lizard story. "The meeting house," he said, "was in the woods and quite a distance from any other house. It was only used once a month. The preacher—an old line Baptist—was dressed in coarse linen pantaloons, and shirt of the same material. The pants manufactured after the old fashion, with baggy legs and a flap in front, were made to attach to his frame without the aid of suspenders. A single button held his shirt in position, and that was at the collar. He rose up in the pulpit and with a loud voice announced his text thus: 'I am the Christ, whom I shall represent today.' About this time a blue lizard ran up underneath his roomy pantaloons. The old preacher, not wishing to interrupt the steady flow of his sermon, slapped away on his legs, expecting to arrest the intruder; but his efforts were unavailing, and the little fellow kept on ascending higher and higher. Continuing the sermon, the preacher slyly loosened the central button which graced the waist line of his pantaloons and with a kick, off came that easy fitting garment. But meanwhile Mr. Lizard had passed the equatorial line of waist band and was calmly exploring that part of the preacher's anatomy which lay underneath the back of his shirt. Things were now growing interesting, but the sermon was still grinding on. The next movement on the preacher's part was for the collar button, and with one sweep of his arm off came the tow linen shirt. The congregation sat for an instant as if dazed; at length one old lady in the rear of the room rose up and glancing at the excited object in the pulpit shouted at the top of her voice: 'If you represent Christ then I'm done with the Bible.'"

In that first election Lincoln voted for candidates for local and state offices, and for a losing candidate for Illinois's single congressional seat. The candidates for the congressional office were the incumbent, Joseph Duncan of Jacksonville, and four others, Alexander Pope Field, Sidney Breese, James Turney, and Lincoln's choice, Edward Coles. Duncan was reelected.

Why Lincoln chose Coles is not recorded. The reelected Congressman had much in common with Lincoln. Born on February 22, 1794, in Paris, Kentucky, Duncan had had little formal schooling but later expressed considerable interest in the cause of public education. He served in the Army during the War of 1812, and moved to Illinois in 1818—the same year it became a state. He purchased land, became a farmer, and began to play an increasingly active role in state politics. First elected to the State Senate in 1824, he worked diligently and successfully for the establishment of a free public-school system in Illinois.

In 1826 Duncan won election to the U.S. House of Representatives, and he continued to serve there until 1834. He ardently supported the sale of public lands in Illinois and other Northwest regions, and the distribution of the proceeds of such sales among the states for the development of internal improvements. Initially a "whole hog" Jackson supporter, he clashed with the administration on several issues—including internal improvements—and returned to state politics. He served as Governor of Illinois from 1834 to 1838, and Lincoln would come to know him well, for these were years in which Lincoln would serve as a State Representative and would become an acknowledged Whig leader. But in 1831, to the young Lincoln, Duncan appeared merely one of four candidates he did not favor.

A month after the election, Offut opened his store in New Salem. An affable, voluble, and outgoing man, he took pride in his clerk and often bragged about Lincoln's physical prowess. This annoyed the Clary's Grove boys, and particularly their leader, Jack Armstrong, who challenged Lincoln to a wrestling match. In a frontier community, refusing a challenge like Armstrong's was the same as admitting cowardice. Lincoln, of course, knew this, and agreed to the match. The whole village turned out to see the local champion and the untested newcomer. As Armstrong began to get the worst of the fight, his gang moved in to help him. Lincoln forestalled the impending disaster. He said he would fight them all, but one at a time. No one accepted. Armstrong and Lincoln declared their match a draw and became fast friends.

The wrestling match with Armstrong gained Lincoln immediate acceptance by the rough-and-tumble Clary's Grove boys. Next he tried to break through the upper crust of New Salem's rudimentary social elite. He joined the New Salem debating society, and to the surprise of its members, who had, according to Rowan Herndon, "anticipated the relation of some humorous story," at his first appearance there, he spoke ably and persuasively: "He pursued the question with reason and argument so pithy and forcible that all were amazed."

He did not want just to impress the local gentry with his speaking ability, however. He was aware of what his education lacked, and with Mentor Graham, Jack Kelso, and a few others, he pursued studies of grammar, mathematics, and other fields. The newcomer quickly and simultaneously became popular and better educated.

Lincoln's political education also advanced while he was in New Salem. Offut's store became the local forum. Around the potbellied stove men of the community gathered to discuss the political issues of the day: the problems of a national bank, the always troublesome tariff question, internal improvements—an issue vital to the New Salem area—land policy, and the latest administration appointments. Here he gauged the political sentiment of his new neighbors.

Lincoln's arrival in New Salem started him on a political career that was destined to outlast by far his mercantile venture. Little more than a year passed between Lincoln's arrival and his first candidacy for public office, the state legislature. From then on, he was always in the public eye—running for office, serving in office, or campaigning for someone else.

On March 9, 1832, Lincoln the candidate was born. He decided to run for the state legislature. In a circular passed around the county, Lincoln addressed the issues of internal improvements, public education, and usury laws. He concluded the circular with this statement:

> Every man is said to have his peculiar ambition. Whether it be true or not, I can say, for one, that I have no other so great as that of being truly esteemed by my fellow men, by rendering myself worthy of their esteem. How far I shall succeed in gratifying this ambition is yet to be developed. I am young, and unknown to many of you. I was born, and have ever remained in the most humble walks of life. I have no wealthy or popular relations or friends to recommend me. My case is thrown exclusively upon the independent voters of the county; and, if elected, they will have conferred a favor upon me for which I shall be unremitting in my labors to compensate. But, if the good people in their wisdom shall see fit to keep me in the background, I have been too familiar with disappointments to be very much chagrined.

Unfortunately for Lincoln's candidacy, the Black Hawk War cut short his campaigning. On April 6, 1832, in violation of the provisions of a treaty that was less than a year old, the Indian chief Black Hawk and approximately five hundred warriors crossed over onto the Illinois side of the Mississippi River. Black Hawk hoped by virtue of alliances with other tribes to regain lands in Illinois. U.S. Army authorities warned him on several occasions to turn back and stay in Missouri. When he refused, Governor John Reynolds of Illinois called for volunteers, and all over the state men eagerly signed up to combat the Indians.

Lincoln was one of them. On April 21, 1832, he enrolled in the state militia. His company consisted mainly of members of the Clary's Grove group and his popularity with them caused him to be the elected captain. Doubtless during the Black Hawk War he became better acquainted with Congressman Duncan, who served as Brigadier General of the volunteer forces. At any rate, when his term of service ended Lincoln reenlisted and served until July 16, 1832. He never engaged in military action against the Indians, but then neither did most of the others. Lincoln later recalled this to political advantage.

Lincoln returned to New Salem from the war with only two weeks left to campaign. In those two weeks he worked hard, and Stephen T. Logan, who later took Lincoln into his law practice, left this impression of Lincoln's stump manner:

> He was a very tall and gawky and rough looking fellow then. His pantaloons didn't meet his shoes by six inches. But after he began speaking I became very much interested in him. He made a very sensible speech. . . .

New Salem Village—*he had received 277 of the 300 votes cast. (Illinois Department of Conservation)*

> He had then the same individuality that he kept all through his life. . . .
> We very soon learned that he was immensely popular. . . . In the election of
> 1832 he made a very considerable impression upon me as well as upon other
> people.

Two weeks simply were not enough. When the election returns came in
Lincoln received 657 votes. He ranked eighth in a field of thirteen candidates
for the four seats to which Sangamon County was entitled. One of the four men
elected was a well-known Methodist preacher named Peter Cartwright, who
later opposed Lincoln in his race for Congress. Although he lost, Lincoln had
reason for satisfaction. He had received 277 of the 300 votes cast in his home
precinct. He knew that with more exposure he would win a seat. Later, he
recalled that the 1832 election was the only one he lost on a direct vote of the
people.

In the meantime, Denton Offut had left New Salem. His store had not
prospered and debts had accumulated, causing Offut to run away to escape his
creditors. Lincoln then went into partnership with William F. Berry, but their
merchandising venture also failed miserably. In April 1833, saddled with debt,
Lincoln disposed of his interest in the store.

For a while his occupations varied. He received the appointment as
Postmaster of New Salem from a Democratic administration. He later explained,
"The office [was] too insignificant, to make [my] politics an objection." He
became the assistant surveyor of Sangamon County and worked odd jobs. Both
the postmastership and the position as assistant surveyor put him in a position to
expand his acquaintance among the electorate of Sangamon County.

Lincoln-Berry store—*saddled with debt, Lincoln disposed of his interest. (Illinois Department of Conservation)*

In the spring of 1834 Lincoln ran again for the state legislature. Though an avowed Clay Whig, he received a great deal of support from Democrats. In fact, a group of them approached him early in the campaign. They said they were willing to drop two of their own candidates and support Lincoln, hoping this would defeat John T. Stuart, the acknowledged Whig leader of Sangamon County. Lincoln reported the offer to Stuart. Justifiably confident of his own strength, Stuart advised Lincoln to accept it. Lincoln did so, with the result that both he and Stuart were elected. Stuart later referred to the incident and observed that "Lincoln acted fairly and honestly about it." The returns showed Lincoln had captured 1,376 votes of the 8,569 that were cast. Of the thirteen candidates in the race, Lincoln came in second. So, at the age of twenty-five, Lincoln left for the state capital at Vandalia in his first elective capacity.

As a capital, Vandalia left much to be desired. The population was about six hundred. The buildings—mostly log cabins—numbered perhaps one hundred. A rundown two-story brick building built in 1824 served as the State House. The Senate occupied the second floor and the House of Representatives the first. If, when he arrived in late November, he expected a teeming metropolis he was sorely disappointed. Nevertheless, Vandalia offered Lincoln a far broader horizon than New Salem. Though he could not have known it, the road to Congress—and the White House—began in Vandalia.

There Lincoln began to meet and cultivate acquaintance with the political leaders of Illinois. Party lines were beginning to solidify, and Lincoln, a Whig, naturally associated principally with other Whigs. Following a time-honored tradition in legislative bodies, Lincoln gave few speeches during his first term. He observed veteran legislators maneuver their bills and learned the lessons of

7

legislative politics. Representative John T. Stuart, whose respect Lincoln had earned during the campaign, took the freshman under his wing and served as his tutor.

Postmastership—*too insignificant to make [my] politics an objection. (Library of Congress)*

(Illinois Department of Conservation)

8

John T. Stuart—Lincoln "acted fairly" in deal with Democrats. *(National Archives)*

State House in Vandalia—*a rundown two-story brick building. (Illinois State Historical Library)*

The legislative session ended on February 13, 1835, and Lincoln returned to New Salem. He had learned a great deal in the brief session, and on the advice of Stuart began to study law. Once back in New Salem, he pursued his legal studies avidly. He frequently visited Springfield to borrow law books from Stuart, argued minor cases, and drew up legal documents for his neighbors. It was in New Salem, on August 25, 1835, that a young neighbor named Ann Rutledge died. While there is no hard evidence that Lincoln and Ann were linked romantically, he mourned for her. He had roomed at the Rutledge tavern and knew Ann at least as a friend.

In the meantime the Governor of Illinois, Joseph Duncan, Lincoln's former Congressman, called a special session of the state legislature. The construction of the Illinois and Michigan Canal had come to a virtual standstill. In addition, the recent census showed population growth sufficient to demand a reapportionment of legislative districts. In December 1835, Lincoln set out again for Vandalia.

In this special session Lincoln played an active role, which contrasts markedly with the previous session. It is likely that Stuart confided to Lincoln his decision to run for Congress and his hope that Lincoln would succeed him at Vandalia as Whig floor manager. In the special session the results of Stuart's grooming began to show. Lincoln introduced a bill relating to debtor insolvency, presented a road-building petition, and maneuvered a bill through the legislature for the incorporation of the Beardstown and Sangamon Canal. He also showed remarkable independence on economic issues such as banking and land policy.

One small matter remained, however, before he could assume leadership of the Whig contingent in the legislature—his reelection. On June 13, 1836, he stated his case in a letter to the editor of the *Sangamo Journal*:

> In your paper last Saturday I see a communication over the signature of "many voters," in which the candidates are called upon to "show their hands." Agreed. Here's mine.
>
> I go for all sharing the privileges of government who assist in bearing its burdens. Consequently, I go for admitting all whites to the right of suffrage who pay taxes or bear arms (by no means excluding females).
>
> If elected, I shall consider the whole people of Sangamon my constituents, as well those that oppose me as those that support me.
>
> While acting as their representative, I shall be governed by their will on all subjects upon which I have the means of knowing what their will is; and upon all others, I shall do what my own judgment teaches me will best advance their interests. Whether elected or not, I go for distributing the proceeds of the sales of public lands to the several states to enable our State, in common with others, to dig canals and construct railroads without borrowing money and paying the interest on it.
>
> If alive on the first Monday in November, I shall vote for Hugh L. White for President.

The campaign got under way, and it had a few moments of drama. Shortly after Lincoln declared his views in the *Journal*, Colonel Robert Allen stated in a campaign speech that he knew some things about Lincoln that, if stated publicly, would destroy his chances of election. In response to this innuendo, Lincoln declared that "if I have done anything . . . which . . . would subject me to a forfeiture of that confidence, he that knows of that thing, and conceals it, is a traitor to his country's interests." Colonel Allen said no more.

Whigs presented themselves ably in Sangamon County, Lincoln most of all. On August 1, he polled 1,716 votes, the highest of all candidates. An added delight came when he learned that all his legislative colleagues elected from Sangamon County were Whigs. Only John Stuart's failure to win the congressional seat marred the Whig sweep.

On December 5, 1836, one of the most historic sessions of the Illinois legislature convened. Several of the new faces on the Whig side later played a large role in Lincoln's life. A new Whig representative from Jacksonville in Morgan County, John J. Hardin, later became Lincoln's rival for the Whig nomination to Congress. A Kentucky émigré, Hardin was handsome, an eloquent speaker, and an idealistic reformer with somewhat cynical views of politics. On the Democratic side of the aisle, Stephen A. Douglas graced the legislative hall. Small but powerful, Lincoln's future opponent for the U.S. Senate and the Presidency was just beginning to enter the limelight.

In July 1837, halfway through the session, English-born Edward D. Baker joined the Whig delegation. Sangamon County Representative Dan Stone had resigned his seat, and a special election made Baker his successor. A florid, persuasive speaker, Baker served with distinction in many public offices during his long career and became Lincoln's close friend. Lincoln named one of his children after him and wept openly when Baker died on the battlefield in the opening months of the Civil War. Like Hardin, Baker became a rival for the congressional nomination.

Lincoln played a leading role in the two most significant pieces of legislation enacted at that session: a massive internal improvements measure and the removal of the state capital from Vandalia to Springfield. It has frequently been charged that Lincoln and the Sangamon County delegation traded their votes on the internal improvement scheme for support to make Springfield the capital. When the votes of Lincoln and his co-workers in the removal campaign are examined, however, there is no evidence of such a trade. Lincoln's support of the internal improvements measure was completely consistent with all his remarks on internal improvements since 1832. It stemmed from his desire to improve the country and thus the opportunities of individuals to better their lives. Indeed he had made internal improvements an important part of his legislative career. He also wanted to see the removal of the capital to Springfield, and he worked hard for it.

State House in Springfield—*the strength of the Sangamon delegation led by Lincoln prevailed. (Illinois State Historical Library)*

Enthusiasm for the internal improvements scheme swept through the state legislature. Each representative sought new roads, bridges, canals, and railroads for his district. A few thoughtful representatives, such as John Hardin, felt that the internal improvements scheme was dangerously large. Enormous expenditures would be required for a long time with no immediate prospect of adequate revenue. Visions of burgeoning commerce, however, made most representatives excessively enthusiastic, Lincoln included, and the measure passed easily in February 1837.

Less enthusiasm greeted the proposal to move the capital to Springfield. Virtually every city of any size clamored to be the capital. The strength of the Sangamon delegation led by Lincoln prevailed, however, and on February 28, 1837, Springfield won the designation.

Appropriately enough, the day after the removal of the capital to Springfield Lincoln was admitted to the bar. John T. Stuart accepted him as a law partner, and on April 15, 1837, Lincoln threw his belongings into his saddlebags, borrowed a horse, and moved to Springfield.

New Salem was a dying town. The hopes of the villagers had been tied to the promise of the Sangamon River being navigable. If navigable, the river could serve as an avenue of commerce that would bring prosperity to the town. When that proved impossible, the settlers of New Salem drifted away, carrying their shattered dreams with them.

Springfield—*the logical place to go. (Library of Congress)*

For Lincoln, Springfield was the logical place to go. He already had many friends there due to its proximity to New Salem, and with the state capital soon to be located there, the prospects for a budding young lawyer and legislator were promising.

Although Lincoln's professional prospects were rising rapidly, his personal life had encountered difficulties. Among the many friends Lincoln had made while in New Salem were Mr. and Mrs. Bennett Abell. On one visit Mrs. Abell mentioned to Lincoln that she was going back to Kentucky to visit her family. She jestingly added that she would bring her sister, Mary Owens, back to Illinois when she returned if Lincoln would marry her. In the same jovial spirit that Mrs. Abell posed the question, Lincoln agreed. Problems began when, indeed, Mrs. Abell did return with her sister. Lincoln had seen Mary three years earlier, in 1833, and had been impressed by her. He remembered her as a rarity on the rough and tumble Illinois frontier: a well-dressed, attractive, educated southern woman. Now, she was back in New Salem, and he had promised to marry her!

A courtship developed between them, but it ran a tempestuous course. Miss Owens, accustomed to a certain degree of pampering, felt slighted by Lincoln's halfhearted attention to her. Years later, in 1866, she recalled one incident for William H. Herndon:

> I thought him lacking in smaller attentions. One circumstance presents itself just now to my mind's eye. There was a company of us going to Uncle Billy Greene's. Mr. Lincoln was riding with me; and we had a very bad branch to cross. The other gentlemen were very officious in seeing that their partners got over safely. We were behind, he riding in, never looking back to see how I got along. When I rode up beside him, I remarked, "You are a nice fellow! I suppose you didn't care whether my neck was broken or not." He laughingly replied (I suppose by way of compliment) that he knew I was plenty smart to take care of myself.

Stormy as the courtship may have been, Lincoln eventually proposed to Mary Owens just before leaving for the opening of the legislative session in Vandalia. She had not replied before he left, so Lincoln pursued the courtship by mail. On December 13, 1836, Lincoln wrote to Mary complaining that he was "mortified" by her failure to write to him. He wrote of the internal improvements issue, the possibility of removing the capital to Springfield, and other political issues. He concluded by saying, "This letter is so dry and stupid that I am ashamed to send it, but with my present feelings I can not do any better." A few additional letters passed between them, but their relationship came to an end. On August 16, 1837, Mary rejected Lincoln's proposal of marriage. By most accounts Lincoln was relieved at the rejection.

In fact, the next April Lincoln wrote in intimate detail concerning Mary Owens to Mrs. Orville H. Browning of Quincy, who, with her lawyer husband, were among his closest lifelong friends. He reviewed the quaint circumstances that led to Mary's return to Illinois and added:

Mary Owens—*"mortified almost beyond endurance." (Lincoln's Other Mary,* Ziff-Davis Publishers)

MARY OWENS

In a few days we had an interview, and although I had seen her before, she did not look as my imagination had pictured her. I knew she was over-size, but she now appeared a fair match for Falstaff; I knew she was called an "old maid," and I felt no doubt of the truth of at least half of the appellation; but now, when I beheld her, I could not for my life avoid thinking of my mother; and this, not from withered features, for her skin was too full of fat, to permit its contracting in to wrinkled; but from her want of teeth, weather-beaten appearance in general, and from a kind of notion that ran in my head, that nothing could have commenced at the size of infancy, and reached her present bulk in less than thirty-five or forty years; and, in short, I was not at all pleased with her. But what could I do? I had told her sister I would take her for better or for worse. . . .

. . . and so I mustered my resolution, and made the proposal to her direct; but, shocking to relate, she answered, No. . . . I tried it again and again, but with the same success, or rather with the same want of success. I finally was forced to give it up, at which I very unexpectedly found myself mortified almost beyond endurance . . . that she whom I had taught myself to believe no body else would have, had actually rejected me with all my fancied greatness; and to cap the whole, I then, for the first time, began to suspect that I was really a little in love with her. . . . Others have been made fools of by the girls; but this can never be with truth said of me. I most emphatically, in this instance, made a fool of myself. I have now come to the conclusion never again to think of marrying; and for this reason; I can never be satisfied with any one who would be block-head enough to have me.

Mary Todd—*single pretty women were in very short supply. (Library of Congress)*

With the Mary Owens matter out of the way, Lincoln prepared for his new life in Springfield. He shared quarters with Joshua Fry Speed, over the latter's store on only a promise of eventual payment. Speed took an instant liking to Lincoln, and the friendship became deep. Over the years they corresponded with an intimacy that made Lincoln's letter to Mrs. Browning seem restrained.

Lincoln's law practice, after a slow start, grew nicely. There were heavy duties when the state legislature was in session. And every other year he had to attend to his reelection. In 1838 Lincoln faced a particularly important contest.

The predictions of John Hardin were coming true. The state of Illinois floundered with financial difficulties caused by its massive internal improvements program. Lincoln had to justify to his constituency the vigorous efforts he had made for the program. He apparently did so to the satisfaction of the Sangamon County citizens, for they returned him for another term. He emerged as undisputed leader of the Whig party in the House. His stature is indicated by his nomination for the speakership. A token gesture because of a large Democratic majority that precluded the election of a Whig, the nomination showed Lincoln's standing in the party.

During this session Lincoln also first came into direct rivalry with Stephen A. Douglas, but on this occasion they fought not for a political office but for a lady's hand.

In the autumn of 1839 Mary Todd, sister of Mrs. Ninian Edwards and a cousin of John Todd Stuart, arrived to grace Springfield society. Like Mary Owens, Mary Todd came from an aristocratic Kentucky family and had been well educated. She had also grown accustomed to the attentions Mary Owens had found so lacking in Lincoln. Single pretty women were in very short supply in Springfield and this alone assured that Miss Todd would have many callers from the numerous young men. In addition, fashionable society centered in her

Stephen A. Douglas—*eloquent, witty, natty, and handsome. (Library of Congress)*

sister's home. The eligible young men from the higher levels of local society attended the parties, cotillions, and entertainments held there. All, it seemed, save one.

The genteel manners Mary Todd brought from Kentucky aristocracy had been successfully transplanted in Springfield, but Abraham Lincoln did not, at that point, feel comfortable in those surroundings. Perhaps his involvement with Mary Owens had made him uneasy about his rustic family background, his unfamiliarity with etiquette, and his lack of formal education. Certainly Lincoln did not eagerly seek acceptance by the Edwards's coterie upon his arrival in Springfield, nor is it likely that he would have gained it quickly if he had. Although he played a role in the removal of the state capital to Springfield and thus the promise of prosperity for the city, and had a partnership with John T. Stuart, Lincoln remained diffident, awkward in the company of ruffled and ribboned femininity. Only gradually did he become a member of Springfield's fashionable young set.

Mary Todd, on the other hand, fit smoothly into Springfield society. Vivacious, lovely, and friendly, she quickly attracted suitors. Among those who courted her were Edwin B. Webb, a widower with two children; Lyman Trumbull, a Connecticut native later destined to go to the United States Senate at Lincoln's expense; and, of course, Stephen A. Douglas. Webb's suit was doomed to failure. Mary "regretted . . . his constant visits, attentions, etc." Nor did Trumbull win her favor, even though, in Mary's words, "he is talented and agreeable and sometimes *countenances* me." Douglas seemed a far more likely match. In 1836 he had been elected to the state legislature after serving as state's attorney first in Morgan and then Sangamon County. His meteoric rise to fame had just begun.

Ninian Edwards—*let Lincoln know in no uncertain terms that he believed Mary to be marrying below her station. (Illinois State Historical Library)*

In addition to these suitors, during the winter of 1839–1840 a new one began to appear in the Edwards's living room—Abraham Lincoln.

Mary could hardly have been attracted by Lincoln's looks, but other things were more important to her. She once confided, "I would rather marry a good man—a man of mind—with a hope and bright prospects ahead for position." Whatever the attraction, Lincoln obviously felt the same. The courtship between the shy lawyer and the charming, fashionable young belle progressed. Perhaps Mary saw in Lincoln "bright prospects" for election to Congress. By the end of 1840 they were engaged to be married.

The impending marriage, however, created dissension in Mary's family. Even though Lincoln and Ninian Edwards had served together on the Whig side in the state legislature, Edwards let Lincoln know in no uncertain terms that he believed Mary to be marrying below her station. Lincoln, whose own social self-esteem was hardly high, probably believed Edwards right and manipulated a breaking of the engagement. Yet Lincoln's affection for Mary persisted. In one of his intimate letters to Joshua Speed, he reflected his concern with his courtship:

> There is still one unhappy whom I have contributed to make so. That still kills my soul. I can not but reproach myself, for even wishing to be happy while she is otherwise.

He severed the engagement believing he was doing the best for Mary, whom he felt to be better than himself.

During their estrangement Mary constantly assured Lincoln that although she accepted the breaking of the engagement her feelings toward him had not changed. She did not share Ninian Edwards's opinion. Gradually Lincoln renewed his courtship of Mary Todd. Dr. Anson G. Henry, a physician and close friend of Lincoln, and Mrs. Simeon Francis, wife of the editor of the Whig *Sangamo Journal,* conspired to bring them together. Dr. Henry carried messages from one to the other and assured each of the other's feelings. Mrs. Francis often provided a rendezvous. Their conspiracy went well, for by September 1842, Lincoln and Mary were again engaged.

That same month Mary Todd and a friend, Julia Jayne, got Lincoln into a problem that could have threatened his chances for Congress—in fact, his entire political future. On September 8 there appeared in the *Sangamo Journal* a letter signed "Rebecca," similar to others that had appeared in previous issues. This particular letter ridiculed James Shields, a prominent state official and a member of the Edwards's clique, and virtually accused him of being a liar. The letter even impugned his manhood. Shields, a short-tempered man, immediately demanded that editor Simeon Francis give him the name of the author of the letter. Francis gave him Lincoln's name.

Lincoln had helped phrase some of the letters, but the portions of the letter that offended Shields were written by Mary and Julia. Lincoln took the responsibility, however, when Shields demanded an apology and a retraction. Lincoln replied with an explanation but not an apology.

This inspired Shields to challenge Lincoln to a duel.

James Shields—*duel to be fought with broadswords. (Library of Congress)*

Intermediaries tried to negotiate a more peaceful settlement than an illegal duel. Still fuming, Shields refused. Arrangements for the duel continued, but Lincoln cleverly turned them to his advantage. As the person challenged, Lincoln had the right to specify the weapons to be used. Much taller and longer of limb than Shields he demanded that the duel be fought with broadswords. Together with seconds they actually went to an island in the Mississippi River near Alton for the duel before Shields finally saw the absurdity of trying to compete with Lincoln's long arms. He realized that he had been outwitted and withdrew his challenge. Shields later distinguished himself as the only person ever to become a U.S. Senator from three states.

Ninian Edwards's home, where thirty-three-year-old Lincoln married his twenty-three-year-old bride on November 4, 1842. *(Illinois State Historical Library)*

The newlyweds made their first home in the Globe Tavern *(left)—room and board for the two came to four dollars a week. (Library of Congress)*

Had they fought, under the law, Lincoln would have forfeited for life the privilege of holding any public office.

The happy ending to the duel was soon followed by the happy ending to Lincoln's courtship of Mary. Their marriage occurred just two months after they renewed their engagement. A month before the marriage, however, Lincoln posed a searching question in a letter to Speed:

> You have now been the husband of a lovely woman nearly eight months. That you are happier now than you were the day you married her I well know; for without, you would not be living. But I have your word for it too; and the returning elasticity of spirits which is manifested in your letters. But I want to ask a closer question—"Are you now, in feeling as well as judgment, glad you are married as you are?" From any body but me, this would be an impudent question not to be tolerated; but I know you will pardon it in me. Please answer it quickly as I feel impatient to know."

On November 4, 1842, in a quiet ceremony in the Edwards's home, thirty-three-year-old Lincoln and twenty-three-year-old Mary Todd became man and wife. They took up residence in the Globe tavern. Room and board for the two came to four dollars a week. Mary had won her man with "bright prospects" and Lincoln looked to his political future as a way to fulfill those prospects.

Two months after his marriage Lincoln showed less candor in commenting about his own marriage than he had sought from Speed. Lincoln wrote: "Mary is very well and continues her old sentiments of friendship. How the marriage life goes with us I will tell you when I see you here, which I hope will be very soon."

All his attention that year had not been focused on his campaign to win Mary's hand. He had decided not to seek another term in the state legislature after completing his present, fourth, term. Instead, he set his sights on a higher goal. Illinois, growing in population, found its representation in Congress had grown from a single Congressman when Lincoln arrived in Illinois, to two in 1833, and to three in 1835. In 1842 Lincoln's friend and former law partner John T. Stuart served as one of the three Congressmen completing his second term. He did not expect to seek another.

Burgeoning immigration, mainly from Tennessee and Kentucky, had boosted the state's population so substantially that Illinois would be entitled to seven Congressmen beginning in 1843.

This meant that Illinois would be divided into seven congressional districts, and the one that included Sangamon County would be favorable to a Whig candidate.

Lincoln resolved to seek the office. So did two of his Whig colleagues in the Illinois legislature: Edward D. Baker, a close friend, who now became a rival as well, and John J. Hardin, Jacksonville's leading Whig. The battle began.

2

"Turn about is fair play . . ."

On May 1, 1843, Whig delegates from eleven Illinois counties assembled in Pekin, Illinois, to select a nominee to seek election as the Congressman from the newly formed 7th Congressional District in the United States House of Representatives. Whigs in each county in the district—Sangamon, Morgan, Scott, Cass, Menard, Logan, Mason, Tazewell, Woodford, Marshall, and Putnam—had held a Whig convention a few weeks earlier to choose delegates and give them instructions.

Abraham Lincoln had been a prime mover in establishing the convention system. He was also a leading candidate for the nomination, fixing election to Congress as his personal goal sometime during the winter of 1842–1843. He worked hard for the nomination right up to convention time, and lost.

The fact that events did not bring him the nomination in 1843 did not deter him from his goal. Instead he skillfully turned the setback to his advantage, maneuvering the convention to endorse unanimously a resolution that had the effect of delivering him the nomination without contest four years later. This accomplishment would have brought applause even from Machiavelli, particularly because in 1843 Lincoln was not the favorite for Congress of Whigs even in his home county, Sangamon, and certainly not in the second largest county of the district, Morgan. And no one had reason to expect that his standing in either of these counties would be improved four years later.

In this noteworthy feat, Lincoln followed a political doctrine which, if not original, he nevertheless refined and applied so effectively throughout his political career that it constitutes one of his most important contributions to statecraft.

That doctrine, simply stated, is: the best way to accomplish a worthy political goal is to reject steps that seem extreme or impractical and concentrate instead on steps that are reachable, small though each may be. In years to come, he applied the doctrine repeatedly as he dealt with slavery and rebellion.

Although Lincoln had already resolved to seek the Whig congressional nomination, so had two other candidates, each with a strong political base. They were Lincoln's Springfield friend Edward D. Baker and John J. Hardin of Jacksonville. All were about the same age: Lincoln thirty-four, Hardin thirty-three, and Baker thirty-two. They had served together in the legislature. Each was ambitious, hardworking. Each eventually served in Congress. Each died violently—Hardin in the Mexican War, Baker in the Civil War, and Lincoln at Ford's Theater.

Lincoln's associations with Baker had always been close and cordial. With Hardin it was different. Lincoln had already clashed with him on the state's internal improvements program, and they seemed to be temperamental opposites as well. The rivalry that developed was not the friendly sort that he had with Baker.

For the moment though, both of them presented serious obstacles to Lincoln's congressional goal. The Morgan County Whigs threw their unanimous support to Hardin. In Sangamon County the party faithful wavered between Baker and Lincoln.

The same day the Illinois legislature passed the act establishing the new congressional districts, Lincoln played a leading role in a Whig meeting that recommended that Whigs throughout the state utilize the nominating convention system. The recommendation was adopted unanimously and Lincoln wrote to Richard S. Thomas, in Virginia, Illinois, his forecast that the convention system, if utilized, would soon make the Whig party dominant in Illinois.

In arguing for the convention system, he looked to the future, not just for himself but for the Whig party. He had noted that the political strength of Democrats mounted steadily since 1835 when they began using a convention system. Conventions produced party unity behind single candidates and kept at a minimum intraparty contests.

A few days later on March 6, Lincoln published his "Address to the People of Illinois," arguing persuasively for the convention system. His appeals were influential with the 7th District Whigs. The district nominating convention met on May 1. The Whigs had postponed the convention from April 5 to accommodate Hardin, who was in Kentucky on a visit.

In preparation for the convention, each county held local conventions in which delegates were chosen and instructed. The Sangamon County convention met on March 20. It climaxed what the Illinois *State Register* referred to as a "deafening" local campaign that featured both Lincoln and Baker. Obviously both had been busy soliciting support, and Baker emerged from the politicking with an advantage. According to the *Register*, Baker's friends arrived early and dominated the morning session, persuading Lincoln to withdraw his name before his real strength became evident. The newspaper intimated that Lincoln supporters were still straggling in during the afternoon and expressed the opinion that by the end of the day they would have "paralyzed" Baker. But after the first few ballots, the convention pledged its support to Baker.

Lincoln had lost. By day's end he found himself in the peculiar position of being elected as a delegate pledged to support his rival. In fact, he became the chairman of the Baker-pledged delegation. Lincoln made a gesture to decline election as a delegate, but the convention insisted. If he had not been a delegate, he would not have been so well positioned to advance successfully his own prospect for future election to Congress.

Edward D. Baker—*groomsman to a man that has cut him out. (Library of Congress)*

The humor of the situation did not escape him. He wryly observed in a letter to Speed: "In getting Baker the nomination, I shall be fixed a good deal like a fellow who is made a groomsman to a man that has cut him out and is marrying his own dear 'gal.'"

The marriage analogy Lincoln used to describe the situation had more than a grain of truth. His failure to get the Sangamon delegation to support him turned in part upon his recent marriage to Mary Todd. Then as now, a wife could help or hinder a political candidate. As a result of his marriage, and other Springfield associations, Lincoln came to be viewed as the candidate of the wealthy and powerful. He remarked on this in a letter to a friend of New Salem days:

> It would astonish if not amuse the older citizens to learn that I (a strange, friendless, uneducated, penniless boy, working on a flat boat at ten dollars per month) have been put down here as the candidate of pride, wealth, and aristocratic family distinction.

The problem related not just to his marriage to Mary Todd. It related also to his association with a group in Springfield called the "Junto," a small group of business and social leaders that included the aristocratic Ninian Edwards.

In the same letter Lincoln added, "There was too, the strangest combination of Church influence against me."

The "strangest combination" consisted of several factors. E. D. Baker, a member of the popular Campbellite denomination (now known as the Disciples of Christ), had preached many a sermon. His popularity in church circles even reached beyond the Campbellites. Lincoln, on the other hand, belonged to no church at all; he was one of the very few nonchurchgoing residents of Springfield. Critics argued that he did not deserve the vote of any churchgoing man. Mrs. Lincoln attended the Episcopal Church, which had a very small membership—hardly a political plus in an area that viewed the Episcopal Church as aristocratic.

Religion remained an issue throughout the rest of Lincoln's life. In 1843 this factor alone could well have given Baker the margin of support he needed to win the endorsement of Sangamon Whigs.

Despite his loss of Sangamon delegates, Lincoln did not give up his candidacy. He successfully pursued support in Menard County, where he still had many friends from New Salem days. He hoped for such a close vote between Baker and Hardin that the delegates from Menard and Mason counties could deadlock the convention.

Lincoln, however, also carefully honored the instructions that bound him to support Baker as a convention delegate from Sangamon County. In a letter to a Menard friend, Martin Morris, he declared, "I would as soon put my head in the fire" as to violate the instructions.

Nevertheless, he felt no compunctions—privately, at least—against keeping his own candidacy alive in other counties. In writing to the same Menard friend, he said:

> You say you shall instruct your delegates to go for me unless I object. I certainly shall not object. That would be too pleasant a compliment for me to tread in the dust. And besides if any thing should happen (which however is not probable) by which Baker should be thrown out of the fight, I would be at liberty to accept the nomination if I could get it. I do however feel myself bound not to hinder him in any way from getting the nomination. I should despise myself if I were to attempt it.

Lincoln did not advertise these initiatives. He closed one of the letters with this admonition, "Don't show or speak of this letter." To another he appended, "You have my permission and even request to show this letter to [James] Short; but to no one else unless it be a very particular friend who you know will not speak of it." In today's parlance, Lincoln kept all his options open.

If Lincoln had moments when he felt his candidacy thwarted by the convention system, he had no one to blame but himself. Lincoln had fought vigorously for the convention system. In its absence he could have run regardless of the candidacy of others like Hardin and Baker.

An exciting and close district convention ensued, but it soon appeared that Hardin had the edge. J. B. Ruggles, a delegate to the convention, described the climactic moments:

> When the convention assembled, Baker was there with his friend and champion delegate, Abraham Lincoln. The ayes and noes had been taken,

and there were fifteen votes apiece, and one in doubt that had not arrived. That was myself. I was known to be a warm friend of Baker, representing people who were partial to Hardin. As soon as I arrived Baker hurried to me, saying "How is it? It all depends on you." On being told that notwithstanding my partiality for him, the people I represented expected me to vote for Hardin, and that I would have to do so, Baker at once replied: "You are right—there is no other way." The convention was organized, and I was elected Secretary. Baker arose, and made a thrilling address, thoroughly arousing the sympathies of the convention and ended by declining his candidacy. Hardin was nominated by acclamation.

John J. Hardin—*Lincoln was ready with his political master stroke. (Illinois State Historical Library)*

But Lincoln was ready with his political master stroke the minute Hardin received the nomination. He had prepared a resolution in advance and quickly offered it to the convention. The resolution stated that the delegates to the convention—as individuals—believed Edward D. Baker to be a sterling Whig and deserving of the nomination at the next Whig district convention.

The Pekin convention could not bind the convention that would succeed it, but the resolution certainly enhanced Baker's position. Actually, the resolution served several important goals, including Lincoln's own self-interest. First of all, it substantially reduced the possibility that Hardin would be nominated for a second term. Second, it laid the foundation for a succession of one-term Whig Congressmen. Third, it put Baker very deeply in Lincoln's debt and virtually assured him of Baker's support when Lincoln's turn as candidate arrived. Fourth, it cemented the unity of Whigs in the 7th Congressional District not only for the current campaign but for several years to come. Fifth, it virtually guaranteed the survival of the convention system of nominee selection. Finally, and most important to Lincoln, the resolution was an important first step toward his congressional goal.

Lincoln paid a small price for these gains. He had already lost the 1843 nomination. He had no assurance that his position in 1844—when the next congressional election would be held—would be any better. By postponing his own ambitions for a short time, he virtually assured the eventual prize for himself and in the meantime he guaranteed greater unity for his party.

There is substantial evidence that Lincoln received verbal assurances in advance of the Pekin convention that, in return for working on Hardin's behalf in the upcoming election and helping to obtain subsequent nomination for Baker, he would not be opposed by either of them for the nomination in 1846.

Some 7th District Whigs grumbled about the establishment of a rotation-in-office practice, but most accepted it. In any case, events proceeded on schedule.

Hardin won the election by a narrow margin. He received Lincoln's support in the campaign—as promised in the bargain—but, curiously, not Lincoln's vote. Lincoln cast his vote for other offices that year but not for Congress. Undoubtedly, this reflected a dusky side of Lincoln's political nature. He did not always forgive and forget. His failure to vote was partly a reprimand to Hardin for getting the prize that year that he had wanted. Still, Lincoln kept the letter of his bargain. He gave Hardin everything he could in the election campaign except his vote.

The 1844 convention was perfunctory. Helped by Hardin's early declaration that he would not seek reelection, and by Lincoln's Pekin resolution, Baker won easy nomination and election. Lincoln supported Baker, of course, but he also worked diligently for another Whig candidate. Henry Clay, Lincoln's "beau ideal of a statesman," won the Whig nomination for the Presidency and Lincoln campaigned as an elector pledged to Clay.

Lincoln politicked prodigiously. He gave speeches, helped organize local "Clay Clubs," and beat the bushes mustering support for the Whig candidate. In a private letter to Hardin, William Herndon assessed Clay's prospects in various Illinois counties, and spoke of the personal equation in politics:

> I know that if you were in Morgan all would go well but I fear that the people of Morgan have lost what they are not able to replace. I know how this goes if Baker or Lincoln is missing at our meetings. It seems that something is lost.

Added evidence of Lincoln's hard work was given Hardin by William L. Long of Jacksonville:

> The loco's [a derogatory term for Democrats] are pretty much down in the mouth. Baker and Lincoln have been engaged the last week in demolishing Calhoun Cavalry [partisans for John C. Calhoun], in which they completely succeeded. The cause is prospering.

Some Whig newspapers began to mention Lincoln and John Hardin as possible Whig candidates for the gubernatorial election to be held in 1846, but Lincoln gave them no encouragement. He had determined to take the congressional seat. He prepared carefully, worked hard, and had no intention of having his well-developed plans scuttled by a hopeless run for state office. Indeed, he may have encouraged those who wanted Hardin to run for Governor.

Between the campaign of 1844 and the Whig convention of 1846, Hardin began to have second thoughts about the Pekin agreement. He had been disappointed in his two short years in Congress but found life out of Congress even less satisfying. He began to weigh the possibility of returning to Congress; at the same time he considered suggestions that he run for Governor. When word of this reached Lincoln, he visited Hardin to find out where he stood. Hardin refused to commit himself, so Lincoln quietly began a campaign to secure enough delegates at the convention to forestall any effort by Hardin to obtain the nomination. He wrote to newspaper editors and others and pleaded his case. He said he did not wish to disparage Hardin in any way and appealed only to justice and the belief that "turn about is fair play." Hardin, meanwhile, remained undecided. Some of his close advisers, such as George T. M. Davis, urged him to run for Governor but his own inclination was to run for Congress. He delayed any public announcement of candidacy, and this delay gave Lincoln time to seek support.

In November 1845, Hardin finally made up his mind. In a letter to the editor of the Tazewell *Whig* in Tremont, Illinois, Hardin firmly declined the gubernatorial candidacy. Although flattered by those supporting him for the governorship, he had decided to reenter politics only as a candidate for the congressional nomination.

In organizing his counterattack Lincoln felt no hesitation about using newspapers to his advantage. He made direct appeals for cooperation from his friends in the Whig press. On November 17, 1845, he wrote to editor Benjamin F. James of the Tazewell *Whig:* "If your feelings toward me are the same as when I saw you (which I have no reason to doubt) I wish you would let nothing appear in your paper which may operate against me." The next day he wrote to Henry E. Drummer in Beardstown, "I wish you would, if you can, see that . . . the Beardstown paper [Gazette] takes no stand that may injure my chance."

While trying to influence the press to give him favorable mention for Congress, Lincoln went to some length to keep out of the newspapers the fact that he and Hardin both had their eyes on the congressional seat. He also avoided appearing critical of Hardin. He wanted no dissension in Whig ranks that could be avoided. To editor James he wrote on December 6, 1845:

> It is my intention to give him [Hardin] the trial, unless clouds should rise, which are not yet discernible. This determination you need not, however, as yet, announce in your paper, at least not as coming from me. . . . In doing

this, let nothing be said against Hardin . . . nothing deserves to be said against him. Let the pith of the whole argument be "Turn about is fair play."

On January 16, 1846, he wrote urgently to editor James with explicit instructions on the editorial message he wanted published in the next issue:

> A plan is on foot to change the mode of selecting the candidate [for Congress] for this district. The movement is intended to injure me. . . . I want you to let nothing prevent your getting an article in your paper, of this week taking strong ground for the old system, under which Hardin & Baker were nominated, without seeming to know or suspect, that any one desires to change it. . . . Don't fail, on any account, to get it in this week.

James came through as directed with an appropriate editorial in the Tazewell *Whig* of January 24.

On the same day he wrote the frantic directive to James, Lincoln used a Democrat to deliver some of his campaign mail to Petersburg in Menard County. The Democrat was State Senator Thomas L. Harris. Lincoln had missed the mail dispatch by a half hour that day, and Harris took Lincoln's letters home with him, posting them in Petersburg.

Quite a few Whigs supported Hardin's nomination to Congress, especially in Jacksonville, but Lincoln had been effective in securing pledges for himself. Hardin's advisers in different parts of the district told him of Lincoln's strength and chided him for not making his ambition clear earlier. P. H. Thompson of Pekin wrote him on January 12:

> I find upon enquiring among our friends that Mr. Lincoln during his journey through the circuit sought and obtained pledges from most of what we call leading men in this vicinity. No one supposed here, until your letter was published that you had any desire to again represent us in Congress. Had such a wish been expressed many would have hesitated before pledging themselves to Lincoln. I know that you have many warm and ardent friends here, who are ready at a suitable time to do all you can reasonably ask of them, as the matter now stands however the common conversation is "Hardin is a good fellow and did us and himself great credit and honor by his course in Congress, Lincoln is also a good fellow and has worked hard and faithfully for the party, if he desires to go to Congress let him go this time, turn about is fair play." This latter remark I hear made in the store daily. . . . Lincoln would at this moment be the choice of probably a large majority of the Whigs [in Tazewell].

Not all the delegates were impressed by the arguments for Lincoln. Of Lincoln's qualifications for the congressional seat, Delegate Ira Fenn said:

> Two or three are endeavoring to impress upon the mind of the people that it is Lincoln's right to have the office the next term. The grounds appear to be that the doctrine of "taking turns" was established by the Pekin convention,

P. H. Thompson to Hardin—*let [Lincoln] go this time, turn about is fair play. (Chicago Historical Society)*

that it has so far been acted on, that it is now Lincoln's turn, that Hardin had had his turn, that it is due to Lincoln on account of his great services to the Whig party on account of his talent and worth, that he is poor & Hardin is rich, that this is the only Whig district, in short that this is the only crumb that a Whig politician can obtain in the State, and that no one deserves more than Lincoln. Indeed all these reasons & perhaps some others were urged to induce me to commit myself for Lincoln. I replied that I had the highest respect for Lincoln and entertained toward him the very best feeling but I supposed the question for us to determine was, who could best advance our interests in Congress.

Nevertheless, the tide appeared to be with Lincoln. It became clear to Hardin that he would have great difficulty obtaining the nomination. Still ambitious for Congress, he pondered the alternatives. On January 16, 1846, he wrote to Lincoln and proposed a new method of selecting a congressional candidate.

Hardin's proposal would have established a nominating procedure similar to the modern primary system. Lincoln adamantly disapproved. In a lengthy letter to Hardin he outlined his objections. He noted that under the convention system both Baker and Hardin had obtained nomination and subsequent election: "I am satisfied with the old system under which such good men have triumphed." He did concede that there might be some vagueness or ambiguity in the old system and indicated he would be amenable to clarifying those provisions. However, he found highly objectionable a provision in Hardin's proposal that candidates could not campaign outside their own counties. "On reflection," he wrote to Hardin, "you will see, the fact of your having been in Congress has, in various ways, so spread your name in the district, as to give you a decided advantage in such a stipulation." Lincoln also objected to Hardin's proposal for apportionment of delegate strength to individual counties. In short, he simply would not support Hardin's proposals.

While trying to talk Hardin out of the race, Lincoln sent a flurry of letters and made a number of personal appearances to keep his own fences mended.

On January 14 he wrote to B. F. James of Tremont: "When this Supreme court shall adjourn . . . it is my intention to take a quiet trip through the towns and neighbourhoods of Logan county, Delavan, Tremont, and on to & through the upper counties." The next day he wrote in alarm to John Bennett of Petersburg: "Nathan Dresser is here and speaks as though the contest between Hardin & me is to be doubtful in Menard county. . . . Don't fail to write me instantly on receiving this, telling me all—particularly the names of those who are going strong against me." On January 21 he wrote to N. J. Rockwell that he did want the congressional seat, and repeated this argument of "turn about is fair play." He added, "I shall be pleased if this strikes you as a sufficient argument."

He spent two full days, January 24 and 25, campaigning in Petersburg.

His correspondence with James remained steady. He wrote to him on January 27 making suggestions about the selection and instruction of delegates to the convention. On February 9 he answered an article in the Morgan *Journal* (Jacksonville) critical of his role in squelching Hardin's candidacy.

James responded by writing in the Tazewell *Whig* of February 21, "We conceive it due to Mr. Lincoln, that the people of this district should pay a substantial tribute to his worth, energy and patriotic exertions in behalf of Whig principles."

Lincoln's adroit maneuvering and tireless efforts made it clear to all that Hardin's chances of securing the nomination for himself were doomed. Accordingly, on February 26, 1846, the *Sangamo Journal* published Hardin's letter withdrawing his name from consideration. The General had been outgeneraled.

Three months later, on May 1, 1846, the Whig district convention was held in Petersburg. In the afternoon presiding officer Stephen T. Logan (Lincoln's former law partner) presented the following resolution to the convention:

> Resolved, that we present to the Whigs of this District Abraham Lincoln as the Whig candidate for Congress; that in his past firm and undeviating attachments to and his active and able support of Whig principles, his abilities and integrity, entitle him to their cordial and active support in the approaching election.

The convention adopted the resolution unanimously. The *Sangamo Journal* observed, "This nomination was, of course, anticipated, there being no other candidate in the field. Mr. Lincoln, we all know, is a good Whig, a good man, an able speaker and richly deserves the confidence of Whigs in District and State." Thus Lincoln won without contest the nomination he had been seeking since 1843. His attention now turned to the campaign.

The Democratic party had selected as its candidate another Sangamon County man, Peter Cartwright, of Pleasant Plains, a Methodist circuit-riding preacher. The same Peter Cartwright had defeated Lincoln in the 1832 state legislative contest. By 1846, however, Lincoln had broadened his political base. He had served four successive terms in the state legislature. Cartwright had served only two terms, the second resulting from his victory over Lincoln. His first was in 1828. In the years since Cartwright last served, Lincoln rose to leadership of the Whig party in the legislature. Cartwright's two terms were undistinguished.

Yet Cartwright had a substantial following. Sixty-two years old in 1846, his reputation had spread throughout the 7th Congressional District because of his circuit-riding ministry. He was a flamboyant, colorful personality. A native Virginian, he had moved with his family to Kentucky while still young. At the age of sixteen he converted to the Methodist Church at a camp meeting. He received his "exhorter's" license in 1802, and for twenty-two years spread the Methodist message in the Kentucky and Tennessee regions. These were slave states and in 1824, largely because of his opposition to slavery, Cartwright transferred to the Sangamon circuit in Illinois. He had a ready wit, dealt with deriders at his meetings with force, and was widely admired and respected—in short, the Reverend Peter Cartwright made a formidable opponent.

Lincoln had been nominated on May 1 and Cartwright on May 13. The campaign began on May 25, when Lincoln delivered a speech in Jacksonville. There is, perhaps, a delicate irony in Lincoln's selection of Jacksonville, John Hardin's home, as the site of his campaign opener. Regrettably, none of the speeches made by either Lincoln or Cartwright have been preserved. From newspaper accounts, as well as other sources, it seems to have been largely lackluster. Lincoln is known to have delivered only seven speeches. He spoke in Springfield, Lacon, Hennepin, Mackinaw, Delavan, Jacksonville, and in Marshall County. This is not surprising because in that period, like today, speeches were not the most important part of congressional campaigning. Personal contact between the candidate and his would-be constituents was far more important. A glimpse of Lincoln in this setting has been provided by J. H. Buckingham, a reporter for the Boston *Courier*. In 1847 Buckingham shared a stagecoach to Springfield with Lincoln, then a Congressman-elect. He reported:

> We were now in the district represented by our Whig Congressman, and he knew, or appeared to know, every body we met, the name of the tenant of every farm house, and the owner of every plat of land. Such a shaking of hands—such a how d'ye do—such a greeting of different kinds, as we saw, was never seen before; it seemed to me as if he knew everything, and he had

a kind word, a smile and a bow for every body on the road, even to the horses, and the cattle, and the swine.

The burning issue of the campaign turned out to be the question of how protective the tariff should be. On this issue Lincoln took middle ground. On July 25, 1846, the Lacon, Illinois *Gazette* reported that in his speech of July 18, "with a logical, argumentative effort he [Lincoln] demonstrated the necessity of a discriminating tariff. " The tariff had been a major issue in American politics for years. Southerners, anxious to obtain cheaply produced foreign goods, advocated a low tariff. Westerners generally took the same position. The plows and other farm implements they needed were produced more cheaply abroad than at home.

Northerners, on the other hand, sought to protect the fledgling industrial development that had begun to replace farming in the rocky soil of New England. They demanded a high protective tariff to encourage the purchase of American-made goods.

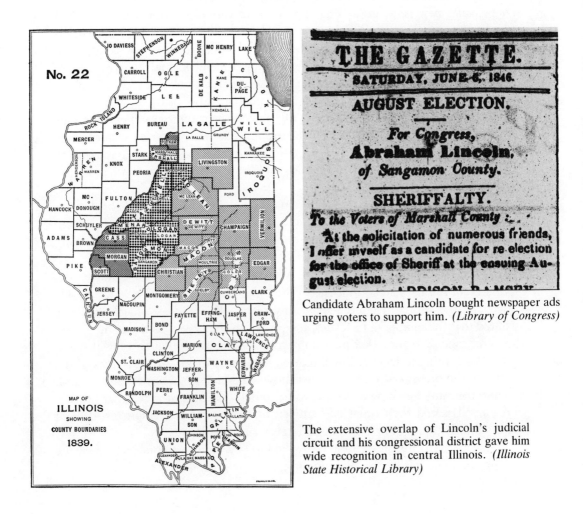

Candidate Abraham Lincoln bought newspaper ads urging voters to support him. *(Library of Congress)*

The extensive overlap of Lincoln's judicial circuit and his congressional district gave him wide recognition in central Illinois. *(Illinois State Historical Library)*

Lincoln favored flexibility. A "discriminating tariff" would fix the import duty at a level that would equalize the competitive position of United States and foreign-made products. For example, if a plow cost twenty dollars more to manufacture in the United States, the duty on a plow imported from Great Britain would be twenty dollars. Given the practical political considerations of his era—when tariffs were the principal source of federal revenue—he had taken a reasonable position. Lincoln believed that politics is the art of the possible, and had he taken a more rigid, inflexible position, he would have jeopardized some of his own support.

Two days after the Lacon speech he crossed the Illinois River to address voters in two precincts of Marshall County. They assembled in a grove on the Bonham farm. On July 22 he spoke in Hennepin, and, according to the Tazewell *Whig,* Lincoln appeared at Mackinawtown the afternoon of July 24 and the next evening at nearby Delavan.

As in his first try for the congressional nomination, Lincoln was criticized for marrying into the aristocratic Todd family.

Then, toward the end of the campaign, when Cartwright's position looked hopeless, a new issue arose. The opposition of various church groups that had worked against Lincoln when he first sought the nomination in 1843 once again emerged. Opponents charged that he had once declared that drunkards were often as honest, generous, and kindly as church members and sometimes more so. A whispering campaign began. Rumors that Lincoln was an infidel—a derider of religion, an atheist—flew throughout the district. In response, Lincoln prepared a handbill detailing his views on religion. Several of his friends convinced him, however, that publishing it would only broaden awareness of the charges and do more harm than good. Lincoln still felt he had to respond to the charges but decided to postpone publishing his response until after the election.

In other ways too religion gave drama to the campaign. Cartwright did not neglect his ecclesiastical endeavors and this was not always to his advantage. Then, as now, some citizens disapproved of preachers in politics—and especially preachers like Cartwright.

The fiery former Chaplain of the War of 1812 assailed unrepentance, the Church of the Latter-Day Saints, Baptists, and Calvinists with equal fervor. He detested the Mormon church in nearby Hancock County so deeply he once stated that the murder of its leader, Joseph Smith, had been justifiable homicide.

The candidate sprinkled his campaign calendar with religious revival meetings. According to legend, Lincoln attended one of these. At the climax of the sermon the preacher-candidate asked those expecting to go to heaven to stand. Then the same for those expecting to go to hell. Cartwright noted that Lincoln remained seated both times and singled him out from the pulpit for a direct question: Did Lincoln plan to go to heaven or to hell?

According to the story, Lincoln replied loudly, and to the merriment of the congregation, that he was planning to go to Congress.

34

Nor did campaign activities occupy all of Lincoln's time. Besides attending to his law practice, he set aside time for several unusual literary pursuits. He wrote poetry and also a true murder mystery. Each appeared in the Quincy *Whig* but without identifying the author.

In these literary endeavors he had the assistance of a Quincy attorney, Andrew Johnston. On February 24, 1846, just before his nomination to Congress, Lincoln sent Johnston several pieces of his favorite poetry, among them William Knox's "Mortality," which Lincoln two months later declared he would give all he was worth to have written. In a letter accompanying the poems, Lincoln wrote, "By the way, how would you like to see a piece of poetry of my own making? I have a piece that is almost done, but I find a deal of trouble to finish it."

By April 18 Lincoln had overcome the "deal of trouble" and sent to Johnston the first ten stanzas of "My Childhood Home I see Again." Obviously, the pace and strain of campaigning had not kept him from finishing off the quatrains. To Johnston he wrote:

> In the fall of 1844, thinking I might aid some to carry the State of Indiana for Mr. Clay, I went into the neighborhood in that State in which I was raised, where my mother and only sister were buried, and from which I have been absent about fifteen years. That part of the country is, within itself, as unpoetical as any spot of the earth; but still, seeing it and its objects and inhabitants aroused feelings in me which were certainly poetry; though whether my expression of those feelings is poetry is quite another question. When I got to writing, the change of subjects divided the thing into four little divisions or cantos, the first only of which I send you now and may send the others hereafter.
>
> Yours truly,
> A. Lincoln

Peter Cartwright—*assailed unrepentance . . . Baptists, and Calvinists with equal fervor. (Library of Congress)*

QUINCY WHIG.

BARTLETT & SULLIVAN.   QUINCY, ILLINOIS, WEDNESDAY, MAY 5, 1847.   VOL. 10—NO. 3.

THE RETURN.

PART I.—REFLECTION.

My childhood's home I see again,
  And sadden with the view;
And still, as memories crowd my brain,
  There's pleasure in it too.

Oh! memory—thou mid-way world
  'Twixt earth and Paradise,
Where things decayed, and loved ones lost,
  In dreamy shadows rise;

And freed from all that's earthly vile,
  Seem hallowed, pure and bright;
Like scenes in some enchanted isle,
  All bathed in liquid light.

As dusky mountains please the eye,
  When twilight chases day—
As bugle notes, that pass us by,
  In distance die away—

As, leaving some grand water-fall,
  We lingering list its roar—
So memory will hallow all
  We've known—but know no more.

* * * * * * * * *

This was the only time Lincoln the poet made it into print during his lifetime. *(Library of Congress)*

My childhood's home I see again,
  And sadden with the view;
And still, as memories crowd my brain,
  There's pleasure in it too.

O! memory—thou mid-way world
  'Twixt earth and Paradise,
Where things decayed, and loved ones lost,
  In dreamy shadows rise;

And freed from all that's earthly vile,
  Seem hallowed, pure and bright;
Like scenes in some enchanted isle,
  All bathed in liquid light.

As dusky mountains please the eye,
  When twilight chases day—
As bugle notes, that pass us by,
  In distance die away—

As, leaving some grand water-fall,
  We lingering list its roar—
So memory will hallow all
  We've known—but know no more.

Near twenty years have passed away
  Since here I bid farewell
To woods and fields, and scenes of play,
  And playmates loved so well.

Where many were, but few remain
  Of old familiar things;
But seeing them, to mind again
  The lost and absent brings.

The friends I left that parting day,
  How changed, as time has sped!
Young childhood grown, strong manhood gray,
  And half of all are dead.

I hear the loved survivors tell
  How nought from death could save,
Till every sound appears a knell,
  And every spot a grave.

I range the fields with pensive tread,
  And pace the hollow rooms,
And feel (companion of the dead)
  I'm living in the tombs.

Lincoln renewed the literary correspondence September 6, just a month after his election to Congress, sending Johnston additional verses inspired by his visit to Indiana. He explained:

The subject of the present one is an insane man. His name is Matthew Gentry. He is three years older than I, and when we were boys we went to school together. He was rather a bright lad, and the son of the rich man of our very poor neighborhood. At the age of nineteen he unaccountably became furiously mad, from which condition he gradually settled down into harmless insanity. When, as I told you in my other letter I visited my old home in the fall of 1844, I found him still lingering in this wretched condition. In my poetizing mood I could not forget the impressions his case made upon me. Here is the result.

But here's an object more of dread
    Than aught the grave contains—
A human form with reason fled,
    While wretched life remains.

When terror spread, and neighbors ran
    Your dangerous strength to bind,
And soon, a howling, crazy man,
    Your limbs were fast confined:

How then you strove and shrieked aloud,
    Your bones and sinews bared;
And fiendish on the gazing crowd
    With burning eyeballs glared;

And begged and swore, and wept and prayed,
    With maniac laughter joined;
How fearful were these signs displayed
    By pangs that killed the mind!

And when at length the drear and long
    Time soothed thy fiercer woes,
How plaintively thy mournful song
    Upon the still night rose!

I've heard it oft as if I dreamed,
    Far distant, sweet and lone,

The funeral dirge it ever seemed
    Of reason dead and gone.

To drink its strains I've stole away,
    All stealthily and still,
Ere yet the rising god of day
    Had streaked the eastern hill.

Air held her breath; trees with the spell
    Seemed sorrowing angels round,
Whose swelling tears in dewdrops fell
    Upon the listening ground.

But this is past, and naught remains
    That raised thee o'er the brute;
Thy piercing shrieks and soothing strain
    Are like, forever mute.

Now fare thee well! More thou the cause
    Than subject now of woe.
All mental pangs by time's kind laws
    Hast lost the power to know.

O death! thou awe-inspiring prince
    That keepst the world in fear,
Why dost thou tear more blest ones hence,
    And leave him lingering here?

If I should ever send another, the subject will be a "Bear-Hunt."
                      Yours as ever,
                         A. Lincoln

On February 25, 1847, Lincoln wrote again to Johnston:

> To say the least, I am not at all displeased with your proposal to publish the
> poetry, or doggerel, or whatever else it may be called, which I sent you. I
> consent that it may be done . . . but let names be suppressed by all means. I
> have not sufficient hope of the verses attracting any favorable notice to
> tempt me to risk being ridiculed for having written them.

He enclosed "The Bear Hunt."

On May 5 the Quincy *Whig* published anonymously the first two groups of
verses, the only time Lincoln the poet made it into print during his lifetime.
"The Bear Hunt" was not printed, doubtless considered by Johnston an
unsuitable companion to the other verses.

Early in the same campaign year, and doubtless through the agency of
Johnston, another literary work of Lincoln's anonymously appeared in the
Quincy *Whig*. Printed April 15, 1846, and copied a week later in the *Sangamo
Journal* in Springfield, it was the following true account of an extraordinary case
involving arrest for murder.

> In the year 1841, there resided, at different points in the State of Illinois,
> three brothers by the name of Trailor. Their Christian names were William,
> Henry, and Archibald. . . . In the neighborhood of William's residence,
> there was, and had been for several years, a man by the name of Fisher, who
> was somewhat above the age of fifty; had no family, and no settled home; but
> who boarded and lodged a while here, and a while there, with the persons
> for whom he did little jobs of work. His habits were remarkably economical,
> so that an impression got about that he had accumulated a considerable
> amount of money. In the latter part of May in the year mentioned, William
> formed the purpose of visiting his brothers at Clary's Grove, and Springfield;
> and Fisher, at the time having his temporary residence at his house, resolved
> to accompany him. They set out together in a buggy with a single horse. On
> Sunday Evening they reached Henry's residence, and staid over night. On
> Monday Morning, being the first Monday of June, they started on to
> Springfield, Henry accompanying them on horse back. They reached town
> about noon, met Archibald, went with him to his boarding house, and there
> took up their lodgings for the time they should remain. After dinner, the
> three Trailors and Fisher left the boarding house in company, for the avowed
> purpose of spending the evening together in looking about the town. At
> supper, the Trailors had all returned, but Fisher was missing, and some
> inquiry was made about him. After supper, the Trailors went out professedly
> in search of him. One by one they returned, the last coming in after late tea
> time, and each stating that he had been unable to discover any thing of
> Fisher. The next day, both before and after breakfast, they went professedly
> in search again, and returned at noon, still unsuccessful. Dinner again being
> had, William and Henry expressed a determination to give up the search and
> start for their homes. This was remonstrated against by some of the boarders
> about the house, on the ground that Fisher was somewhere in the vicinity,

and would be left without any conveyance, as he and William had come in the same buggy. The remonstrance was disregarded, and they departed for their homes respectively. . . . On the Friday, week after Fisher's disappearance, the Postmaster at Springfield received a letter from the Postmaster nearest William's residence in Warren county, stating that William had returned home without Fisher, and was saying, rather boastfully, that Fisher was dead, and had willed him his money, and that he had got about fifteen hundred dollars by it. The letter further stated that William's story and conduct seemed strange; and desired the Postmaster at Springfield to ascertain and write what was the truth in the matter. The Postmaster at Springfield made the letter public, and at once, excitement became universal and intense. . . . A purpose was forthwith formed to ferret out the mystery in putting which into execution, the Mayor of the city, and the Attorney General took the lead. To make search for, and, if possible, find the body of the man supposed to be murdered, was resolved on as the first step. . . . This search, as has appeared, commenced on Friday. It continued until Saturday afternoon without success, when it was determined to dispatch officers to arrest William and Henry at their residences respectively. . . . On Monday, the officers sent for Henry, having arrested him, arrived with him. The Mayor and Attorney Gen'l took charge of him, and set their wits to work to elicit a discovery from him. He denied, and denied, and persisted in denying. They still plied him in every conceivable way, till Wednesday, when, protesting his own innocence, he stated that his brothers, William and Archibald had murdered Fisher; that they had killed him, without his [Henry's] knowledge at the time, and made a temporary concealment of his body; that immediately preceding his and William's departure from Springfield for home, on Tuesday, the day after Fisher's disappearance, William and Archibald communicated the fact to him, and engaged his assistance in making a permanent concealment of the body . . . [in] Hickox's mill pond. . . . Archibald . . . was seized and thrown into jail; and, indeed, his personal security rendered it by no means objectionable to him. And now came the search. . . . In attempting to follow the track of the buggy . . . it was found to proceed in the direction of the mill pond, but could not be traced all the way. At the pond, however, it was found that a buggy had been backed down to, and partially into the water's edge. Search was now to be made in the pond; and it was made in every imaginable way. . . . About noon of this day, the officer sent for William, returned having him in custody; and a man calling himself Dr. Gilmore, came in company with them. . . . This Dr. Gilmore arrived, stating that Fisher was alive at his house; and that he had followed on to give the information, so that William might be released without further trouble; [but] the officer, distrusting Dr. Gilmore, refused to release William. . . . Gilmore's story was communicated to Henry Trailor, who, without faltering, reaffirmed his own story about Fisher's murder. Henry's adherence to his own story was communicated to the crowd, and at once the idea started, and became nearly, if not quite universal that Gilmore was a confederate of the Trailors, and had invented the tale he was telling, to secure their release and escape.

Excitement was again at its zenith. About 3 o'clock the same evening, Myers, Archibald's partner, started with a two horse carriage, for the purpose of ascertaining whether Fisher was alive, as stated by Gilmore, and if so, of bringing him back to Springfield with him. On Friday a legal examination was gone into before two Justices, on the charge of murder against William and Archibald. Henry was introduced as a witness by the prosecution, and on oath, re-affirmed his statements, as heretofore detailed. . . . Dr. Gilmore was then introduced by the defendants. . . . [He] stated that he had known Fisher for several years, and that he had understood he was subject to temporary derangement of mind, owing to an injury about his head received in early life. There was about Dr. Gilmore so much of the air and manner of truth, that his statement prevailed in the minds of the audience and of the court, and the Trailors were discharged; although they attempted no explanation of the circumstances proven by the other witnesses. On the next Monday, Myers arrived in Springfield, bringing with him the now famed Fisher, in full life and proper person. Thus ended this strange affair; and while it is readily conceived that a writer of novels could bring a story to a more perfect climax, it may well be doubted, whether a stranger affair ever really occurred. Much of the matter remains in mystery to this day. . . . It is not the object of the writer of this, to enter into the many curious speculations that might be indulged upon the facts of this narrative; yet he can scarcely forbear a remark upon what would, almost certainly have been the fate of William and Archibald, had Fisher not been found alive. It seems he had wandered away in mental derangement, and, had he died in this condition, and his body been found in the vicinity, it is difficult to conceive what could have saved the Trailors from the consequence of having murdered him. Or, if he had died, and his body never found, the case against them, would have been quite as bad, for, although it is a principle of law that a conviction for murder shall not be had, unless the body of the deceased be discovered, it is to be remembered, that Henry testified he saw Fisher's dead body.

It is curious that while he was campaigning for Congress Lincoln was unwilling to have the poetry and murder story appear under his own name. Perhaps his reluctance was based only on undue modesty, but the likelihood is that it was something more; he must have felt that the association of his name with these literary efforts might in some way complicate his candidacy. He had waited long for his turn for Congress and he was not about to jeopardize the opportunity on the chance that voters might think his verse either silly or beneath the dignity of the office he sought.

He had good reason to avoid unnecessary complications. He faced not just the nominee of the Democratic party, but a third candidate in the field, Elihu Walcott of the Liberty party. Walcott busily scoured the countryside for votes, spreading the gospel of abolitionism. He and his party represented the first stirrings of the slavery issue that would rock the nation with civil war in two short decades. Of course, everyone knew Walcott had no chance of winning, or even coming in second. But there was always the possibility that he might take just enough votes away from one candidate to give the election victory to the other. And the likely loser in that case would be Lincoln.

The only strongholds of antislavery sentiment in the 7th Congressional District were in Putnam and Marshall counties. In 1838 Benjamin Lundy, the famous abolitionist, had moved to Hennepin, in Putnam County, and there for a year published a newspaper called the *Genius of Universal Emancipation.* Lundy died the next year but he had begun to develop a fervent group of antislavery advocates in the area.

A small but steady stream of immigrants from northern states moved into northern Illinois bringing new support to the antislavery forces. In each election since the 7th District was formed, the Liberty party had fielded a candidate for the congressional seat. Its candidate never received a substantial vote and 1846 was no different. Walcott snared a mere 249 votes. Still, that represented an increase from the 82 Liberty votes in 1844.

On August 3 men in the 7th District cast their votes. Lincoln voted Whig for all offices except Congress. Following the curious custom of that era he voted for his principal opponent, Cartwright.

When the votes were counted Lincoln had garnered 56 percent, a 1,511 vote margin over Cartwright. He carried nine of the eleven counties in the district—all except Woodford and Marshall. In Sangamon County he received 1,535

Election results from the *Gazette.* (Library of Congress)

THE GAZETTE.

SATURDAY, AUGUST 15, 1846.

Two interesting articles, copied from a New York Magazine, are on our first page.

THE ELECTION.

Returns come in so slowly that we are not yet prepared to form any definite opinion as to the general result.

No doubt is entertained of the election of French and Wells.

CONGRESSMEN.

1st District—Robert Smith is elected by a majority of from 5 to 700.

2d District—John A. M'Clernand.

3d and 6th Districts—Doubtful.

4th District—John Wentworth.

5th District—S. A. Douglass.

7th District—Abraham Lincoln, by a majority of about 1400.

41

votes for a margin of 64 percent (see table below). His victory exceeded the margins by which Hardin and Baker had won. This was the largest Whig plurality ever in the state. The Democratic Illinois *State Gazette* said editorially:

> We had hoped better results would have followed the nomination of Mr. Cartwright. But "General Apathy" seems to have controlled the Democratic Party—and wherever he is commander-in-chief, defeat ensues as a natural consequence. Better luck next time.

The campaign experience clearly was not one of Cartwright's favorites. In 1856 he published his autobiography. It contained over five hundred pages but curiously no reference to Lincoln, the man who had defeated him ten years before. Nor does it mention Cartwright's congressional candidacy.

With his seat in Congress assured, Lincoln waited for the first session of the 30th Congress to convene. He had a long wait, for Congress would not meet until December 1847—sixteen months hence.

Results of the 1846 Congressional Election

County	Lincoln	Cartwright	Walcott
Cass	546	489	—
Logan	390	166	—
Marshall	252	323	21
Mason	330	294	
Menard	456	336	—
Morgan	979	949	18
Putnam	216	213	139
Sangamon	1,535	845	14
Scott	602	478	—
Tazewell	819	436	42
Woodford	215	300	15
TOTAL	6,340	4,829	249

3

"The new party had no principle."

THE PRESENCE OF A Liberty party candidate in the 1846 congressional election for Illinois' 7th District may not have concerned Lincoln or Peter Cartwright, but it was a portent of the future. While the issues of tariffs, a National Bank, and internal improvements dominated politics through the early 1840s, slavery began rapidly to emerge as a key center of political controversy. That issue ultimately led to the virtual destruction of the existing major political parties.

Antislavery sentiment was not particularly new. There had been opponents of slavery for as long as there had been slaves. Initially, however, most of the opposition to slavery sprang from deeply held moral beliefs, articulated primarily by religious groups—most notably the Society of Friends, or Quakers. As the years passed, antislavery sentiment grew slowly but steadily. A watershed came during the Revolutionary War period when the lofty rhetoric of revolution espoused the enlightenment concepts of liberty and freedom. More than a few colonists perceived the paradox of a thriving institution of slavery in a country striving to set itself free.

In the years that followed the Revolution, as a new nation struggled to establish an enduring government, the problem of slavery came up again and again. Most of the New England states had enacted emancipation measures, but that involved little sacrifice since slavery was economically unsuited for the small rocky farms that dotted the northern countryside. The South, however, insisted on maintaining its slave system. During the debates at the Constitutional Convention, northern and southern delegates clashed constantly on the problem.

Eventually, the delegates hammered out a compromise. Slavery could continue, but only three-fifths of the slaves were to be counted in determining how many representatives a state would be entitled to in Congress. And, significantly, Article V of the Constitution provided that after 1808 the African slave trade could be abolished. It seemed clear that the delegates, while willing to accommodate the South to some extent, envisioned the eventual extinction of slavery in the not-too-distant future. And even in the South, slavery had become less and less economical as a system of labor. Agricultural processes that drained the soil were limiting the crops that could be produced. Cotton, the primary cash crop, required a great deal of labor, particularly in removing seeds, and even the use of slaves for this work made less and less economic sense.

The cotton gin—*drastically changed the economics of slavery. (Smithsonian)*

The invention of the cotton gin in 1791, however, drastically changed the economics of slavery. By providing a mechanical means of removing seeds, a large number of slaves could be freed to pick the cotton, enabling planters to grow larger and larger cotton crops. In the wake of this development, the institution of slavery flourished anew. Interstate slave trading grew, and natural increases in the slave population kept a thriving market supplied. The withering of slavery anticipated by the framers of the Constitution never materialized.

Opponents of slavery were still few in the early nineteenth century and still associated for the most part with churches. Several religious denominations split over the issue of slavery. Congregations of individual churches often divided into pro- and anti-slavery factions. In fact, at one time Thomas Lincoln ended his affiliation with a church when his personal antislavery convictions conflicted with the opinions of the majority of his fellow churchmen. At the time his son Abe was an impressionable lad of seven.

The only substantial nonreligious organization with antislavery leanings to emerge in this period was the American Colonization Society. Founded in 1816 by such prominent men as Daniel Webster, James Monroe, Lincoln's political idol Henry Clay, and John Marshall, the society had as its object the voluntary freeing of slaves by willing owners, and the relocation of the freed men to Africa. While the society sought to encourage emancipation and colonization, its philosophy was nonetheless predicated on racism. Believing blacks to be inferior, the society sought to remove them entirely from the United States. As a side benefit, it hoped colonized blacks would begin to Christianize Africa. During the administration of James Monroe, the colony of Liberia came into being, and the society began its work of repatriation. Congress helped this work along by passing a law providing that slaves captured in the illegal slave trade would be sent to Liberia. Still, the venture obviously could never fulfill its objectives. The cost of transporting blacks to Liberia was high, and while dues, bequests from conscience-stricken slaveholders, and other fund-raising activities provided funds for the colonization of thousands of blacks, the society had set itself an impossible goal. Nevertheless, for all its racism and limitations, the Colonization Society became the starting point for the antislavery careers of many of the prominent abolitionists of the 1830s and 1840s.

Meanwhile, the religious sects that gave birth to the antislavery movement continued to exert a pervasive influence. Evangelical proselytizing in the West led to thousands of revivals and religious meetings, and the stream of converts turned with zeal to a wide variety of reform movements. Naturally the institution of slavery became a target of their moral and religious fervor.

As the antislavery sentiment developed in the West in the wake of the revival movement, it began to sweep eastward. By 1829 the antislavery cause had enlisted a young man from Massachusetts, William Lloyd Garrison, destined to become the most strident voice in the abolitionist camp. In Ohio a young Salmon P. Chase began a public career by speaking out against slavery, and in New York William H. Seward, future Governor and Secretary of State in Lincoln's presidential administration, attracted attention with his antislavery sentiments. Several state abolition societies formed, and the antislavery movement rapidly gained momentum.

By 1833 the antislavery movement had reached a point that required some national institutionalization in order to harness effectively the energies of the growing band of hard-working zealots. Accordingly, in December 1833, sixty-two antislavery men held a meeting in Philadelphia and formed the American Anti-Slavery Society. At this early stage there were several different antislavery philosophies, and all were represented in the society. Some wanted gradual, compensated emancipation; others added colonization to those aims; more radical abolitionists sought immediate, uncompensated emancipation; and a few pushed for the extension of suffrage to blacks as well. But these diverse elements united in one thing—opposition to slavery.

In the years that followed its founding, the American Anti-Slavery Society established a network of state and local chapters, wrote tracts, petitioned Congress frequently, and tried to publicize the inhumanity of slavery through lectures, slave narratives, and the columns of antislavery newspapers. These developments did not go unnoticed by slave owners and their supporters. Several southern states enacted laws prohibiting the sale or distribution of abolitionist tracts and providing for stiff fines or harsh penalties for offenders. Frequent bonfires in the South were made when abolitionist literature came to the local post office. Slave codes, which generally prohibited teaching slaves to read or write, were enforced with greater determination than ever.

Southern resistance and opposition to abolitionist doctrines could also be attributed to growing restiveness among slaves. In 1822 evidence of a massive slave revolt under the leadership of Denmark Vesey, a free Negro, was uncovered in South Carolina.

Just two years before the creation of the American Anti-Slavery Society, slave owners were struck with terror when Nat Turner led a slave uprising in Southampton, Virginia. Turner, a slave preacher, and a small group of disciples roamed the countryside for two or three days and killed over sixty whites. In retaliation, twenty blacks were hanged and a dozen others were removed from

The American Anti-Slavery Society—*united in one thing . . . (Library of Congress)*

. . . the inhumanity of slavery. (Library of Congress)

Discovery of Nat Turner.

Nat Turner—*grim specter of rebellion. (Library of Congress)*

the area. The grim specter of rebellion and uprising fueled the vigor with which slave owners resisted the spread of abolitionist teachings.

Slave owners were not the only ones standing against the abolitionists. Antiabolitionist demonstrations and riots broke out in the North and border states as well. On October 2, 1833, over a thousand New Yorkers mobbed a church in the wake of abolitionist lectures by William Lloyd Garrison and Lewis Tappan. In 1833 in Connecticut and in New Hampshire, mobs thwarted abolitionist efforts to establish integrated schools. In 1836 James G. Birney, editor of the abolitionist Cincinnati *Philanthropist,* had to wade through mobs angered by his antislavery editorializing in order to reach his office.

Perhaps the most notorious antiabolitionist incident of the 1830s was the murder of Elijah Lovejoy in Alton, Illinois. Lovejoy, a native of Maine, edited the Alton *Observer,* an unyielding abolitionist newspaper. On several occasions angry townsmen had thrown Lovejoy's presses into the Mississippi River. Proslavery sentiment was strong in Alton, and Lovejoy's vehement abolitionism did not sit well with his fellow citizens. Finally, on November 7, 1837, a mob set Lovejoy's plant on fire and a member of the mob shot and killed Lovejoy as he tried to protect his property. Shortly afterward, in a speech to the Young Men's Lyceum in Springfield, Illinois, Abraham Lincoln delivered an address deploring the murder as an example of "mobocratic spirit," the increasing lawlessness that

47

Elijah Lovejoy—his *vehement abolitionism did not sit well with his fellow
citizens. (Alton Telegraph)*

The Mob attacking the Warehouse of Godfrey Gilman & Co. Alton Ill. on the Night of the 7th Nov. 1837

Lovejoy was killed by "mobocratic spirit." *(Library of Congress)*

was spreading throughout the country. Editorials nationwide condemned the
murder of Lovejoy, although seldom expressing support of his antislavery views.

Yet the violence with which the abolitionists were attacked yielded some
surprising dividends. The attacks—widely reported in the public press as well as
in abolitionist papers—earned the abolitionists some sorely needed sympathy
from less radical critics of slavery. In addition, the violence prompted several
hitherto reluctant abolitionists to throw in their lot with the American Anti-
Slavery Society. The most significant convert was Gerrit Smith, a wealthy

Gerrit Smith—*poured thousands of dollars into abolitionist coffers. (Library of Congress)*

philanthropist who afterward poured thousands of dollars into abolitionist coffers.

Thus far the American Anti-Slavery Society had made little effort to inject its cause into politics. Antislavery men belonged to both major political parties, the Whigs and the Democrats (though it should be noted that there were more antislavery adherents in the Whig party than in the Democratic party), and several noted abolitionists had been elected to Congress. In Congress antislavery members raised the issue of slavery. John Quincy Adams unrelentingly fought the gag rule that prevented the presentation of antislavery petitions; Joshua R. Giddings lashed out continually at the proslavery forces in the House of Representatives, as did John Parker Hale in the Senate. All these men played their antislavery roles while retaining their identification with traditional political parties.

Neither major party took a strong position on slavery, however, and inevitably the abolitionists began to consider the possibility of creating a third party devoted solely to abolitionist principles. This caused the abolitionists to split into two factions. One group, nettled by the radical rhetoric of William Lloyd Garrison, wanted to try and effect change through political action. Garrison and his followers, on the other hand, were completely devoted to the somewhat contradictory causes of immediate emancipation and the need for moral persuasion to change people's attitudes on the question of slavery. They felt that entering the political arena would lead to excessive compromise and possibly corruption.

These factions had their showdown at an American Anti-Slavery Society convention in 1840. At the end, Garrison had won. The defeated faction withdrew from the society and created a separate group, the American and Foreign Anti-Slavery Society under the leadership of Lewis Tappan, and embarked on a course of political activism.

In April 1840, a convention met in Albany, New York, and nominated James G. Birney and Thomas Earle as candidates for President and Vice-President respectively. As an abolitionist nominee for the Presidency, Birney was an admirable choice. Born in 1792 in Kentucky, the son of a wealthy slave owner, he attended Princeton and then returned to the South to establish his own plantation in Alabama. Active in Alabama politics, he came to oppose slavery and became an agent for the American Colonization Society. His views continued to shift, however, and he came to believe in immediate emancipation, became a local agent in Kentucky for the American Anti-Slavery Society, and shortly afterward a Vice-President of the society. In 1835 he moved to Cincinnati due to the hostility he encountered in Kentucky, and there began publishing the *Philanthropist*. Even there angry mobs surrounded his offices, threatening his life. He finally moved to New York to take a position as corresponding secretary for the American Anti-Slavery Society. His nomination reflected his long-standing and bitter opposition to the radicalism of Garrison. Thomas Earle, Birney's running mate, was a Philadelphia merchant and lawyer. A vigorous proponent of extending the franchise to Negroes, he occasionally served as the editor of the *Columbian Observer* and other antislavery newspapers.

A new party had been created, and presented its candidates. Dubbed the Liberty party by supporter Gerrit Smith, the fledgling party set out on its first political foray. The 1840 campaign, however, turned into a disaster for it. Inexperienced in politics, the men who conducted the campaign were generally inept. Too, the wide popularity of Whig candidate William Henry Harrison's Log Cabin and Hard Cider campaign vastly overshadowed abolitionist appeals. Nonetheless, the Liberty party did salvage something from the campaign. If they were inexperienced when the campaign began, the abolitionists surely learned a great deal. They renominated Birney early in 1841 for the 1844 presidential race, and with three years to organize, prepare, and campaign, they hoped for a more respectable vote than the meager 7,000 that Birney received in 1840.

Birney accepted the second nomination, and in the 1844 election he garnered 62,000 votes of the 2,600,000 cast. In spite of this slim showing, the Liberty party was having a profound impact on the American political scene. The campaign in 1844 had pitted Henry Clay against dark horse candidate James K. Polk. If Birney had not been a candidate, the Liberty party votes would undoubtedly have gone to Whig candidate Clay, and in New York these votes made a crucial difference. In that state the Liberty party siphoned just enough support away from Clay to send New York's electoral votes—and thus the close election—to Polk.

Beyond this, antislavery men in the Whig and Democratic parties were becoming increasingly adamant in their demands that their own parties take a stand on slavery. If the parties failed to do so, there was now another party to which they could turn.

At the same time the Liberty party had internal problems. While virtually all

Neither major party took a strong position on slavery. *(Library of Congress)*

William Lloyd Garrison—*radical rhetoric* *(Library of Congress)*

James G. Birney—his 62,000 votes were slim but profound. *(Library of Congress)*

Free-Soiler Martin Van Buren—Lincoln campaigned against "spoiler" antislavery parties. *(Library of Congress)*

the Liberty men agreed that slavery should be abolished, on most other issues they aligned with either the Democrats or Whigs. This created some confusing—and amusing—contradictions. Among proposals for the Liberty party platform were suggestions that the party support prohibition and that it oppose prohibition; that suffrage be extended and that it be restricted; that internal improvements be expanded or ignored. Clearly the Liberty party suffered from its inability to agree on anything but the slavery issue.

As the 1848 elections approached, disagreement even over the slavery issue arose within the Liberty party. The Mexican War had resulted in the acquisition of substantial territory from Mexico, and the question of the extension of slavery into the new territories became an immediate issue. Within the Liberty party there were members who wanted to focus their efforts on ensuring that slavery did not spread. They were opposed by doctrinal purists who maintained that the party should not be diverted from its efforts to push for immediate abolition everywhere.

In addition, dissension within the major parties over the slavery issue grew as the campaign approached. The Whig party nominated Zachary Taylor for the Presidency. His major asset lay in his appeal as a Mexican War military hero, but abolitionists within the party were appalled by the fact that he was also a Louisiana slaveholder. Democratic antislavery men were increasingly disturbed by the continued southern dominance of their party. On August 9, 1848, disaffected Whigs, antislavery Democrats (frequently referred to as Barnburners), and various Liberty party members assembled in Buffalo, New York, and created a new party, the Free-Soil party, so-called because of its slogan "Free Soil, Free Speech, Free Labor and Free men."

The Free-Soilers were more moderate than the Liberty party. They opposed the extension of slavery but stopped short of calling for immediate abolition. This moderated antislavery viewpoint was bound to have a broader appeal than simply clamoring for instant emancipation. In a pointedly symbolic act, the convention nominated a Democrat, former President Martin Van Buren, for President and a Whig, Charles Francis Adams, for Vice-President. Seeing the broader appeal of the Free-Soil party, the Liberty party, which had nominated Gerrit Smith for President several months earlier, withdrew its own candidate and threw its support to the Free-Soil party. Election day proved the wisdom of this course of action. The Free-Soilers received nearly 300,000 votes—almost five times as many as the Liberty party in 1844.

The significance of the Free-Soil vote in 1848 escaped no one. Zachary Taylor won the election by fewer than 150,000 votes. Had the Free-Soil party chosen a more attractive candidate than Van Buren, enough votes might have been taken away from Taylor to have thrown the election to Lewis Cass, his Democratic opponent. The antislavery movement, if not yet strong enough to win a presidential election, had proven once again that it could be a "spoiler" for other candidates.

To a devoted party man like Lincoln, the politicization of the antislavery movement between 1840 and 1848 was disturbing. Lincoln had seen firsthand the virtues of unification in politics and the disaster that splinter groups and factions could cause. Lincoln spelled out his reactions to the new party in a letter to a Putnam County Liberty man, Williamson Durley, shortly after the defeat of Henry Clay in 1844, in an election in which Lincoln worked diligently on behalf of Clay:

> If the Whig abolitionists of New York had voted with us last fall, Mr. Clay would now be President, Whig principles in the ascendant, and Texas not annexed; whereas by the division, all that either had at stake in the contest, was lost. And, indeed, it was extremely probable, beforehand, that such would be the result. As I always understood, the Liberty-men deprecated the annexation of Texas extremely; and, this being so, why they should refuse to so cast their votes as to prevent it, even to me, seemed wonderful. What was their process of reasoning, I can only judge from what a single one of them told me. It was this: "We are not to do *evil* that *good* may come." This general proposition is doubtless correct; but did it apply? If by your votes you could have prevented the *extention*, &c. of slavery, would it not have been *good* and not *evil* so to have used your votes, even though it involved the casting of them for a slaveholder? By the *fruit* of electing Mr. Clay would have been to prevent the extension of slavery, could the act of electing have been *evil?* . . .
>
> To recur to the Texas question, I understand the Liberty men to have viewed annexation as a much greater evil than I ever did; and I, would like to convince you if I could, that they could have prevented it without violation of principle, if they had chosen.

In the 1848 campaign, in which he spoke frequently in Maryland, Massachusetts, and Illinois, Lincoln returned again and again to this theme; in his view, voting for a Liberty or a Free-Soil candidate had virtually the same effect as voting for the Democratic candidate. Time and again, according to the Boston *Daily Advertiser*, he charged that "the new party had no principle."

Ultimately Lincoln failed, not because of any lack of wisdom in his viewpoint, but because the issue of slavery became paramount, and both major political parties tried to avoid it. By failing to take a stand on the slavery issue, the Whig and Democratic parties created a void. That void demanded the creation of a new political party, a party that addressed the single issue that men cared most about—slavery. First came the Liberty party, then the Free-Soilers, and, finally, the Republican party.

Still, as Lincoln prepared to go to Congress, the struggle over slavery lay in the future. For the moment other events demanded his time.

4

"Being elected . . . has not pleased me."

SIXTEEN MONTHS ELAPSED between Lincoln's election to Congress and the day he actually took office. It was a long interlude. It could have been much shorter, only four months, instead of sixteen.

Lincoln could have been sworn in as Congressman a full year ahead of schedule. The opportunity came because of a resignation. His friend and political ally Congressman Edward D. Baker became caught up in the Mexican War fever that struck the nation. At the end of the first session of the 29th Congress, he resigned his seat in Congress to lead a regiment of Illinois volunteers in Mexico.

The vacancy had to be filled; a successor had to be chosen in a special election.

On December 30 Whig Members of the legislature from Sangamon County met in the office of the *Sangamo Journal* to select a candidate. They asked Lincoln if he wanted the nomination. Recently voted a full term in Congress by an unprecedented margin, he would have easily won the special election. Lincoln declined.

Why he rejected the offer stands as one of the great mysteries of his life. No explanation appears in his correspondence nor in the notes of others. The *Journal* was silent on the question.

Sangamon Whigs then proposed Judge William Brown of Springfield for the vacancy. This brought protests from Whigs in Morgan County and Brown withdrew.

John Henry of Jacksonville, one of those who objected to Brown, eventually won approval by a caucus of Whigs in the legislature. In the special election on January 20 Henry defeated Democrat J. W. Crosby and Liberty candidate Arch Job. Henry had presented himself in the campaign as a poor man who badly needed the congressional mileage allowance. He became known derisively in some quarters as the "mileage Congressman." Lincoln voted for Henry. Thus Henry, not Lincoln, went off to Washington for the second session of the 29th Congress.

Why did Lincoln decide not to go? No single reason, or combination, seems adequate.

Was it the pressure of legal business? He certainly spent much of the sixteen-month interlude traveling the judicial circuit and practicing before the Illinois Supreme Court in Springfield. Assumpsit cases, damage suits, and an occasional divorce claimed his time. Perhaps he did not want to leave this business in the

John Henry pleaded poverty and was chosen to succeed E. D. Baker in Congress. *(Illinois State Historical Library)*

hands of his partner, Billy Herndon, but he never before—nor after—allowed the pressure of legal business to deter him from political activity.

Perhaps he had made a promise to Mary. This too is unlikely. Why would Mary wish to delay the "bright prospects" for her man? In fact, soon after his election, Mary was going about Springfield confidently predicting her husband one day would be President. If there were domestic reasons—health, financial, or otherwise—to justify the delay in going to Washington such does not appear.

Other things needed attention. Lincoln wanted to clear away the attack on his religious beliefs. He had to rent his house, make travel plans. None of these suffice to explain why he turned down the extra year in Congress.

The Lincoln home—*palatial when contrasted with the other places he had called home. (Library of Congress)*

Had he accepted the offer to go to Washington in 1846, the extra year would have given Lincoln a distinct advantage over those who were to enter office for the first time with the 30th Congress. He would have had the year to learn the procedures and traditions of the House of Representatives, the physical layout of the Capitol, the departments of government, and the city itself.

Most important of all he would have been able to establish in that year a valuable acquaintance with the personalities of the Congress and their differing reactions to the issues confronting the nation.

This extra year would have brought other advantages. For that extra twelve months he would have been Congressman, not just Congressman-elect. Capitol Hill would have provided him with a national platform from which to advance his ideas. All that year he would have been able to use the considerable advantages of office, and particularly the mailing privilege—the congressional frank. This would have given him unlimited use of the postal service to distribute his correspondence, printed copies of speeches, and other public documents. When Lincoln finally took office a year later, he was among the most avid users of the frank.

Perhaps the decision not to go to Washington a year early was made during one of the periods of deep depression and melancholy that occasionally seized him. For three long years he had focused all his energies on getting elected to Congress. Now that he had reached this goal, perhaps he had second thoughts. He enjoyed his life in central Illinois. He had a growing law practice and a family. His house on 8th and Jackson was better than average for Springfield—palatial when contrasted with the other places he had called home.

Washington was a long way off—a different, unknown world. Would he really like life there? Would Mary and the boys like it? Would he be a nobody, of little recognition and influence in Washington? Would he get along? Questions like these may have given him pause.

In October, just a few weeks after his election, he observed in a letter, "Being elected to Congress . . . has not pleased me as much as I expected." This may have been because his election had been anticlimactic. After Hardin withdrew there had been no real contest. The letdown may have been deep, perhaps inspiring a lingering melancholy, a troubled questioning of whether he really wanted to go to Congress after all.

Or, perhaps, "turn about is fair play" restrained him. He had argued forcefully that the office should be passed around and now he may have felt obligated to let the year of Baker's term go to someone else.

In any event, he kept busy during the long interlude. Immediately after the election he arranged for the publication of his handbill responding to the scurrilous rumors of his atheism. On August 15 it appeared in the Illinois Gazette. It is the only public statement Lincoln ever made regarding his religious views:

> A charge having got into circulation in some of the neighborhoods of this District, in substance that I am an open scoffer at Christianity, I have by the advice of some friends concluded to notice the subject in this form. That I am not a member of any Christian Church, is true; but I have never denied the truth of the Scriptures; and I have never spoken with intentional disrespect of religion in general, or of any denomination of Christians in particular. It is true that in early life I was inclined to believe in what I understand is called the "Doctrine of Necessity"—that is, that the human mind is impelled to action, or held in rest by some power, over which the mind itself has no control; and I have sometimes (with one, two or three, but never publicly) tried to maintain this opinion in argument. The habit of arguing thus however, I have entirely left off for more than five years. And I add here, I have always understood this same opinion to be held by several of the Christian denominations. The foregoing is the whole truth, briefly stated, in relationship to myself, upon this subject.
>
> I do not think I could myself, be brought to support a man for office, whom I knew to be an open enemy of, and scoffer at, religion. Leaving the higher matter of eternal consequences, between him and his maker, I still do not think any man has the right thus to insult the feelings, and injure the morals, of the community in which he may live. If then, I was guilty of such conduct, I should blame no man who should condemn me for it; but I do blame those, whoever they may be, who falsely put such a charge in circulation against me.

Lincoln did not, however, blame Cartwright or his family for the accusation. He was convinced that Cartwright had never approved of its circulation. In fact, the campaign left him with no grudge or bitterness toward Cartwright. Years after his congressional campaign, in 1859, Lincoln defended Cartwright's grandson against a murder charge. In an 1885 letter to Jesse Weik, William H. Herndon described the case:

> About 1859 there lived in a village about 17 miles west of [Springfield] two young men of the first families. One of the young men was named Quinn Harrison, grandson of the Reverend Peter Cartwright. The other was named Greek Crafton, a young lawyer who studied law with Lincoln and Herndon. . . . There seemed to be a long-existing feud between the families . . . at least between the boys. . . . The young men met in a store in Pleasant Plains one day by accident and some hot words passed between the two. Crafton struck and gathered Quinn Harrison and threw him. Harrison in the scuffle got out his knife, cut and stabbed Crafton fatally. . . . Harrison was arrested and a grand jury found an indictment against Harrison for murder. Lincoln, Logan and others were employed by Harrison. Governor Palmer and the State's attorney prosecuted. The lawyers on both sides were among the most able in the state. . . . During the trial . . . the court . . . decided a question against Lincoln's view of the law. . . . Lincoln could not stand the absurd decision . . . and in his anger he rose up and seemed inspired with indignation. . . . He . . . spoke fiercely, strongly, contemptuously of the decision of the court. . . . I shall never forget that scene. Lincoln had the crowd, the jury, the bar in perfect sympathy and accord. The court's decision was ridiculed, scoffed and kicked out of court. Lincoln was mad, vexed and indignant. When a great big man of mind and body gets mad he is mad all over, terrible furious, eloquent.

The Illinois *Gazette* approved of Lincoln's response to the charge that he was an infidel. *(Library of Congress)*

MR. LINCOLN.

We are gratified to be able, this week, through our columns, to repel the imputation cast upon the moral character of Mr. Lincoln, our congressional Representative elect, to injure his election—we refer to the charge against him of infidelity. But few in this county were apprised of the story prior to the election—it was generally rumored soon after. We, in common with most of Mr. L.'s friends, did not believe the charge; and we felt confident that the *enquiry* respecting it, in our last paper, would lead to its refutation. In this we were not mistaken, for we have received a letter, together with a handbill, denying the charge, which we spread before our readers.

Mr. Lincoln is right in supposing that Mr. Cartwright circulated the story in this county, and also that he, Mr. L., lost some votes thereby. It appears the Rev. gentleman circulated the same story in other parts of the District. Well, this is novel business for a minister of the Gospel. It is quite bad enough for one sustaining that high office to meddle with politics at all; but when in the canvass he descends from the arena of honorable warfare to revel in the filth of defamation and falsehood, what shall we say of his character as a man, and what the world of the religion he professes?

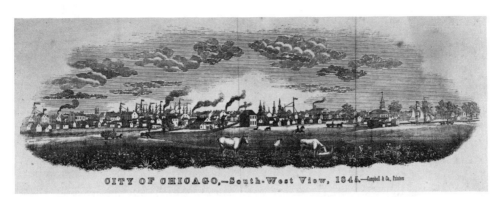

City of Chicago—denied a harbor due to Polk's veto. *(Library of Congress)*

Lincoln's persuasiveness carried the day, and the jury acquitted Cartwright's grandson on the grounds of self-defense.

Matters of public concern, as well as legal business, took up some of Lincoln's time too.

The summer of 1847 provided Lincoln an opportunity to mingle with the great and near great before leaving for Washington.

Among the issues of deep concern to Illinois and other western states were internal improvements. Even though these improvements had virtually bankrupted the state of Illinois, Lincoln remained a staunch advocate. A river and harbor bill containing additional internal improvements for Illinois and the rest of the nation had been passed by the 29th Congress but vetoed by Democratic President James K. Polk. A ground swell of opposition to Polk's decision resulted in the calling of a river and harbor convention to protest the veto. It was held in Chicago where eight thousand dollars for improvement of the harbor had been lost because of the veto. Learning of the convention, Lincoln hurriedly purchased stock in a proposed railroad between Springfield and Alton, and the directors of the railroad made him a delegate to the convention.

On July 1, 1847, Lincoln left Springfield to attend the convention and visit Chicago for the first time. Horace Greeley, covering the event for the New York *Tribune* reported that it was probably the largest meeting ever held in the United States. About five thousand attended, a number greater than the population of the host city. It convened on July 5 and adjourned on July 7. Although it did not last long, the convention drew a distinguished group of participants. Included were Lincoln's future Attorney General, Edward Bates; U.S. Senator Thomas Corwin of Ohio; and Judge David Dudley Field of New York.

Not all the delegates agreed on policy. On July 6 Field spoke to the convention and criticized the enormity of some of the internal improvements endorsed by the convention. As the New York *Tribune* reported: "In the afternoon, Hon. Abraham Lincoln, a tall specimen of an Illinoisan . . . was called out, and spoke briefly and happily in reply to Mr. Field."

The river and harbor convention also gave Lincoln his famous nickname "Old Abe." Elihu B. Washburne recalled years later that:

> One afternoon, several of us sat on the sidewalk under the balcony of the Sherman House, and among the number was the accomplished scholar and unrivaled orator, Lisle Smith. He suddenly interrupted the conversation by exclaiming "There is Lincoln on the other side of the street. Just look at 'Old Abe.'" No one who saw him can forget his personal appearance at that time. Tall, angular and awkward, he had on a short-waisted, thin swallowtail coat, a short vest of the same material, thin pantaloons scarcely coming to his ankles, a straw hat and a pair of brogans with woolen socks.

Before going to Chicago, Lincoln had made at least two trips to a dry-goods store in Springfield. On June 23 he bought two and one-half yards of black cloth for $15 and coat trimmings for $2.62. On June 29 he bought a pair of suspenders for $1.25. If these items were in the wardrobe that Lincoln displayed at the convention they did not have their intended effect.

After he returned from Chicago, Lincoln had the more somber duty of attending the funeral of his recent rival, John J. Hardin. Deprived of the opportunity of a second term in Congress, Hardin had, like his successor, Congressman Baker, sought adventure on the battlefields of Mexico. There he died a hero's death in a gallant charge at the battle of Buena Vista in February 1847. Lincoln conducted a meeting in Jacksonville in April offering resolutions of sympathy and regret for Hardin's death and doubtless attended the funeral. If the occasion was somber, however, the activities of the townspeople belied that fact. In the frontier community of Jacksonville residents eagerly seized almost any occasion as an excuse for festivities. J. G. Buckingham, Mr. Lincoln's stage companion, witnessed Hardin's funeral and left this impression:

> This day is devoted to the *solemn* duty of depositing in the grave the remains of Colonel Hardin, which have been brought from Mexico for that purpose. . . . But it is in fact *a gala day*. There is no solemnity. A country muster in old times, was as nothing to it. This is a temperance town, and no liquor is allowed to be sold in its precincts, but yet drunken men and boys are abundant, and noisy. Last night a military company marched into town from Springfield, and to-day it has marched off to the strains of gay music, towards the former residence of the dead, to take up and escort the procession. . . . The square is over-run with mounted marshals, dressed with enormous white sashes, who are curvetting and galloping about in every direction, apparently with no other object in view than to show themselves off.

Perhaps a rival had been eliminated, but Lincoln had lost in Hardin's death a close political associate as well.

Temperance exhortation also occupied part of his time. During the spring and summer of 1847 Lincoln spoke, with mixed results, at meetings of the Sangamon

County Temperance Union. On May 30 he and J. B. Weber provided the program. According to the minutes of the meeting, the attendance was fair. Most of those present had already signed a pledge of abstinence, but three new converts were enrolled.

On June 20 he joined S. S. Brooks on the platform. According to the minutes, "Interesting meeting. Mr. Lincoln made an excellent address—none signed pledges." On August 30 he shared the program with H. Robinson. One listener signed up.

The year 1847 also found Lincoln busy with his law practice. Damage suits, divorce and larceny cases, writing contracts, and mortgages occupied his time. In addition to taking part in the trial of cases throughout the circuit, he practiced before the state supreme court and the United States district court, the latter conveniently located on the floor below his law office.

On April 15 he defended George Kerr, Sr., and J. Randolph Scott against charges of aiding a fugitive slave. The judge dismissed the case when Lincoln argued that the Negro in the case could not be proved to be a slave.

On June 16 the Springfield circuit court ruled that his clients Reynolds and Walker had to pay a nine hundred dollar debt but owed only one cent in damages. How much Lincoln's fee exceeded the amount of damages was not recorded.

Not until autumn did Lincoln direct his attention to the coming trip to Washington. On October 23 he signed a lease under which D. Ludlum rented the Lincoln house in Springfield for one year beginning November 1. Ludlum paid ninety dollars for the entire year, but the Lincolns reserved the "north up stairs room" for the storage of furniture. The house at that time had only one full floor with two attic rooms upstairs.

Two days later, October 25, Lincoln, Mary, and the children boarded a stagecoach for Saint Louis. Their departure was noted in the Lacon, Illinois, *Gazette* on October 30:

> Mr. Lincoln, the member of Congress-elect from this district has just set out on his way to the city of Washington. His family is with him; they intend to visit their friends and relatives in Kentucky before they take the line of march for the seat of government. Success to our talented member of Congress! He will find many men in Congress who possess twice the good looks, and not half the good sense, of our own representative.

Stagecoach journeys in Illinois imposed many hardships on travelers. Even a two- or three-day journey would tax the patience of Job. One observer noted that "strangers in Buffalo complained of the impositions, the lies, and the impudence of . . . steamboat captains, but I will put an Illinois stage agent or driver against anything that I ever saw before, in Europe or America, and bet odds upon him for impudence and imposition." Usually overcrowded, stages made uncertain progress, and accommodations along the way were uneven at

61

At St. Louis, the Lincolns boarded a steamboat . . . (Missouri Historical Society)

best. The route from Springfield to St. Louis included stops at Jacksonville and White Hall, although it is not known whether the Lincolns stopped at either. If they did, it probably was at White Hall. The facilities there, according to one contemporary account, were:

> Neat and clean, everybody is attentive, the supper has been well got up, and abundant in variety, as well as excellent in quality. The name of the landlord is Tracy, and he and his wife deserve to be remembered and to be made known to the traveling community.

From White Hall, the stage route led to Alton and then across the Mississippi River by ferry to St. Louis.

The Lincolns spent the night of October 27 at the Scott Hotel on the corner of 3rd and Market streets. Also spending the night there was Joshua F. Speed, the man who had welcomed Lincoln to Springfield years before, provided him with his first Springfield sleeping quarters on credit, and had been his confidant during periods of melancholy and romantic stress. Now he had taken the trouble to go to St. Louis to see the Lincolns off on their momentous journey to Washington.

At St. Louis the Lincolns boarded a steamboat to Frankfort, Kentucky. The boat provided relief from the stagecoach. Conditions were less crowded, the river less jolting than the roads, and if the captains were surly they could not have been worse than the stage drivers. The journey lasted about a week, and about November 2 the Lincolns arrived in Lexington. Mary Todd's half sister, Emilie, later recalled her first encounter with the future President:

> The whole family stood near the front door with welcoming arms and, in true patriarchal style, our colored contingent filled the rear hall to shake hands with the long absent one and "make a'miration" over the babies. Mary came in first with little Eddie, the baby, in her arms. To my mind she was lovely; clear, sparkling blue eyes, lovely smooth white skin with a faint, wild rose color in her cheeks, and glossy light brown hair, which fell in soft short curls behind each ear. She was then about twenty-nine years of age.
>
> Mr. Lincoln followed her into the hall with his little son, Robert Todd, in his arms. He put the little fellow on the floor, and as he arose, I remember thinking of "Jack and the Bean Stalk," and feared he might be the hungry giant of the story—he was so tall and looked so big with a long, full black cloak over his shoulders, and he wore a fur cap with ear straps which allowed but little of his face to be seen. Expecting to hear the "fe, fi, fo, fum," I shrank closer to my mother and tried to hide behind her voluminous skirts. After shaking hands with all the grownups, he turned and, lifting me in his arms, said "So this is little sister." His voice and smile banished my fear of the giant.

The Lincolns stayed in Lexington for about three weeks, the first real vacation in years. But Lincoln did not merely rest and relax. In Lexington he renewed and expanded his limited acquaintance with the institution of slavery. He took advantage of the opportunity to examine it closely.

Whether by stagecoach or steamboat—*journeys in Illinois imposed many hardships on travelers. (Library of Congress)*

Slavery had been in existence in North America for roughly two hundred years. During that period a wide number of beliefs, customs, practices, and traditions had developed that had been incorporated into "Black Codes" adopted by the slaveholding states. Most provided, for example, that slaves should not be permitted to learn to read or write; their marriages were not recognized by law; they were not permitted to gather in groups or travel at night without a pass from their owner. Enforcement of the codes was sometimes lax, but always harsh and strict following a slave insurrection or the threat of one.

Main Street in Lexington, where the institution of slavery—*did not coincide with the cruel picture of bondage . . . circulated by the abolition societies. (Mrs. William H. Townsend)*

Robert S. Todd residence—*in true patriarchal style. (Transylvania University Library)*

Slave cabins in Kentucky like those on the Todd plantation. *(J. Winston Coleman, Jr.)*

The treatment slaves received at the hands of their overseers and owners varied from plantation to plantation. On some, slaves received consideration and kindness. They had adequate food, clothing, shelter, and medical care. Punishment was meted out judiciously and temperately. On other plantations, however, a darker picture emerges. Slaves lived in hovels, had inadequate clothing, and were fed just enough to sustain life. Cruel whippings and beatings were frequent and slaves occasionally died under the lash. Children could be sold apart from their parents as soon as they were old enough to travel. Between these two extremes, there were many gradations.

Yet no direct correlation between the harshness of treatment and the urge to seek freedom existed. Some of the best treated slaves ran away, tried to poison their masters, or plotted insurrection. Some of the most harshly treated slaves seemed to be the most docile and contented. Still the surface cheerfulness, the melodic spirituals, and the subservient demeanor can all be attributed to the

Lexington's slave auction—*where Lincoln's father-in-law bought and sold. (University of Kentucky Library)*

practice of "puttin' ole massa on." The fugitive slave laws and the repressive slave codes all testify mutely to the slave owner's fears of his slaves.

On the Todd plantation, Lincoln saw the more benevolent side of the slave system. The Todds owned numerous slaves, and treated them well. The house servants became in many ways a part of the family. The institution of slavery Lincoln saw in Lexington did not coincide with the cruel picture of bondage that appeared in the slave narratives circulated by the abolition societies— particularly the eloquent condemnation of the institution by a Baltimore slave named Frederick Douglass that appeared shortly after Lincoln took his seat in Congress. Yet beneath the serene façade that Lexington presented, there were troubling undercurrents.

In the middle of the public square in Lexington stood a slave auction block. Nearby, a public whipping post reminded the slaves of the punishment they would receive if they overstepped boundaries—if they failed to "stay in their place." News articles in the Lexington papers revealed the deep but submerged hostility between slave and owner. A young slave girl named Cassily, for example, had been indicted for mixing an ounce of ground glass with the gravy for dinner and serving it to her master. A few days after Lincoln arrived in Lexington, the death of Mrs. Elizabeth Warren received widespread publicity. Most of the town thought she had been murdered by slaves. Reports of similar incidents in other towns appeared frequently in the newspapers Lincoln read during his Lexington vacation.

The slavery question must have occupied much of Lincoln's thought. Surely he met—or even visited—his hero, Henry Clay, then in residence at his Ashland estate. Clay, himself the owner of many slaves, advocated colonization as the solution to racial difficulties. Free the slaves, he said, and then return them to Africa. An early member of the American Colonization Society, he was an articulate, eloquent spokesman for the movement. Lincoln eventually embraced the colonization proposal. He did not advance it prior to or during his congressional term, but later he repeatedly advocated emancipation and colonization. It became the mainstay of his racial ideology. As President, he even tried unsuccessfully to establish colonies of former slaves in both Panama and Haiti. Perhaps the beginning of Lincoln's commitment to colonization occurred in Lexington. Clearly he concluded there, if not sooner, that slavery would emerge as an increasingly troublesome national issue.

While Lincoln pondered the slavery issue he also became better acquainted with his wife's relatives and cemented their family relationships. Mary enjoyed a renewal of the comfort and relaxation she had known as a child. The contrast between the tranquil, genteel atmosphere of the Todd mansion and the still rustic prairie capital in Illinois must have been great.

One development of a political nature is worth recording. In the months between Lincoln's election and the time he took his seat, antiwar sentiment grew substantially across the nation, articulated mainly by the Whig party. On November 13 Lincoln heard Henry Clay give a speech in Lexington. Lincoln's father-in-law, Robert Todd, served as vice-chairman of the event. In the speech Clay denounced the Mexican War as one of aggression instigated by President

Henry Clay—his Lexington speech inspired Lincoln to speak out as a war protestor. *(Library of Congress)*

Clay's Ashland estate—*free the slaves, he said, and then return them to Africa.* (*Kentucky Historical Society*)

Polk. The speech had a profound impact on Lincoln. Undoubtedly it inspired him to speak out as a war protestor soon after he arrived in Washington.

In Lexington Lincoln also found time to read. He remained sensitive to the deficiencies in his education and took advantage of every opportunity to improve them. The Todd home contained an extensive library and Lincoln spent many pleasant hours perusing the books there. Several have marginal notes in Lincoln's handwriting, indicating his reading matter while there. He read an anthology of poetry, memorized William Cullen Bryant's "Thanatopsis," which had a theme similar to his favorite poem, "Mortality." He also enjoyed Cowper, Pope, Blair, and a number of lesser poets. Though a hardheaded pragmatist in politics, Lincoln nurtured a strain of romanticism. This strain grew in Lexington, and accounts in part for the magnificent prose style Lincoln developed and the lyrical beauty of the Second Inaugural, the Gettysburg Address, and other speeches.

Lincoln probably spent a great deal of time in the courthouse around Lexington. He felt at home among lawyers. He enjoyed entertaining them with his droll, earthy stories, just as he had done on the judicial circuit and in the State House in Illinois. Here too he could have observed a number of slave cases. Perhaps he met John C. Breckinridge, whom fate later cast as his opponent in the 1860 presidential election.

After three weeks in Lexington, Lincoln and his family packed for the last stage of their trip. On November 25 they said their good-byes and the Congressman-elect and his family set off for the nation's capital.

To reach Washington, the Lincolns had several choices. It isn't known for certain how they traveled, but they likely took a stagecoach from Lexington to Winchester, and the Potomac railroad to Harpers Ferry. At Harpers Ferry the Baltimore and Ohio Railroad could take them to Relay Station, Maryland, and from there to Washington. As an alternative, they could have taken the stage from Lexington to Maysville, and connected with a steamboat traveling on the Ohio River. At any rate, their journey lasted a week, and was, without question, demanding and draining—perhaps enough to stir moments of doubt and melancholy in the Congressman-elect.

5

"A City of Magnificent Intentions"

THE CAPITAL CITY TO WHICH the Lincolns traveled was a far cry from the tourist mecca of today. Travel by train, car and plane has made the city of Washington and the federal government accessible to everyone. A thriving tourist industry is one of Washington's biggest businesses, and beginning at cherry blossom time each year the streets, monuments, and public buildings are thronged with visitors.

In the 1840s though, travel was arduous and the demands of a growing nation kept citizens at their homes and farms. Still, if the Washington of the 1840s pales next to the metropolis of today it was then a city of grandeur compared to Springfield. Fifty thousand residents—36,000 white, 10,000 free Negroes, and 4,000 slaves—occupied the city. Marble, granite, and sandstone government buildings foreshadowed the development of government sprawl that characterizes Washington today. Hotels, theatres, markets, and restaurants were far more plentiful than in Springfield, and the soirees, levees, and dinners that attended the functioning of government were much more glittering and sophisticated than in the Illinois capital.

Then as now, Washington served first and foremost as the location of the federal government. The site for the seat of government had been the result of a compromise. In return for their acquiescence on several key provisions at the

The city out of wilderness was slowly turning into a city of grandeur. *(Library of Congress)*

At opposite ends of Pennsylvania Avenue, the Congress and the President held forth in the Capitol and the White House—shown in these previously unpublished photographs. *(Library of Congress)*

Constitutional Convention, southern delegates demanded that the seat of government be located in the South. Thus, in 1791, George Washington selected a site not far from his Alexandria home and appointed commissioners to lay out the city and erect public buildings to house the offices of the government.

Washington selected as well a French engineer who had served under him, Pierre Charles L'Enfant, to plan the city. L'Enfant meandered through the area and then made a schematic drawing. Logical and grandiose in conception, it formed the basis for the development of the city even after L'Enfant was dismissed in 1792 for failing to work rapidly enough.

The city grew slowly, but by the 1840s government buildings, congressional boardinghouses, and diplomatic residences took up a good proportion of the city's acreage. At opposite ends of Pennsylvania Avenue, the Congress and the President held forth in the Capitol and the White House. In between, several buildings housed the agencies and departments that carried on the business of government.

The Capitol building, of course, overlooked the downtown area from Capitol Hill. With ambitious plans for enlargement even then, the Capitol boasted the paintings and sculpture that adorned the Rotunda and the House and Senate chambers. Spacious grounds were filled with trees and intricately arranged flower gardens. The famous statue of George Washington by Horatio Greenough occupied a prominent place in the eastern Capitol garden. Nearby, congressional boardinghouses provided lodging and meals for the Representatives and

Senators when Congress was in session. Sweeping below the Capitol's west front was the Mall. Elaborate plans for its development—plantings, gardens, promenades—had been made and discarded several times. It remained a swampy marsh with slave pens along one side—an eyesore for the new capital.

Down the avenue, the Executive Mansion was the showplace. Though far smaller then than now, even in the 1840s the White House could claim a luxuriousness befitting the nation's chief executive. Elegantly papered walls, crimson drapes, a sparkling chandelier, two huge mirrors, and marble mantels over the fireplace characterized the reception room. The East Room provided an admirable setting for meetings and parties. Impeccably furnished with damask-covered sofas and chairs and exquisitely ornamented with three chandeliers and marble tables, this room was the principal attraction of the White House, even as it is today.

This previously unpublished 1850s photograph shows the Bulfinch gates to the Capitol that Lincoln entered each day. *(Library of Congress)*

The Greenough statue of Washington dominated the entrance to the Capitol. *(Kiplinger Washington Collection)*

The Mall—*elaborate plans for its development . . . had been made and discarded several times. (Library of Congress)*

White House—*luxuriousness befitting the nation's chief executive. (White House Collection)*

The White House gates, through which Lincoln walked to see President Polk, and later as President himself. *(Library of Congress)*

The Post Office—*the most beautiful and magnificent government building in the city.* *(Library of Congress)*

The National Observatory—*one of the finest astronomical facilities in the world.* *(Kiplinger Washington Collection)*

The Post Office, considered by many to be the most beautiful and magnificent government building in the city, covered the entire block between 7th and 8th streets, and fronted on E Street. The impressive marble building displayed stately and ornate Corinthian columns, and its three stories loomed to what was then an awesome height.

Nearby stood the Patent Office. Built along neoclassical lines, its graceful Doric columns and architectural simplicity made it stand out. In addition to housing the papers and models of patents, in the 1840s the Patent Office served as the repository for the collections of the National Institute. Displayed in the hall on the second floor were the Declaration of Independence, the Constitution, and other national treasures.

The sciences were represented in official Washington by the National Observatory and the Smithsonian Institution. The Observatory, part of the Navy Department, provided the government with one of the finest astronomical facilities in the world. And as Lincoln was getting ready to go to Washington, construction of the Smithsonian was just about to get under way. The result of the bequest of an Englishman, James Smithson, the institution has since become one of the world's finest museum complexes.

The military occupied the War Department, the Navy Department, and the Navy Yard. Located in a building on the west side of the White House, the War Department had spread out to nearby buildings leased by the government. The Navy Department had its quarters in a building just behind the War Department building, but had control of the Navy Yard as well. Located near the eastern branch of the Potomac River, the Navy Yard employed hundreds of men keeping its boats in order.

To the east of the White House stood the Treasury Department. Then still under construction, plans for the completed building called for a mammoth length of 457 feet. Within this Greek Revival structure, scurrying accountants and auditors looked after the economic well-being of the country.

The State Department occupied several houses near the White House. The work space was cramped, and clerks continually had to shuffle between several buildings. There were frequent complaints that the department needed to be housed in a single building, but that was far in the future.

In addition to these public buildings, there were numerous homes that served as diplomatic residences, and several attractive private houses. Hotels, such as Brown's Indian Queen and the National Hotel, served the transient population of the capital. Boardinghouses dotted the Capitol Hill area to provide board and lodging for members of Congress, and private residences frequently boasted a Congressman or Senator as guests.

The spiritual needs of the city were met by thirty-seven churches, including Catholic, Baptist, Lutheran, Methodist, Episcopalian, Presbyterian, and Unitarian. There was even a Quaker meetinghouse in the city. Mixed in with the churches though were numerous dramshops, saloons, and brothels. The needs of the flesh were just as demanding as the needs of the soul.

As a city as well as the national capital, the District of Columbia had its own government; or, rather, three governments. The ten-square-mile area originally comprising the District of Columbia encompassed three distinct cities: Washington, Georgetown, and Alexandria. Alexandria was retroceded to Virginia in 1846 (ironically, because it was felt that the federal government would never grow so large as to need all the space originally set aside), but Georgetown and Washington remained, each with a separate municipal government.

Washington city was governed by an elected city council and a mayor chosen by the council. So too was Georgetown. Residents grumbled that these bodies were not responsive to their needs. The streets were ill-kept, and few streets were lit. In fact, the year the Lincolns arrived, the House of Representatives was lighted with gas for the first time, but the only streetlights were along Pennsylvania Avenue and only for the time Congress met. They were fueled with kerosene.

Then as now, the relationship between the federal government and the city government was a testy one: the city felt that the federal government should help bear the cost of street paving, lighting, policing, and other municipal services, but the federal government balked. As a result, the police force consisted of federally paid guards, charged only with the protection of federal property. Other municipal services lagged far behind the city's needs.

To meet the medical needs of Washington, the city had only the Washington Asylum, a building initially erected as a poorhouse. Even though there were periodic outbreaks of cholera and other deadly diseases, the city refused to spend money for the construction of up-to-date medical facilities. Nor was there any public library, or any of the multitude of city services that people take for granted.

There were some signs of progress, however. In 1811 Georgetown approved the use of local taxes to establish public schools. But in most other respects, Washington still lagged far behind the other major cities on the East Coast.

In the 1840s Washington did serve as an educational center. The capital boasted two institutions of higher learning. Columbian College, today George Washington University, had been incorporated in 1821. With its medical college, it occupied five buildings. In Georgetown, the Jesuit-run Georgetown University had several buildings overlooking the Potomac River. Just a few years before Lincoln came to Washington, in 1843, the university had erected its own observatory. By the standards of the 1840s the educational facilities in Washington were almost unsurpassed.

Literate Washingtonians supported three newspapers. The *Union* espoused Democratic causes and the *National Intelligencer* voiced Whig sentiments. A new newspaper, the *National Era* risked the wrath of the predominantly southern town by embracing abolitionism; but editor Gamaliel Bailey was used to that—he had previously edited an abolitionist paper in St. Louis, Missouri. The firm of

War Department and Navy Yard—*employed hundreds of men. (Kiplinger Washington Collection and Library of Congress)*

The Department of State and Treasury buildings are shown in this previously unpublished photograph. *(Library of Congress)*

Saint Matthew's Catholic Church (shown in this previously unpublished photograph) was located across from the White House. It was also used for political meetings. *(Library of Congress)*

Church of the Epiphany, which still had its remarkable tower when this previously unpublished photograph was taken, was a prominent Protestant church in Washington in 1848. *(Library of Congress)*

Alexandria—*retroceded to Virginia because the federal government would never grow so large as to need all the space originally set aside. (Library of Congress)*

Blair & Rives published the *Congressional Globe,* an abbreviated record of the proceedings of Congress. Tracts, pamphlets, and a wide variety of miscellaneous literature were also published in Washington.

There was also a literary organization in Washington. The Union Literary and Debating Society had been organized in 1818, and in the 1840s met each Thursday. Politics and religion were deliberately eliminated as subjects of discussion, and a greater degree of decorum was thereby ensured. In view of his burgeoning poetic interests, it seems likely that Lincoln may have attended some of their meetings after his arrival.

Another cultural oasis could be found on 12th Street, between E and F. There Charles King exhibited paintings (mostly his own) for the edification of Washingtonians and his own enrichment. There was then no National Gallery of Art, or National Collection of Fine Arts, or any other art gallery in Washington.

Historical sites were within easy reach too. Just a few miles downriver from Washington, the Virginia home of George Washington, Mount Vernon, lured a great many visitors. On the Maryland side, the site in Bladensburg where Washingtonians fought approaching British troops served as a reminder of how close Washington had come to destruction during the War of 1812. A dueling ground at Bladensburg had achieved additional fame as the site of the Decatur-Barron duel, and, even in the 1840s, matters of honor were still settled there.

To reach any of the public buildings, diplomatic residences, historical or educational sites, Washingtonians depended on a system of public transportation consisting of horse-drawn omnibuses and carriages for hire, and vessels that plied the Potomac. The omnibuses wended their way between the major hotels, the Capitol, the Navy Yard, and the Georgetown wharves. Rates, which were set by the city government, ran as high as thirty-one cents for a trip between Capitol Square and the Navy Yard Bridge, and after eight o'clock at night drivers could demand fifty cents in addition to the regular fare. Visitors to Alexandria or Mount Vernon, or points either north or south along the Potomac, depended upon regularly scheduled sailing vessels.

More practical and immediate necessities were supplied by a wide variety of stores. Produce came from Virginia and Maryland in carts driven by slaves. A market occupied ground just south of Pennsylvania Avenue between the White House and the Capitol. Several other stores occupied places just off Pennsylvania Avenue, and furniture was sold at auction in an open area at 7th Street and Pennsylvania Avenue. Prices were reportedly reasonable.

Beyond the stores, commerce and industry in Washington were limited. Still, aspiring Washingtonians cherished fond hopes of luring more and more employment to the city. A thriving fishing business, a glassworks, and one or two other successful commercial enterprises, combined with an abundance of space and cheap waterpower, led the city to hold a commercial fair in 1846. Each day a special fair newspaper appeared lauding the advantages of Washington. Unfortunately, the Mexican War came along to still, at least temporarily, the hopes of developing commerce in the city.

Despite the contrast between Springfield and Washington, to more sophisticated observers the capital was a disgrace. Marian Gouverneur recalled Washington in that era as "an ill-contrived, ill-arranged, rambling, scrambling village." Only two streets were paved, and cattle, pigs, and other livestock roamed the streets and meandered through backyards. Garbage piled up in the streets, and sanitary conditions in general were quite crude. All the houses were provided with water from wells. The parks and circles laid out in Pierre L'Enfant's ground plan for the capital city were unplanted and barren; small wonder that Charles Dickens called Washington "a city of magnificent intentions."

Georgetown—*ill-kept, and few streets were lit.(Library of Congress)*

Jackson Monument, located across Pennsylvania Avenue from the White House, was a familiar landmark. (*Library of Congress*)

Georgetown College—*the educational facilities in Washington were almost unsurpassed. (Kiplinger Washington Collection)*

National Intelligencer office—*voic Whig sentiments. (Library of Congres*

A few miles downriver from Washington, the Virginia home of George Washington, Mount Vernon, lured a great many visitors. *(Library of Congress)*

George Washington's grave, located at Mount Vernon. *(Library of Congress)*

Aqueduct Bridge—this remarkable structure helped supply the Capitol with drinking water. *(James Goode Collection; Library of Congress)*

Capital—*"ill-arranged, rambling, scrambling village." (State Department)*

View of Washington overlooking Capitol Hill stables. *(Library of Congress)*

The social life in Washington—an important element to visiting diplomats—was limited. To be sure, there were levees, parties, and receptions at the White House and other official functions, but beyond that the prospects were grim. A few saloons provided entertainment but, as more than one visitor noted, it was necessary to dodge the expectorations of the incessant tobacco chewers who thronged Washington. On 10th Street a converted Baptist Church provided a home for the well-known Christy Minstrels, a building that later became the Washington theatre of impresario John T. Ford.

In the summer anyone with sense left Washington. Sweltering heat and high humidity made the city as stifling as any in the United States. (Today air conditioning helps, but the summers in Washington remain nightmarish—the explanation is that Washington was built on what was once swampy marshland, and, in fact, during the construction of a new building on Capitol Hill workers uncovered a petrified cypress log, a tree that grows today mostly in the Florida Everglades.) Winter was better, but still unpredictable. Summer and spring rains turned the roads into muddy quagmires, and during every season the odor drifting from the Potomac belied one of its chief purposes as the city's sewer system. Small wonder that diplomats assigned to Washington bitterly complained that it was nearly the worst place in the world to work.

Another sight that frequently bothered foreigners—as well as many natives—was the traffic in slaves. Washington became a principal slave trading and transportation area in the years following the end of African slave trade in 1808. As early as 1809 James Madison's secretary commented on the adverse effect on foreign representatives of the coffles of slaves marching through the city.

The slaves who were traded in Washington were only transient however. There remained a substantial population of both slaves and free blacks. Their lot was markedly different from that of white Washingtonians. Restrictions on blacks in Washington were far less severe than in most southern states, but still stultifying. The city's first ordinance concerning blacks was enacted in 1808; it provided a five-dollar fine for any black found on the streets or in a drinking establishment after ten o'clock at night. Soon afterward, ordinances designed to limit the immigration of free blacks into the District were enacted. Certificates of freedom were required of every free black. Laws limiting the right of blacks to own property were passed, and Congress instructed the Commissioner of Public Buildings to prohibit blacks from the Capitol unless they were there on business.

At the same time blacks in Washington enjoyed what were then unparalleled opportunities in Washington. There were schools where they could learn to read and write (most notably the schools of John F. Cook and, later, Myrtilla Miner), and the prohibition on owning property was not enforced. Several blacks accumulated wealth, a few black-owned businesses thrived, and occasionally a black received a salaried job with the government, usually as a messenger.

Too, blacks may have been heartened by the early formation of an abolition society in Washington. Far in advance of most of the rest of the country,

Pennsylvania Avenue was deeply rutted up to Capitol Hill. *(Kiplinger Washington Collection)*

Washington had an antislavery society established by 1827. Many thoughtful residents as well as foreigners deplored the thriving slave trade in the capital, and there was a constant agitation for the elimination of both the trade and slavery itself in the District. However, with a southern-dominated Congress it was inevitable that the institution remain.

In the 1840s, then, Washington was a curious city. A mixture of grandeur and of squalor characterized the capital. Vistas of magnificent buildings and private homes intermingled with rutting hogs and mired roads. Promise and potential for the future lay soundly grounded in Pierre L'Enfant's visions, but for the moment they had been set aside. Still, to the Congressman-elect from Illinois, it was a far step up the ladder from the State House in Springfield.

6

"Delightful and grand . . ."

LATE IN THE EVENING OF DECEMBER 2, 1847, Abraham Lincoln, his wife, and their sons—Bobby, four, and Eddy, not yet two—arrived by train in Washington. Weary from the long journey from Kentucky, they took temporary rooms in Brown's Indian Queen Hotel, a well-known establishment located on Pennsylvania Avenue.

They stayed there only a day or so, long enough to find permanent lodgings at the boardinghouse on Capitol Hill operated by Mrs. Anna G. Sprigg. For the new Congressman, Mrs. Sprigg's boasted an ideal location. It stood directly across from the Capitol itself in a row of houses on the ground now occupied by the Library of Congress.

Lincoln was one of the few Members of Congress who brought his family to Washington. Suitable private homes were almost nonexistent. Only nine Members of the 30th Congress, House and Senate combined, occupied separate houses. Most stayed, wifeless, in small boardinghouses like Mrs. Sprigg's.

The tract of land on which the Sprigg house stood had originally been owned by Charles Carroll (who also once owned much of the land on which the Capitol was erected), and the row of houses became known as Carroll Row or sometimes Duff Green Row, honoring the fiery political editor of the U.S. *Telegraph* who lived in the Sprigg boardinghouse. Perhaps Green, a distant relative of Mary's, had suggested that the Lincolns stay there.

Several of Lincoln's congressional colleagues also boarded at Mrs. Sprigg's. Joshua R. Giddings, the radical antislavery representative from the Western Reserve of Ohio, stayed there. In addition Abraham McIlvane, James Pollock, and John Blanchard from the Pennsylvania delegation roomed there along with Jacob Thompson of Mississippi. All were Whigs.

An idea of what the Lincolns found at Mrs. Sprigg's comes from a letter written by Theodore D. Weld, a prominent abolitionist, to his wife:

> I will tell you now how I am situated. Mrs. Sprigg's is directly in front of the Capitol and about as far from it as from our home to Mr. Holmes. . . . The iron railing around the Capitol Park comes within fifty feet of our door. Our dining room overlooks the whole Capitol Park which is one mile around and filled with shade trees and shrubbery. I have a pleasant room on the second floor with a good bed, plenty of covering, a bureau, table, chairs, closets, and clothes press, a good fireplace, and plenty of wood to burn in it.

After a long train ride, arriving in Washington was a welcome relief. *(Library of Congress)*

RAILROAD DEPOT, WASHINGTON, D. C.

Train depot near the Capitol. *(Kiplinger Washington Collection)*

Brown's Indian Queen Hotel—*located on Pennsylvania Avenue. (Library of Congress)*

Mrs. Sprigg's, in the middle of a series of row houses—*most stayed, wifeless, in small boardinghouses. (Architect of the Capitol)*

In his next letter home, Weld described the bill of fare at the house, and some of the housekeeping arrangements:

> In my letter yesterday I did not state how I get along as to diet. Well 1st. We have always upon the table Graham bread and corn bread. A pitcher of milk is always set by my plate and deep soup plate for a bowl so that I can always have a good diet, *good enough.* The milk by the way is *very good.* Mush we always have once and generally twice a day; apples always once a day; at dinner potatoes, turnips, parsnips, spinnage with eggs, almonds, figs, raisins, and bread; the puddings, pies, cakes, etc. I have of course nothing to do with. My anti-meat, butter, tea, and coffee, etc. ism excites some attention but no sneers. . . .
>
> Mrs. Sprigg, our landlady is a Virginian, *not* a slaveholder, but hires slaves. She has eight servants all colored, 3 men, 1 boy and 4 women. All are free but three which she hires and these are buying themselves.

To the family just arrived from Springfield, their new accommodations probably seemed adequate if somewhat cramped. Moreover, Washington—and particularly Capitol Hill—had an air of glamour. Another freshman Congressman from a farming area in upstate New York left this first impression in a letter to a daughter:

> The city of Washington is more of a place than I had anticipated. After ascending 73 stone steps in front of the Capitol we could look over almost the whole city. The sight or view, from this point is delightful and grand, taking in at the same time, the city—the Potomac River—and an extent of level ground as far as the eye can extend.

In addition, Washington was a social center. Frequent balls, parties, and levees were held by the President, Cabinet members, Senators, and members of Congress. Perhaps the first festivities the Lincolns attended were the celebrations that ushered in the New Year of 1848. Artemas Hale, a second-term Whig Member of the 30th Congress from Massachusetts, described a New Year's holiday in his diary:

> This day has commenced a new Year—and has been passed in the customary manner for this city—at 12 o'clock in company with Messrs. Hudson and King I called at the President's and passed through the ceremony of going with the crowd through the house and shaking hands with the President, who was stationed in one of the rooms.
> From the President we went to Mrs. Madison—the widow of the late President. She is a venerable good looking old lady—then to J.Q. Adams— Mr. Seaton's & several other places, among which was Mr. Poor's. . . . In the evening we called upon Mr. Speaker Winthrop and spent some time with Mr. Thomas H. Benton—found him extremely sociable, but very vain.

A few days later, very early in January, Lincoln and Mary attended a performance by the Ethiopian Serenaders at Carusi's Saloon, and the Whig newspaper, the *National Intelligencer,* duly noted their attendance. Carusi's was anything but a saloon. The smartest of Washington's elite were seen there regularly and for a quarter of a century most of the presidential inaugural balls were held there. The internationally famous Ethiopian Serenaders had just returned from Europe where they had performed before Queen Victoria and the royal family.

Julia Dean, a celebrated New York actress, had just started her brilliant career in 1848, and one of her early appearances occurred in Washington. The Lincolns attended, and enjoyed the performance. In 1860 Mrs. Lincoln saw her again, and gave this assessment: "About the time of her debut I saw her in Washington; she has failed greatly since then."

The Lincolns also attended marine band concerts on the White House lawn and the Capitol grounds.

Other activities that Mrs. Lincoln enjoyed included shopping; Washington had enough stores and markets to satisfy Mrs. Lincoln's well-known penchant for bargain hunting. A contemporary from New York State described the Washington shopping scene:

> I am disappointed in finding goods so reasonable here. I supposed everything was higher than we see at home but I do not find it so. I have witnessed a good deal of shopping here. The goods are very handsome. The stores are not large—not near so large as the large stores in Rochester—but I have never seen anywhere near so handsome silks and dress goods generally at one place as I see in the stores here and all are very moderate in price. The best of the calicos seem to be a levy and you get quite a pretty collar for two levys and a pip which means in our vocabulary ⅜. There are a great many establishments of ready made clothing here and the vests and cravats are very showy. A great business is done here in white kid gloves. I have not seen more than four or five stores off from *the* Avenue (Pa.). . . . There are several furniture establishments there/on seventh street/. The furniture is made in the North and is generally made peculiarly to sell. There is an open area where seventh street crosses the avenue where auctions are held and where more or less of furniture is sold almost every day as well as other property.

It is easy to imagine Mary Todd Lincoln, with Robert and Eddy in tow, browsing among the yard goods, and looking for fashionable clothing.

Mrs. Lincoln did not altogether enjoy life in Washington however. In Springfield and in Lexington she had been a social leader, accustomed to receiving a great deal of attention. She had the comfort of a large house. In Washington, as the wife of a very junior Congressman with no place to entertain, she received little attention. In addition, the confines of a boarding-house were hardly suitable for active boys like the Lincolns. Several of the boarders at Mrs. Sprigg's commented on the lack of discipline the Lincoln children received. These were, no doubt, among the forces that led Mrs.

Duff Green, a distant relative of Mary Todd's, probably recommended Mrs. Sprigg's, located on Duff Green Row. *(Library of Congress)*

Jacob Thompson, who boarded with Congressman Lincoln at Mrs. Sprigg's, was charged eighteen years later with complicity in President Lincoln's assassination. *(Library of Congress)*

Prominent abolitionists like Theodore Weld were also among the boarders at Mrs. Sprigg's. *(Library of Congress)*

Earliest known photograph of Capitol—taken just before Congressman Lincoln arrived. *(Library of Congress)*

Washington Birth-Night Ball—*Lincoln and Stephen A. Douglas would be the Illinois managers. (Lincoln National Life Foundation, Fort Wayne)*

Lincoln to return to Lexington after a brief time. Apparently she joined other congressional wives in her dislike for Washington. Another Congressman's wife of that period wrote to a friend, "I do not believe Washington is very pleasant to any of the Member's wives. I have conversed with several whom I have met and all seem tired of it and wish to go home."

The Lincolns nevertheless had a social life. Several balls and ceremonies were held, and often it was obligatory for Congressmen to attend. In February 1848, for example, the Washington Monument Association scheduled a Washington Birth-Night Ball to raise funds. On February 15 the *National Intelligencer* reported that Lincoln and Stephen A. Douglas would be the Illinois managers for the ball. The next day the managers met at City Hall and made the plans. These unfortunately had to be changed because of John Quincy Adams's seizure on the House floor in February 21 and his subsequent death. The ball had to be postponed until March 1 out of respect for the former President.

By mid-April Mary and the boys had returned to Kentucky. In Washington life went on for Lincoln.

The Birth-Night Ball preceded the dedication of the Washington Monument on July 4, 1848. Most Members of Congress attended the ceremony. Congressman Artemas Hale recorded the festive occasion in his diary:

> The morning was ushered in by the ringing of bells and the firing of cannon. At eleven o'clock a procession was formed at the city hall, consisting of a large number of companies of troops, cavalry, artillery, infantry, and rifle men. Free Masons, Odd Fellows, fire companies, &c &c &c and proceeded to the site of the erection of a national monument to the memory of George Washington, the cornerstone of which was to be laid in due form this day. The services were commenced by a prayer . . . after which Mr. Winthrop, speaker of the House of Representatives, delivered a very eloquent and appropriate address. The ceremony of laying the cornerstone was then performed by the Grand Lodge of Washington City—B.B. French the G-master acting in behalf of the Lodge. In the evening there was a very good display of fireworks.

Several other public dinners and parties claimed a portion of Congressman Lincoln's time. On June 13, 1848, he attended a dinner in honor of Senator John J. Crittenden at the National Hotel. On December 20, 1848, the citizens of Washington gave a complimentary dinner "to a portion of the two houses of Congress and one or two other guests." No list of the guests has survived, but Lincoln may well have attended. Lincoln frequently visited the stag breakfasts given Saturday mornings by Senator Daniel Webster. Invitations were much coveted, and Lincoln got more than his share.

Lincoln also helped plan the Inaugural Ball for Zachary Taylor, which occurred at the end of his term as Congressman. He had worked hard for Taylor's election and that earned his selection as a manager of the ball. Among Lincoln's co-managers, interestingly enough, were Jefferson Davis and Robert E.

Laying the cornerstone of the Washington Monument—*the ringing of bells and the firing of cannon. (Library of Congress)*

Lee. Elihu Washburne attended the ball with Lincoln and later recalled that they stayed until nearly 4:00 A.M., and that Lincoln seemed absorbed by the people who attended, and perhaps a bit saddened at the thought of leaving such things behind as the time for his retirement approached. When the celebrants got ready to leave just before sunup, they discovered that the servants had already gone and left most of the coats and hats in a large pile in the lobby. Fistfights broke out as everyone tried to locate the right garment, and Lincoln never did find his hat.

Yet the balls and parties comprised only a small part of Lincoln's spare-time activities. At Sprigg's boardinghouse Lincoln entertained his messmates at dinner by reenacting the forensic efforts of his colleagues on the House floor that day. He delighted his small but attentive audience. Samuel C. Busey, a fellow boarder at Mrs. Sprigg's and only nineteen at the time, recalled the Lincoln of the 30th Congress:

> I soon learned to know and admire Lincoln for his simple and unostentatious manners, kind-heartedness, and amusing jokes, anecdotes and witticisms. When about to tell an anecdote during a meal he would lay down his knife and fork, place his elbows upon the table, rest his face between his hands and begin with the words "that reminds me," and proceed. Everybody prepared for the explosion sure to follow. I recall with vivid pleasure the scene of merriment at the dinner after his first speech in the House of Representatives, occasioned by the descriptions, by himself and other of the Congressional mess, of the uproar in the House during its delivery.
>
> Congressman Lincoln was always neatly but very plainly dressed, very simple and approachable in manner, and unpretentious. He attended his business, going promptly to the House and remaining till the session adjourned, and appeared to be familiar with the progress of legislation.

A prominent boardinghouse that had been home to Clay and Webster, and where President Polk stayed during the renovation of the White House. *(James Goode Collection, Library of Congress)*

Senator Daniel Webster gave stag breakfasts Saturday mornings in his home, and Lincoln got more than his share of invitations. *(James Goode Collection, Library of Congress)*

Congressman Lincoln was very fond of bowling and would frequently join others of the mess, or meet other members in a match game, at the alley of James Casparis, which was near the boarding house. He was a very awkward bowler, but played the game with great zest and spirit, solely for exercise and amusement, and greatly to the enjoyment and entertainment of the other players and bystanders by his criticisms and funny illustrations. He accepted success and defeat with like good nature and humor and left the alley at the conclusion of the game without a sorrow or disappointment. When it was known that he was in the alley, there would assemble numbers of people to witness the fun that was anticipated by those who knew of his fund of anecdotes and jokes. When in the alley, surrounded by a crowd of eager listeners, he indulged with great freedom in the sport of narrative, some of which were very broad. His witticisms seemed for the most part to be impromptu, but he always told the anecdotes and jokes as if he wished to convey the impression that he had heard them from some one; but they appeared very many times as if they had been made for the immediate occasion.

A typical day for Congressman Lincoln began around 8:00 A.M. with breakfast at the boardinghouse table. Between breakfast and noon, he would answer his mail, read the local papers and the Louisville newspaper, to which he subscribed in order to keep in touch with the life Mary and the boys were living. Just before noon he would descend the stairs, cross First Street and the Capitol Plaza, enter the Capitol, and walk into the House chamber in time for the noontime opening ceremony.

Lincoln naturally spent much of his working day in the Capitol. Although substantially smaller than today, the Capitol building was still one of the most breathtaking sights in the nation. The wife of Congressman Jerediah Horsford described the seat of government in a letter to her children in New York:

> I have no words to express the beauty of the Capitol and the grounds and walks about it. I had formed no conception of its exceeding beauty or grandeur. After entering the gate admitting us to the grounds of the Capitol we walk for some distance up a gradual ascent paved to the base of the foundation of the Capitol, here we ascend some 65 or 70 stone steps where we land on a terrace where there is a broad walk around, then we ascend another flight of steps to another terrace or rather embankment where there is a broad pavement which extends around the building.
>
> Near the front of the Capitol just below this upper terrace is a set of marble figures commemorating the battle of Tripoli in which Commodore Decatur obtained the victory over Tripoli and freed the United States from paying tribute to the Barbary States. . . . I believe there is a fountain connected with these figures, but I have seen so much since I looked at that, that my memory does not retain an exact recollection about the fountain or fountains.

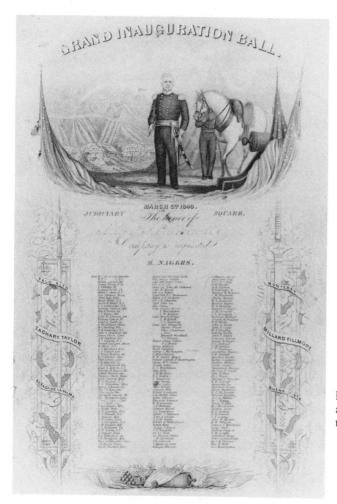

Lincoln earned Taylor's selection as manager of the Grand Inauguration Ball. *(Smithsonian)*

Tripoli Monument—Lincoln passed the monument on the west front of the Capitol when he walked down B Street to see the Smithsonian under construction. *(Library of Congress)*

Huge oil paintings of Washington and Lafayette hung in the House chamber in 1848, as they do today, a constant inspiration to Congressman Lincoln and other members. *(Architect of the Capitol)*

From this terrace we looked over the city and far beyond it. The sun was very bright and the air as clear as possible, not a particle of fog or cloud to obscure the prospect.

The day-to-day activity in the House Chamber is similarly described:

The confusion and noise of the House of Representatives is wearying, you can have no conception of it; I never saw a district school dismissed at noon so rude and noisy, noise perhaps not quite so loud, more like a hundred swarms of bees,—varied by the continuous cries of "Speaker"—"Speaker"— "Speaker" in all manner of tones rising higher and higher. The President's message was received and read by the Clerk—here pronounced "Clark." For a few minutes the house was comparatively still but very soon each Member began and continued to rap for the messenger boys and rustle their papers and converse in a buzz like tone all over, the noise was so deafening that I could not hear but a very little of the message. I was seated in the gallery over the speaker. . . . The seats are stuffed and covered with crimson damask and the window curtains and drapery back of the pillars are of the same material. . . . There seems too little room for the number of occupants.

"I never saw a district school dismissed at noon so rude and noisy." (Kiplinger Washington Collection)

The Senate Chamber. *(Kiplinger Washington Collection)*
Lincoln also frequented the Library of Congress. (Library of Congress)

Lincoln also frequented the Library of Congress. (Library of Congress)

Lincoln had a choice of places where he could find refuge from the clamor on the floor. The noted Washington journalist Ben Perley Poore recounted one of Lincoln's favorite Capitol spots:

> Mr. Lincoln found his way into the small room used as the Post Office of the House, where a few jovial raconteurs used to meet every morning, after the mail had been distributed into the members' boxes, to exchange such new stories as any of them might have acquired since they had last met. After modestly standing at the door for several days, Mr. Lincoln was reminded of a story, and by New Year's he was recognized as the champion story teller of the Capitol. His favorite seat was at the left of the open fireplace, tilted back in his chair, with his long legs reaching over the chimney jamb. He never told a story twice, but appeared to have an endless repertoire of them always ready, like the successive charges in a magazine gun, and always pertinently adapted to some passing event. It was refreshing to us correspondents, compelled as we were to listen to so much that was prosy and tedious, to hear this bright specimen of western genius tell his inimitable stories, especially his reminiscences of the Black Hawk war. . . . He made no mark as a legislator.

Lincoln also frequented the Library of Congress, which then occupied most of the second and third floors of the Capitol, and the library of the Supreme Court, located in the basement. He visited both often, and selected books to take to his room. He usually carried them by wrapping the books in a bandanna, thrusting a stick between the knotted ends of the kerchief, and carrying them away over his shoulder. He studied the six books of Euclid during this period, and renewed his acquaintance with Shakespeare and several of the romantic poets.

He ate some of his meals in the Capitol dining room reserved for Members of Congress. The dining room, located in the basement of the Capitol, served a variety of food. An 1834 Capitol guidebook published the following menu:

> Refectory rules, established by the Commissioner of Public buildings:— Beefsteak, for one, 25 cents; partridge, 25; mutton chop, 12-½; bowl soup, 12-½; one dozen roasted oysters, 18-⅔; half pint stewed oysters, 25; one dozen raw oysters, 12-½; half dozen raw oysters, 6-½; cup coffee, 12-½; small glass punch, 12-½; glass spirits, gin, brandy, whiskey, etc., each 6-¼; bottle of porter or cider, 12-½; half bottle of porter or cider, 6-¼; draught of beer, per pint, 6-½.

By the time Lincoln entered Congress, however, the sale of "intoxicating liquors" had been prohibited within the Capitol. The restriction imposed no inconvenience on Lincoln the teetotaler.

Congress usually adjourned around 3:00 P.M., at which time the main meal of the day would be served at the boardinghouse. Lincoln had the rest of the evening to himself. Perhaps an occasional constituent would visit him and have to be taken to some of the city's showplaces, but only rarely. He spent time addressing copies of the *Congressional Globe* and speeches—his or others—to Billy Herndon and other friends back in Illinois.

Yet the pleasant hours he spent at the library, the post office, or the restaurant were no substitute for the warmth and affection of his family. How much Lincoln missed his wife and children is clearly revealed in the letters they exchanged, only five of which have been preserved. On April 16, 1848, he wrote:

> Dear Mary:
>
> In this troublesome world, we are never quite satisfied. When you were here, I thought you hindered me some in attending to business; but now, having nothing but business—no vanity—it has grown exceedingly tasteless to me. I hate to sit down and direct documents, and I hate to stay in this room by myself. You know I told you in last Sunday's letter that I was going to make a little speech during the week, but the week has passed away without my getting a chance to do so, and now my interest in the subject has passed away too. Your second and third letters have been received since I wrote before Dear Eddy thinks Father is "gone tapila" [child's pronunciation of Capitol]. . . . I went yesterday to hunt the little plaid stockings as you

wished, but found that McKnight has quit business and Allen had not a single pair of the description you give and only one plaid pair of any sort that I thought would fit "Eddy's dear little feet." I have a notion to make another trial tomorrow morning. . . . All the house or rather all with whom you were on decided good terms send their love to you. The others say nothing. . . . And you are entirely free from head-ache? That is good—good—considering it is the first spring you have been free from it since we were acquainted. I am afraid you will get so well, and fat, and young, as to be wanting to marry again. Tell Louisa I want her to watch you a little for me. I did not get rid of the impression of that foolish dream about dear Bobby till I got your letter written the same day. What did he and Eddy think of the little letters father sent them? Don't let the blessed fellows forget father.

In the same letter he made a gentle request: "Suppose you do not prefix the 'Hon' to the address on your letters to me any more. I like the letters very much, but I would rather they should not have that upon them. It is not necessary, as I suppose you have thought, to have them to come free." Clearly, he felt a bit embarrassed to have his wife use "Honorable" in addressing letters to him. Could it be that his joke-telling cronies at the House post office had been poking fun at the formality of his correspondence from Mary? An observer said he was an unaffected person, totally without airs. This made it natural for him to carry books bundled in a colored handkerchief to and from Sprigg's and to ask his wife to drop the pretentious prefix in addressing mail to him.

His second letter was written May 24, 1848. The message was brief: "My dear wife: Enclosed is the draft as I promised you in my letter of Sunday. It is drawn in favor of your father, and I doubt not, he will give you the money for it at once. I write this letter in the post-office, surrounded by men and noise, which, together with the fact that there is nothing new, makes me write so short a letter. Affectionately, A. Lincoln."

Mary wrote a letter dated May 1848 in Lexington which is touched with longing. At the same time it glows with the luxury of her life at her southern home. Ironically, while Lincoln drafted a bill aimed at abolishing slavery in the District of Columbia, his wife enjoyed in Kentucky a life in which slaves provided the basic comforts.

The letter—the only one surviving from Mary to her husband written during the pre-Civil War years—begins with a recitation of the daily chores of raising two boys without the presence of a father and ends with a poignant suggestion that she would like to return to Washington.

Lexington May—48—

My dear Husband—

You will think indeed, that old age, has set its seal, upon my humble self, that in few or none of my letters, I can remember the day of the month, I must confess it as one of my peculiarities; I feel wearied & tired enough to know, that this is Saturday night, our babies are asleep, and as Aunt Maria B[ullock] is coming in for me tomorrow morning, I think the chances will be rather dull that I should answer your last letter tomorrow—I have just received a letter from Frances W[allace], it related in an especial manner to the box I had desired her to send, she thinks with you (as good persons generally agree) that it would cost more than it would come to, and it might be lost on the road, I rather expect she has examined the specified articles, and thinks as Levi says, they are hard bargains—But it takes so many changes to do children, particularly in summer, that I thought it might save me a few stitches—I think I will write her a few lines this evening, directing her not to send them—She says Willie is just recovering from another spell of sickness, Mary or none of them were well—Springfield she reports as dull as usual. Uncle S[amuel Todd] was to leave there on yesterday for Ky—Our little Eddy, has recovered from his little spell of sickness—Dear boy, I must tell you a story about him—Bobby in his wanderings to day, came across in a yard, a little kitten, your hobby, he says he asked a man for it, he brought it triumphantly to the house, so soon as Eddy, spied it—his tenderness, broke forth, he made them bring it water, fed it with bread himself, with his own dear hands, he was a delighted little creature over it, in the midst of his happiness Ma came in, she you must know dislikes the whole cat race, I thought in a very unfeeling manner, she ordered the servant near, to throw it out, which, of course, was done, Ed screaming & protesting loudly against the proceeding, she never appeared to mind his screams, which were long & loud, I assure you—Tis unusual for her now a days, to do any thing quite so striking, she is very obliging & accommodating, but if she thought any of us, were on her hands again, I believe she would be worse than ever—In the next moment she appeared in a good humor, I know she did not intend to offend me. By the way, she has just sent me up a glass of ice cream, for which this warm evening, I am duly grateful. The country is so delightful I am going to spend two or three weeks out there, it will doubtless benefit the children—Grandma has received a letter from Uncle James Parker of Miss[ouri] saying he & his family would be up by the twenty fifth of June, would remain here some little time & go on to Philadelphia to take their oldest daughter there to school, I believe it would be a good chance for me to pack up & accompany them—You know I am so fond of sightseeing, & I did not get to New York or Boston, or travel the lake route—But perhaps, dear husband, like the irresistible Col Mc, cannot do without his wife next winter, and must needs take her with him again—I expect you would cry aloud against it—How much, I wish instead of writing, we were together this evening, I feel very sad away from you—Ma & myself rode out to Mr Bell's splendid place this afternoon, to return a call, the house and grounds are magnificent, Frances W. would have died over their rare exotics—It is growing late, these summer eves are short, I expect my long scrawls, for truly such they are, weary you greatly—if you come on, in July or August I will take you to the springs—Patty Webb's school in S[helbyville] closes the first of July, I expect Mr Webb, will come on for her. I must go down about that time & carry on quite a flirtation, you know we, always had a penchant that way. With love I must bid you good night—Do not fear the children, have forgotten you, I was only jesting—Even E[ddy's] eyes brighten at the mention of your name—My love to all—

Truly yours

M L——

Lincoln responded quickly and enthusiastically to the suggestion.

Washington, June 12, 1848
My dear wife:
On my return from Philadelphia, yesterday, where, in my anxiety I had been led to attend the Whig convention I found your last letter. I was so tired and sleepy, having ridden all night, that I could not answer it till today; and now I have to do so in the H.R. [House of Representatives]. The leading matter in your letter, is your wish to return to this side of the Mountains. Will you be a good girl in all things, if I consent? Then come along, and that as soon as possible. Having got the idea in my head, I shall be impatient till I see you. You will not have money enough to bring you; but I presume your uncle will supply you, and I will refund him here. By the way you do not mention whether you have received the fifty dollars I sent you. I do not much fear but that you got it; because the want of it would have induced you [to] say something in relation to it. If your uncle is already at Lexington, you might induce him to start on earlier than the first of July; he could stay in Kentucky longer on his return, and so make up for lost time. Since I began this letter, the H.R. has passed a resolution for adjourning on the 17th July, which probably will pass the Senate. I hope this letter will not be disagreeable to you; which, together with the circumstances under which I write, I hope will excuse me for not writing a longer one. Come on just as soon as you can. I want to see you, and our dear—dear boys very much. Every body here wants to see our dear Bobby.

Affectionately, A. Lincoln

The last of Lincoln's letters gives other glimpses of the warm, deep, and affectionate relationship he and Mary shared. It also gives a vignette of life on Capitol Hill, suggesting that social life then may have had a side as shady as 130 years later. Black fur bonnets were the trademark of ladies of ill repute. In the letter Lincoln gently chided Mary for duns that came from two merchants and for delaying her departure for Washington, but urged her quickly to get a replacement for a nursemaid who had left.

My dear wife: Washington, July 2. 1848
Your letter of last sunday came last night. On that day (sunday) I wrote the principal part of a letter to you, but did not finish it, or send it till tuesday, when I had provided a draft for $100 which I sent in it. It is now probable that on that day (tuesday) you started to Shelbyville; so that when the money reaches Lexington, you will not be there. Before leaving, did you

make any provision about letters that might come to Lexington for you? Write me whether you got the draft, if you shall not have already done so, when this reaches you. Give my kindest regards to your uncle John and all the family. Thinking of them reminds me that I saw your acquaintance, Newton, of Arkansas, at the Philadelphia Convention. We had but a single interview, and that was so brief, and in so great a multitude of strange faces, that I am quite sure I should not recognize him, if I were to meet him again. He was a sort of Trinity, three in one, having the right, in his own person, to cast the three votes of Arkansas. Two or three days ago I sent your uncle John, and a few of our other friends each a copy of the speech I mentioned in my last letter; but I did not send any to you, thinking you would be on the road here, before it would reach you. I send you one now. Last wednesday, P.H. Hood & Co. dunned me for a little bill of $5.38 cents, and Walter Harper & Co, another for $8.50 cents, for goods which they say you bought. I hesitated to pay them, because my recollection is that you told me when you went away, there was nothing left unpaid. Mention in your next letter whether they are right.

Mrs. Richardon is still here; and what is more, has a baby—so Richardson says, and he ought to know. I believe Mary Hewett has left here and gone to Boston. I met her on the street about fifteen or twenty days ago, and she told me she was going soon. I have seen nothing of her since.

The music in the Capitol grounds on saturdays, or, rather, the interest in it, is dwindling down to nothing. Yesterday evening the attendance was rather thin. Our two girls, whom you remember seeing first at Carusis, at the exhibition of the Ethiopian Serenaders, and whose peculiarities were the wearing of black fur bonnets, and never been seen in close company with other ladies, were at the music yesterday. One of them was attended by their brother, and the other had a member of Congress in tow. He went home with her; and if I were to guess, I would say, he went away a somewhat altered man—most likely in his pockets, and in some other particular. The fellow looked conscious of guilt, although I believe he was unconscious that every body around knew who it was that had caught him.

I have had no letter from home, since I wrote you before, except short business letters, which have no interest for you.

By the way, you do not intend to do without a girl, because the one you had has left you? Get another as soon as you can to take charge of the dear codgers. Father expected to see you all sooner; but let it pass; stay as long as you please, and come when you please. Kiss and love the dear rascals. Affectionately

A. LINCOLN

Toward the end of July the family reunited when Mary, Robert, and Eddy arrived from Kentucky. In the months that followed, Lincoln kept frantically busy with the business of the House of Representatives and with the campaign to elect Zachary Taylor President. He made several speeches in the Washington area, attended meetings of the local Rough and Ready club, and worked with

When Moses led Israel . . . Niagara was roaring here. (Library of Congress)

other Whig members of Congress promoting Taylor. After the first session adjourned, Mrs. Lincoln and the children accompanied him on a speaking tour of New England.

The Lincolns left Washington on September 9.

Like the journeys that took them to and from Washington earlier, this trip was arduous for the young family. Three days were required to travel from Washington to Lincoln's first speaking date at Worcester, Massachusetts. They made most of the trip by railroad, going first to Baltimore on the B & O Railroad, then to New York using en route four different railroads which were later incorporated into the Pennsylvania system; then by boat from New York to Norwich, Connecticut; and at last by the Worcester rail line to the first speaking event.

From then until September 25—thirteen days—they were lodged in eleven different cities, with much travel between stops. The stops: New Bedford, Boston, Lowell, Dorchester, Chelsea, Dedham, Cambridge, Taunton, back to Boston, then Springfield, Albany, and Buffalo. How many hotels and railway cars they entered, and how many times the traveling cases had to be repacked is not recorded, but the effect must have been exhausting.

After Lincoln had finished his tour to plead the cause of Whig unity, he and his family started back to Springfield. They stopped at Buffalo, booked passage for a leisurely steamboat return to Illinois, and then visited Niagara Falls on September 28.

Lincoln was so impressed by the volume of water, roar, mist, and rainbows that he began an essay on the tremendous natural phenomenon:

> Niagara Falls! . . . Its power to excite reflection, and emotion, is its great charm. The geologist will demonstrate that the plunge, or fall, was once at Lake Ontario, and has worn its way back to its present position; he will

ascertain how *fast* it is wearing now, and so get a basis for determining how *long* it has been wearing back from Lake Ontario, and finally demonstrate by it that this world is at least fourteen thousand years old. A philosopher of a slightly different turn will say Niagara Falls is only the lip of the basin out of which pours all the surplus water which rains down on two or three hundred thousand square miles of the earth's surface. He will estim[ate with] approximate accuracy, that five hundred thousand [to]ns of water, falls with its full weight, a distance of a hundred feet each minute—thus exerting a force equal to the lifting of the same weight, through the same space, in the same time. And then the further reflection comes that this vast amount of water, constantly pouring *down,* is supplied by an equal amount constantly *lifted up,* by the sun; and still he says, "If this much is lifted up, for *this one* space of two or three hundred thousand square miles, an equal amount must be lifted for every other equal space; and he is overwhelmed in the contemplation of the vast power the sun is constantly exerting in quiet, noiseless operation of lifting water *up* to be rained *down* again.

But still there is more. It calls up the indefinite past. When Columbus first sought this continent—when Christ suffered on the cross—when Moses led Israel through the Red-Sea—nay, even, when Adam first came from the hand of his Maker—then as now, Niagara was roaring here. The eyes of that species of extinct giants, whose bones fill the mounds of America, have gazed on Niagara, as ours do now. Co[n]temporary with the whole race of men, the older than the first man, Niagara is strong, and fresh to-day as ten thousand monstrous bones, alone testify, that they ever lived, have gazed on Niagara. In that long, long time, never still for a single moment. Never dried, never froze, never slept, never rested.

Lincoln never finished the essay. Instead he and the family boarded the steamer *Globe* for the trip to Chicago. The journey of 1,047 miles usually took just sixty hours. This time it took somewhat longer as the boat went off the normal route to dock at Milwaukee.

The voyage inspired Lincoln to invent a device for lifting boats over shoals. Later that year he perfected the design, and in 1849 with Daniel Webster's help received a patent. The device never found a practical application.

The *Globe* docked at Chicago on October 5, where the Lincolns stayed two nights at the Sherman House, long enough for Lincoln to speak at a large campaign rally. Then they went by rail to Peoria for another rally and finally arrived home in Springfield on October 10.

It had been a hard but exciting year, filled with new vistas—political and scenic—for the Lincolns. Now they had two months together in Springfield.

In December Lincoln returned alone to Washington for the second session of Congress. Mary and the boys remained in Springfield. Initially Lincoln again boarded at Mrs. Sprigg's, although in a different room, but soon he departed for other quarters. Just why he moved or where remains unknown.

March 3, 1849, was an important day. The 30th Congress adjourned and it

With Daniel Webster's help [Lincoln] received a patent. The device never found a practical application. (National Park Service)

proved to be the last day Lincoln would act as a legislator. After adjournment he lingered in Washington to deal with patronage opportunities—for himself and others.

The congressional years had been a strain on family ties, but the ties remained firm.

7

"Men of promise . . ."

THE HOUSE OF REPRESENTATIVES in the 30th Congress consisted of 232 Members, about half the number today.

Lincoln's colleagues reflected the diverse and often conflicting interests of the North, South, East, and West. Votes often divide today on the same sectional lines as in the 30th Congress. Yet, like yesterday, on many issues geographical differences melt away totally.

New issues build new alliances, putting the old out of sight. Sometimes the old disappear only for the moment, other times permanently. Each Member—as in Lincoln's day—has a deep and undeniable allegiance to the interests of his own constituency, but he also claims—and occasionally asserts—a role that rises beyond his constituency. Every Congressman, at least now and then, thinks of himself as a United States Congressman, deciding issues that know no sectional or local character and transcend his district. Yet on the next vote he may find himself wearing a mantle that is totally provincial or partisan. To a tourist in the gallery, or an analyst checking voting records, the effect is bewildering. It is as if the legislative process is an immense but strange game of checkers, with the men changing colors and objectives from play to play.

Except for its role in presidential succession, the House of Representatives now occupies exactly the same fundamental role under the Constitution as in Lincoln's day. Today, as yesterday, it controls the purse strings of government, claiming under the Constitution the exclusive authority to originate all measures to raise and spend revenue. Today, as yesterday, it shares with the Senate the most awesome of all authority, the war powers. Its procedures have changed little over the years. They serve to protect minority rights while assuring that a determined majority can always work its will. Many of the rules and precedents cited by today's Speaker of the House date back to the 30th Congress and before. They are intended to guarantee that no one—not even the most radical and offensive—can be denied his right to speak and vote. In practice, the guarantee does not always hold. In pre-Civil War days the discussion of slavery was effectively prohibited. For years before Lincoln came to Congress John Quincy Adams fought to abolish this gag rule. Since then no comparable denial has occurred.

Lincoln must have marveled at this parliamentary system. He must have seen it as critical to the survival of our most basic liberties. So long as the Speaker protected unreservedly the rights of the most obscure or the most unpopular

Robert Winthrop—the Massachusetts Whig for whom Lincoln cast his vote for Speaker of the House of Representatives. *(Architect of the Capitol)*

The patriarch was John Quincy Adams . . . viewed . . . with awe, veneration, and sometimes resentment. (Library of Congress)

member, Lincoln must have felt confident that every citizen of the nation could be sure his rights too would ultimately find protection.

In Lincoln's Congress, as more recently, the House of Representatives was the training ground for executive branch responsibility. Sixteen of the first thirty-nine Presidents of the United States served in the U.S. House of Representatives. Presidents John F. Kennedy, Lyndon B. Johnson, Richard M. Nixon, and Gerald R. Ford each served in the House. So too did James Madison, John Quincy Adams, Andrew Jackson, William Henry Harrison, John Tyler, James K. Polk, Millard Fillmore, Franklin Pierce, James Buchanan, Andrew Johnson, Rutherford B. Hayes, James A. Garfield, and, of course, Lincoln. All but Adams served in the House before attaining the Presidency.

In the 30th Congress Lincoln first made acquaintance with both of the men who were to become his presidential running mates, as well as with several men destined to be in his Cabinet and others who were to be prominent in the Confederacy. Lincoln's most esteemed colleague in the 30th Congress, Adams, had already served as President.

The political crosscurrents in Lincoln's Congress were as unpredictable as today. Some of Lincoln's closest friends in the 30th Congress later took prominent roles against him in the Civil War. And some of those with whom he disagreed most sharply in his congressional days became loyal supporters when he became President.

The issues that absorbed the 30th Congress bear remarkable resemblance to those of the recent past: human rights and a controversial war. The greatest issues of Lincoln's Congress revolved around the status of that most odious form of human degradation—slavery. Second only in importance, at least to Lincoln, was the controversy over the war with Mexico. These issues occupied much of Lincoln's energies and certainly marked his congressional career.

Congressman Lincoln actively criticized the presidential war-making of James K. Polk. His arguments and words echoed in the House years later during the Vietnam era when other war protesters and critics spoke up.

Whether by design or accident, the Mexican War was an expression of the spirit of "Manifest Destiny" that was to dominate United States policy for the next seventy years. Succeeding generations of leadership embraced the notion that the United States was destined by God to expand and, some believed, eventually encompass all of North America—a self-righteous notion and one heavy with militaristic overtones. This powerful theme persisted, grew, and drove men to extreme action. It led the nation into the Spanish-American War and to the construction of the Great White Fleet. Vestiges of "Manifest Destiny" enlivened the House debates of the Vietnam era, and perhaps that high-blown notion exploded for good only when the unvictorious United States troops came home from Vietnam.

In Lincoln's Congress the budding issue of "Manifest Destiny" and the ugliness of slavery were beginning to tear at the fabric of American society.

Lincoln's work to check the growth of slavery is inseparably linked with the great debates and votes in the House in the 1960s that helped to bring blacks to full citizenship.

In Lincoln's Congress slavery posed an agonizingly difficult problem. The Constitution provided in Article 1, Section 9, that Congress could not outlaw the African slave trade before 1808, just one year before Lincoln's birth. Thomas Jefferson incorporated strong language against slavery in his draft of the Declaration of Independence but it was struck out at the insistence of southern delegates to the Continental Congress. But by the time Lincoln went to Congress, most northern states had abolished slavery.

When new territory joined the United States, the slave states sought to extend the institution while the free states worked to exclude it. Until 1847 compromise after compromise had been made as new territory was acquired.

In the 30th Congress, however, a spirit of compromise was lacking. Antislavery Whigs and Democrats both suspected that President James K. Polk had deliberately provoked the Mexican War in order to gain new slave territory. In the closing days of the 29th Congress, forces determined to contain slavery— led by antislavery Pennsylvania Democrat David Wilmot—tried to prevent the extension of slavery into territory acquired as a result of the Mexican War. Wilmot created havoc on the floor of the House when he introduced an amendment to an appropriations bill—the Wilmot Proviso—forbidding the extension of slavery.

Antislavery forces also raised questions concerning slavery in the District of

Columbia. Abolitionists viewed the presence of slavery in the national capital as particularly odious since Congress had unquestioned authority to abolish it there. Throughout the 30th Congress, antislavery Members presented petitions, introduced bills and resolutions, and voiced long tirades against slavery in the District, and even Lincoln drafted a bill to abolish it. The paradox of slavery in the capital of a country committed to liberty was emphasized in 1848 by the fulsome speeches delivered in the wake of European revolutions that year; as Congressmen praised the spirit of liberty that had led to revolution in Europe, slaves chained together in coffles shuffled past the United States Capitol.

The lesser issues of the 30th Congress also find their echo today. Lincoln battled for internal improvement, mainly waterways, as did his colleagues from the West. In recent years the district Lincoln served has been absorbed in the same cause—specifically the improvement of river locks to facilitate commerce by barge. Western Congressmen were naturally concerned with internal improvement. Contrasted with the East and South, the West contained great stretches of primitive wilderness. Its economic development depended upon the expansion of markets for western produce. This in turn required better transportation. Western Congressmen persistently demanded federal support for massive improvements—road building, bridge construction, canal excavation, river and harbor projects, and railroads.

Congressmen from the Northeast, just as naturally, tended to be against such measures. They saw them serving mainly the sectional interests of the sparsely populated West at the expense of those in the East and North. President Polk echoed their views and, when he vetoed a River and Harbor bill that had passed the 29th Congress, kicked up a controversy that raged on during the 30th.

Lincoln's Congress also dealt with other issues still familiar in the House— benefits for veterans, complaints about postal service, and the publication of military documents. Mileage allowances for Congressmen became a scandal, at least to the readers of Horace Greeley's New York *Tribune*. It even resulted in some bad press for Congressman Lincoln (see chapter 8).

The men who confronted these issues were from a wide variety of back- grounds.

Lincoln found many fellow attorneys among his colleagues in Congress. But other occupations were represented. The 30th Congress consisted of 74 percent lawyers, 16 percent businessmen, 1 percent educators, 7 percent farmers, 1 percent clergymen, and 1 percent other occupations. The breakdown in the 95th Congress (1977–1979): 50 percent lawyers, 26 percent businessmen, 16 percent educators, 3 percent journalists, 3 percent farmers, 1 percent clergymen, 1 percent other occupations.

In two major respects the House has changed. Of the 232 Members of the 30th Congress, not one was female. Not one was black. Neither women nor blacks occupied a single position of prominence or responsibility in the entire Capitol. Blacks were not admitted to the House gallery. They could enter the

Horace Greeley—*an exceptional journalist, but . . . a poor prophet. (Library of Congress)*

Capitol only to perform menial duties.

It would be thirty-five Congresses—seventy years—before the first woman would sit as a Member of the House. It would be eighty-three years before a black would serve as a Member, except for a fleeting period after the Civil War. In the 95th Congress, by contrast, seventeen Members of the House are women and seventeen Members are black.

Not a single female voted in the election that put Lincoln and his 231 colleagues in the House. Women would vote in federal elections for the first time in 1920—seventy-four years after the adjournment of the 30th Congress. The first woman elected to the House won the office in 1916, four years before she—or any other woman—could vote in a Congressional election. Lincoln's campaign call in 1836 for suffrage "by no means excluding females" had no visible effect on national politics, except perhaps to convince Lincoln to drop the proposal. He never again spoke up for women's rights.

Clearly, women's rights were nowhere on the agenda when the 30th Congress convened. It was a man's world and a man's House.

A journalist, who himself became a Member of the House before Lincoln's two-year term ended, gave readers his appraisal of the new men on Capitol Hill. Horace Greeley, editor of the New York *Tribune*, looked over the newcomers in 1847 and wrote:

> The 30th Congress has terminated the daily sessions of its first week—and quite satisfactorily. . . . I have watched the new House anxiously this week, and I think it a decided improvement on its . . . predecessor—in intellect, in character and in manners. . . .
>
> The West has sent us some "new men" who in due time will make themselves heard. Among these on the Whig side are Abraham Lincoln of Ill., William P. Haskell of Tenn., George G. Dunn and Elisha Embree of Ind. and Patrick W. Tompkins of Miss.—all (I think) Clay electors and effective canvassers in '44; all in the early prime of manhood; heretofore State legislators and men of sterling qualities to whom the floor of Congress (no matter if they never make speeches) affords liberal opportunities of usefulness.

Greeley also later gave a brief description of Lincoln of the 30th Congress:

> He was then not quite forty years old; a genial, cheerful, rather comely man, noticeably tall, and the only Whig from Illinois—not otherwise remarkable to the best of my recollection. . . . There were men accounted abler on our side of the House . . . yet I judge no other was more generally liked and esteemed than he.

The word comely as used then meant acceptable appearance rather than handsome.

Who were these men with whom Lincoln served in the House of Representatives? What did they do later in life, when the nation was torn by Civil War and the storyteller of the House post office sought to unite them behind the common cause of the Union?

Here is what happened to those Greeley mentioned as "men of promise" from the West.

William Haskell, a Whig, never fulfilled Greeley's prophesy. Born in Murfreesboro, Tennessee, in 1818, he had been educated by a private tutor and later at the University of Nashville. He fought in the Seminole Wars, studied law, and served in the state legislature of Tennessee. His first and only venture into national politics came in the 30th Congress. After a single term, he resumed his law practice. In 1859, at the age of forty, he died in an asylum in Hopkinsville, Kentucky.

Nor was there a bright future in sight for George Dunn of Indiana. He served in only one other Congress, the 34th, and died at the age of forty-four just after completing that term.

Elisha Embree, another Member of the Indiana delegation on whom Greeley pinned his hopes, lost a bid for reelection in 1848 and resumed his law practice. He died in 1863, leaving unrecorded any thoughts he may have had regarding his former House colleague who had risen to the Presidency.

The last Whig colleague in whom Greeley saw great potential was Patrick Tompkins of Mississippi. Tompkins served but a single term, and left for California, apparently bitten by the gold bug. He died in obscurity in the California minefields.

Greeley may have been an exceptional journalist, but, aside from his prediction of Lincoln's ascendancy, a poor prophet.

There were other men in the House of Representatives and in the Senate, omitted from Greeley's prophecy, who were destined to help shape the days ahead and with whom Lincoln's life would become closely intertwined. Some of them had familiar names, even if he had never seen them before. And there were, of course, a few he knew well, such as his fellow colleagues from Illinois. Although he was the "lone star" Whig from Illinois, even in the nineteenth century, the common interests of state delegations often overrode political differences and united Congressmen on issues that benefited their states.

Six men represented Illinois in addition to Lincoln. From Alton, Robert Smith served. A lawyer, but more a merchant, Smith had also served as a captain in the Black Hawk War and as a member of the Illinois legislature. He and Lincoln always worked for internal improvement measures.

Gutsy John Wentworth also supported Lincoln on the internal improvements issue. Representing Chicago, he had a deep interest in federal legislation that would strengthen Chicago's revenue as a port. Lincoln's trip to Chicago protesting President Polk's veto of a river and harbor bill may have brought them together, and their deep interest in Illinois' future assured that they would from time to time work together.

John McClernand of Shawneetown in southern Illinois continued his friendly opposition to Lincoln in the 30th Congress. A Democrat in the state legislature, McClernand had moved up to the United States House of Representatives in 1843, and this was his third term. Ironically, and perhaps a stinging reminder to Lincoln, McClernand was elected to the 36th Congress to fill a vacancy created by the death of Thomas L. Harris, the Democrat who wrested the 7th District from Whig control in the election of 1848. The friendship between Lincoln and McClernand continued until Lincoln's assassination. McClernand served as one of Lincoln's generals in the western theatre of operations. Like Lincoln, he brought to his career a rugged frontier background that cemented their mutual respect for each other despite political differences.

A perpetual splinter in Lincoln's political side was Orlando Ficklin from Charleston, representing a district to the east of Lincoln's. Ficklin, a staunch Democrat, and Lincoln had tousled on everything except internal improvements in the Illinois legislature. Yet they too shared a similar background. Both had been born in Kentucky and were of the same age. They had both turned to law, although Ficklin picked up his judicial education in a university, and both served in virtually the same sessions of the state legislature. Ficklin had been elected to the 29th Congress, so his only advantage was a two-year head start on Lincoln in his congressional career.

Surprisingly, even when the seeds of Civil War were sown, Ficklin did not go over to the newly formed Republican party. He remained a Democrat and served as a presidential elector in the Democratic convention of 1864. Yet these were years far in the future for these colleagues of the 30th Congress.

Lincoln's colleague from Quincy, Illinois, William Richardson, was also a former member of the state legislature. Richardson had won an enviable reputation as a captain in the Mexican War, and Stephen A. Douglas's election as Senator opened the way for Richardson to aim at the House of Representatives. He naturally cashed in on his war reputation and succeeded Douglas, a step that foreshadowed as well his accession to the Illinois Senate seat in 1861.

The far northwest counties of Illinois were represented by Thomas Turner. An Ohioan by birth, Turner had moved to Illinois in 1838, and established himself as an able attorney and probate judge. In addition he founded a newspaper, the *Prairie Democrat,* and even served as Postmaster of Freeport. The 30th Congress was for him, as for Lincoln, his first and last service in the federal legislature.

Ironically, Lincoln and his colleagues from Illinois stood united on an issue—internal improvements—which provided them almost no opportunity for common action in the 30th Congress. President Polk's veto of the River and Harbor bill in the 29th Congress made it clear that no bill in Lincoln's Congress would be enacted into law to provide federal assistance for land development and transportation measures that would benefit Illinois and the rest of the western United States.

Nevertheless, on several occasions Lincoln and his Illinois associates pushed forward for more modest measures. Lincoln and Wentworth worked together on a bill that would provide federal money for clearing the Savannah River for navigation. Lincoln also rounded up congressional support for assistance to the Illinois and Chicago Railroad.

Among Lincoln's congressional colleagues, the patriarch was John Quincy Adams. Eighty years of age when the 30th Congress convened, the former President had acquired a reputation in the House as an unceasing champion of the antislavery movement. He had defended, eight years before, the famous slave mutineers from the ship *Amistad.* Soon thereafter he succeeded in persuading the House to remove a gag rule that for years had prevented the presentation of antislavery petitions. His colleagues viewed him with awe, veneration, and sometimes resentment.

This was to be his last Congress. He served as Lincoln's colleague for less than three months. Few moments in the history of the House of Representatives have been more dramatic than the sudden collapse of John Quincy Adams on the House floor. Massachusetts Representative Artemas Hale vividly recorded the incident in his diary:

> Monday Feby. 21. At ¼ past one o'clock p.m. Mr. John Quincy Adams was seized of a paralysis, in his seat & while in the act of falling was caught by Mr. Fisher of Ohio who sat next to him—a rush from all parts of the House was immediately made towards him—and he was taken to the Rotunda, laid on a sofa and carried to the Room of the Speaker—as soon as he was taken the House adjourned—Soon after he was carried into the Speakers Room he was distinctly understood by Dr. Newell of New Jersey to say "the last of earth" and "satisfied" and to ask for his wife—In a few minutes he became entirely unconscious—and remained so until Wednesday evening 17 minutes past 7 o'clock without a groan or a struggle—and thus ended the mortal life of one who had from his youth been almost constantly employed in the public service of his country—filling in succession most of the highest offices in the government, with an ability, integrity, and fidelity which even his enemies could not call in question—he was born July 11, 1767.

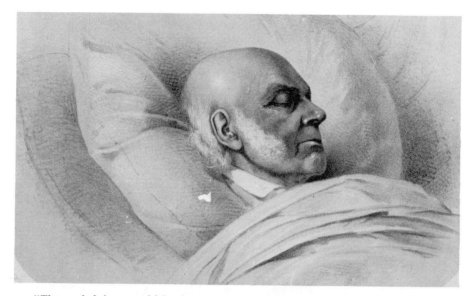

"Thus ended the mortal life of one who had from his youth been almost constantly employed in the public service of his country." (Library of Congress)

> Thursday, 24th. The House met at 12—the Speaker in a few impressive remarks announced the death of Mr. Adams—Mr. Hudson moved the usual resolutions prefaced with appropriate remarks. . . . A Committee of 30 was appointed to make the arrangements for the funeral & the House adjourned to Saturday.

Lincoln probably witnessed Adams's fall from his back-row desk. Appointed as a member of the committee of thirty to make the funeral arrangements, he did not participate actively since most of the details were left to a subcommittee of five. But he did march in the funeral procession the following Saturday.

The death of this champion of freedom stirred deep emotions within Lincoln. Adams was a close friend of Joshua Giddings and visited at Mrs. Sprigg's where both Giddings and Lincoln boarded. His path and Lincoln's crossed many times in the ten weeks between the convening of the first session of the 30th Congress and the day Adams was stricken.

In addition to the patriarch, there was a pesky gadfly in the House. A southern Democrat, this Congressman boomed a "no" to almost every proposal for a government expenditure. He opposed the establishment of the Smithsonian Institution, berated government departments that wanted to expand to provide new services, and even objected to the erection of a monument to John Quincy Adams in the congressional burial grounds. He did not want the streets in the capital graveled, and strenuously objected to bills that commissioned artists to paint portraits of the Presidents. He also opposed antislavery activity of any form and spoke often of the dangers of racial amalgamation. Virtually every measure that Lincoln supported, this Congressman opposed. Andrew Johnson of Tennessee—the gadfly of the 30th Congress—became Lincoln's running mate in

1864, and the next year, President. Years later, when a bill was considered to commission his own presidential portrait, he could not object.

A southerner drew Lincoln's praise. On February 2, 1848, Lincoln wrote to his law partner, William H. Herndon:

> I just take up my pen to say that Mr. Stephens of Georgia, a little, slim, pale faced, consumptive man, with a voice like Logan's, has just concluded the best speech of one hour's length I ever heard. My old withered dry eyes are full of tears yet.

"Mr. Stephens" referred to Alexander H. Stephens, a third-term Whig with a distinguished background. A graduate of the University of Georgia and a well-known lawyer, he had served six years in the Georgia legislature before being elected to Congress. He, like Lincoln, became a leading figure among the "Young Indians," an informal group of Whig members working for the election of Zachary Taylor. Stephens served in the House of Representatives until 1859. The sectional issues that cleaved party alignments forced Stephens to change parties and he became a Democratic presidential elector in 1860.

It is rumored that Lincoln offered Stephens a Cabinet post in 1860 in the hope of keeping the Union intact. If actually offered, Stephens turned it down. He did plead, however, both in private correspondence and in public statements, for the South not to secede. He wrote, "I knew Mr. Lincoln, thought well of him personally, believed him to be a kind hearted man." When Georgia's legislature voted to leave the Union, Stephens remained loyal to his state. He became a Member of the Confederate Congress and subsequently the Vice-President of the Confederacy.

Lincoln also worked closely with a fellow "Young Indian" named Howell Cobb from Georgia. Like Stephens, Cobb had been well educated and had seen prior service as a state legislator. Like Lincoln he opposed the Mexican War and worked hard to secure Zachary Taylor's election. He later became a Major General in the Confederate Army.

Lincoln had an entirely different relationship with John Gorham Palfrey of Massachusetts. A Harvard-educated minister and former editor of the prestigious monthly the *North American Review*, Palfrey had served in the Massachusetts legislature, and had just been elected to the House of Representatives. One of the few radical antislavery Members of Congress, he served only one term. Although a Whig, important differences separated him from Lincoln.

Palfrey belonged to the so-called "conscience Whigs" while Lincoln associated with the "cotton Whigs." The slavery issue divided the two. Palfrey out of "conscience" unyieldingly demanded the abolition of slavery, while Lincoln expressing a sentiment linked with the interests of the southern cotton states wished merely to contain slavery to its present boundaries. They personified the growing internal rift that ultimately destroyed the Whig party.

John Quincy Adams's funeral procession wound its way to the congressional burial grounds, where he was interred until the spring when the body was taken to its final resting place in Massachusetts. *(Library of Congress)*

Andrew Johnson—the gadfly of the 30th Congress—opposed virtually every measure that Lincoln supported. *(Library of Congress)*

Alexander Stephens—*"the best speech of one hour's length I ever heard." (Library of Congress)*

Howell Cobb—*a fellow "Young In-dian." (Library of Congress)*

Horace Mann—*a cause even larger than public education. (Library of Congress)*

The conscience Whigs were willing to bolt from the regular Whig party and support an avowed antislavery candidate of the Free-Soil or Liberty party stripe. They refused to acquiesce in the presidential nomination of Zachary Taylor, a slaveholder. One of the main reasons Lincoln accepted an invitation to speak in New England during the presidential campaign of 1848 was to help unify the Whig party and stem the tide of defection to Free-Soil or Liberty candidates. Palfrey with equal zeal supported defection. In Congress and in the campaign of 1848, Lincoln and Palfrey often differed; during the Civil War they were united, and Lincoln appointed Palfrey Postmaster of Boston.

Lincoln must have been impressed by his colleague Horace Mann. Elected to succeed John Quincy Adams, Mann pursued a lifelong commitment to the principle of public education. So did Lincoln. As far back as 1832, in his first campaign for the state legislature, Lincoln had espoused free public education, though as a state legislator he did not support it. Rumors circulated that Mann hoped to use his congressional seat to promote the establishment of a national Department of Education, with himself as Secretary. He also ardently opposed slavery. Mann's opposition had been at the time of his election to Congress largely a private matter. He had expressed his views to his friends, in personal gatherings, but had not publicly denounced the institution. He knew well the divisive emotional nature of the subject and did not want it to jeopardize his hope to extend public education.

Early in the 30th Congress, however, Mann had to make a choice. In April 1848, he was asked to defend Daniel Drayton, accused of stealing eighty slaves to take them north. He accepted the case, despite the risk it posed to his effectiveness in advancing his cherished goal. He wrote to his wife that he felt he was fighting for a cause even larger than public education when he opposed slavery. A man of deep principle and persuasion, he successfully defended Drayton. He did not live to see slavery abolished nor the educational reforms he sought enacted, for he died in 1859.

On the other side of the Capitol, one of Lincoln's future Cabinet members served in the Senate. Simon Cameron, a Pennsylvania Whig, was finishing the unexpired term of James Buchanan, who had resigned from the Senate to accept appointment as Secretary of State. Cameron served in the Senate until March 3, 1849. Both he and Lincoln left Washington at the end of the 30th Congress. They returned together in 1861—Lincoln as President and Cameron as Secretary of War.

Another future member of Lincoln's Cabinet, Whig Caleb Blood Smith served his third and last term as Lincoln's colleague in the House. At the close of the 30th Congress, President Zachary Taylor appointed Smith as a member of a board investigating claims of American citizens against Mexico. Smith later joined the Republican party and rose to prominence. In 1861 Lincoln selected him to be his Secretary of the Interior, a post he held until 1863 when Lincoln appointed him judge of the United States District Court for Indiana.

As the 30th Congress began, Lincoln's Civil War counterpart also sat in the Senate. Two years earlier Jefferson Davis had resigned his seat in the House of Representatives to serve in the Mexican War. He served with distinction in the siege of Monterrey and in the battle of Buena Vista. Covered with laurels, he would easily win appointment in 1847 to fill a Senate vacancy. His term lasted until 1851, when he waged an unsuccessful campaign for the governorship of Mississippi. In 1853 President Franklin Pierce appointed him Secretary of War. He held the post until 1857 when the Mississippi legislature returned him to the Senate. He served there until the outbreak of the Civil War. He and Lincoln had been born a year apart within a few miles of each other in Kentucky. Davis headed the Confederate cause, taking office as President of the Provisional Confederacy the same year Lincoln became President of the United States.

The lofty rhetoric of Daniel Webster and John C. Calhoun filled the Senate Chamber of the 30th Congress. The *Congressional Globe*, a predecessor of the *Congressional Record*, chronicled spirited speeches and debates on fundamental principles of government, the definition of liberty, and the relationship between state and federal governments. Yet, despite the fact that the words of these two giants occupied page after page of the *Globe*, most of the sentiments, lofty or otherwise, were those of Members of Congress as relatively unknown and unassuming as Lincoln was then.

Many of Lincoln's friendships in the Congress were with the lesser known, never-to-be-famous Members whose lives or careers up to then had similarities to his own. In a letter written in 1854, Lincoln recalled "with Col. Crozier . . . I formed quite an intimate acquaintance, for a short one, while at Washington."

Simon Cameron—future Secretary of War. *(Library of Congress)*

Jefferson Davis—*Lincoln's Civil War counterpart. (Library of Congress)*

He referred to John Hervey Crozier, a second-term Whig representative from Tennessee. Like Lincoln, Crozier was a lawyer, former state legislator, and sometime presidential elector. The 30th Congress marked the end of his public service. He resumed his law practice in 1849, and continued arguing cases until 1866. He took no part in the Civil War, although in 1856 he switched to the Democratic party. After his retirement from the law, he devoted the remaining years of his life to literature and historical research.

Lincoln also knew Artemas Hale, a fifty-five-year-old Whig from Massachusetts. Like Lincoln, Hale had a background of limited schooling and farm labor. He served several terms as a state legislator prior to 1842. In 1845 he had been elected to Congress and he served for two terms. After leaving the House, he resumed agricultural pursuits and had only one other political office—presidential elector for the Lincoln-Johnson ticket in 1864.

These were the men important to Congressman Lincoln's current tasks—and to his future.

8

"Abolitionist doctrines . . ."

MYTHS DEVELOP ABOUT GREAT MEN, and they are often hard to shake. One of the most persistent about Lincoln is that he had a burning passion to abolish slavery since early manhood and missed no opportunity to proclaim his conviction. He, of course, deserved to be called the "Great Emancipator," but the notion that he earned the title early in his political career is without foundation. It was not until he became a Congressman that Lincoln decided to make slavery a political campaign issue. In none of the campaigns in which he had participated before his congressional career did he speak out against it. After he came to Congress he made slavery an issue in every campaign. Something happened to Lincoln on Capitol Hill. Behind him lay an era in which he generally avoided slavery as a topic of political discussion. Ahead was a totally different part of his life, one in which he missed no opportunity to identify himself as an antislavery disciple.

Until his election to Congress, Lincoln had never lived with slavery. He was born in Kentucky, a slave state, but left there at the age of six. Those childhood years were spent in a rural farm setting where few slaves lived. Lincoln's recollections give no sign that he ever saw a slave in those years.

From the age of seven on, he lived in free states. His boyhood was spent in Indiana and his adult years in Illinois. In both, fugitive slaves and slaves in transit would only occasionally be seen or discussed. Yet in both, public sentiment for slavery was substantial and vocal. The reason for the existence of proslavery sentiment in these states could be found in immigration patterns. At this point most of the population lived in the southern portion of each state and had settled there as immigrants from Kentucky and Tennessee where slavery was common.

Before his election to Congress, Lincoln's only real encounter with slavery occurred on his flatboat trips down the Mississippi River. At New Orleans he saw slaves in chains. It made a lasting impression, but the experience itself had been fleeting.

Riding the judicial circuit, Lincoln often had to take whatever cases were available. Consequently, he occasionally took part in trials involving slaves. Once he represented a slave owner who sought to recover custody of his property—a former slave whose residence in Illinois made him legally free. It was not one of Lincoln's better moments and he knew it. He never collected a fee for his legal services. If he had been paid, the money would have burned his conscience.

Slave auction within sight of the Capitol. *(Library of Congress)*

PUBLIC SALE.

THE Subscriber will sell, to the highest bidder, on a credit of six months, for approved paper, seventy valuable NEGROES. Any person wishing to buy at private sale, by applying to the Subscriber, can be informed of their price, and see the slaves, before Monday the 12th day of December; on which day, if not previously sold, I shall offer them, at my farm near Bladensburg, if fair, if not, on the next fair day. Sale to take place at 12 o'clock.

WILLIAM DUDLEY DIGGES.

Washington, Nov. 14, 1825.

Slave sale poster.
(Library of Congress)

In Illinois slavery troubled him but it was out of sight most of the time and therefore more of an abstract moral issue than a concrete problem that had to be faced.

In the District of Columbia Lincoln confronted slavery every day. The move to Washington put Lincoln and his family right in the midst of slavery and a thriving slave trade. He could not put it out of sight except by closing his eyes. It flourished. It was an everyday, ugly reality. Slaves worked in Mrs. Sprigg's boardinghouse where the Lincolns lived. If Lincoln walked east from the boardinghouse, in five minutes he could watch slaves being bought and sold at an auction block. If he walked westerly, past the Capitol, in ten minutes he could see the slave pens on the mall. In a speech given six years later, in 1854, Lincoln recalled for his audience one aspect of slavery in Washington:

> In view from the windows of the Capitol, a sort of Negro-livery stable, where droves of Negroes were collected, temporarily kept, and finally taken to Southern markets [was] openly maintained.

The "Negro-livery stable" that Lincoln mentioned was easily seen from the west windows of the Capitol. The pen closest in view was the one that looked the most like a penitentiary. There slaves were kept inside a two-story building that was tightly enclosed by a fence about fifteen feet high. Posts and other framing for the fence were on the outside, making the inside surface smooth and difficult to scale.

Under construction just across B Street, S.W.—now Independence Avenue—was the red brick structure that would house the Smithsonian exhibits. It was the most impressive cultural advance ever to come to Washington, and perhaps to the nation. While the bricks were being put in place for this edifice of learning, slaves in the pens across the street could get glimpses of the new superstructure by peering through openings high enough in the main building to permit a view over the fence.

Only seven blocks separated the Capitol and the nearest slave pen, an easy stroll for Lincoln's long legs. The juxtaposition of these establishments—the pens for the worst form of human degradation and the Smithsonian for a high cultural purpose—must have troubled him. He probably covered the half-mile often to ponder this mixture of humanity and inhumanity.

Actually the closeness of these contradictory institutions was a physical symbol of the compromise of freedom that had been written into the United States Constitution sixty years earlier. The document—in all other respects so totally devoted to the object of equality and justice—contained a provision that allowed the African slave trade to continue for twenty years. With slavery thus guaranteed in the basic charter of individual liberty, it seemed appropriate that slave pens be located in the nation's capital directly across the street from a center for human enlightenment. No more shocking and enduring evidence of a nation half-slave and half-free existed. No one who lived or worked on Capitol

Hill could ever put this evidence out of mind. And upon some, like Lincoln who both lived and worked there, it made a deep and lasting impression.

Robey's Pen was the "Negro-livery stable" to which Lincoln referred. It was located on the east side of 7th Street, just off B. One block west, on the southeast corner of 8th and B, a Mr. Williams operated another slave pen called the Yellow House. An English writer, Mr. Abdy, described his 1835 visit to Robey's Pen:

> One day I went to see the "slave pen"—a wretched hovel right against the Capitol, from which it is distant about half a mile, with no house intervening. The outside alone is accessible to the eye of the visitor, what passes within being reserved for the exclusive observation of its owner, a man by the name of Robey, and his unfortunate victims. It is surrounded by a wooden paling fourteen or fifteen feet in height, with the posts outside to prevent escape, and separated from the building by a space too narrow to permit of a free circulation of air. At a small window above, which was unglazed and exposed alike to the heat of summer and the cold of winter, so trying to the constitution, two or three sable faces appeared looking out wistfully to while away the time and catch a refreshing breeze, the weather being exceptionally hot. In this wretched hovel all colors except white, both sexes, and all ages, are confined, exposed indiscriminately to the contamination which may be expected in such society and under such seclusion.

Walter C. Celephane, in a report published later by the Columbia Historical Society, described an Alexandria slave depot and a schooner used for the shipment of slaves:

> Slaves were frequently sold at auction, together with furniture, carpets and household goods, at the regular auction houses of the city.
>
> The greater number of the slaves brought into this District were taken into Alexandria, where the principal depot was kept by the firm of Franklin & Armfield. A member of this firm made a statement to one Mr. Leavitt in January, 1834, which statement appears in a letter published in New York, that the number of slaves carried from the District in one year before was about one thousand, but that it would be much greater during 1834; and he expected their house alone would ship at least eleven or twelve hundred. We learn that the net profit of this firm for the preceding year had been $33,000.
>
> These slaves were mostly shipped away in schooners. While the United States Government had been careful to join with the other governments in suppressing the seizure of slaves in Africa and their transportation to this country, it was a common thing for free negroes to be seized in the District of Columbia and transported from here to other places in these slave vessels. A description of one of them is taken from the source just above referred to. It reads thus:
>
> "The hold is appropriated to slaves and is divided into two apartments. The after hold will carry about eighty women, and the other about one hundred men. On either side were two platforms running the whole length,

Robey's Pen—*"In view from the windows of the Capitol, a sort of Negro-livery stable." (Kiplinger Washington Collection)*

Smithsonian Institution—*slaves in the pens across the street. (Library of Congress)*

Sale of free citizens in the District of Columbia—"the very seat and center" of slave trade in the United States. *(Kiplinger Washington Collection)*

one raised a few inches, and the other half way up to the deck. They were about five or six feet deep. On these the slaves lie as closely as they can be stowed away."

A writer whose father was closely linked with Lincoln's entire span of national prominence gave a glimpse of slavery in Washington during the 30th Congress. John G. Nicolay first met Lincoln during the circuit-riding days, served as his private secretary during the Civil War, and later became his biographer. His author-daughter, Helen Nicolay, recorded the slave atmosphere:

> The tramp of leaden feet crossing Chain Bridge on a journey into bondage might be heard any month in the year; or a slave-driver on horseback, with pistols and whip, might march his captives straight past the Capitol, actually in the shadow of the dome, the men in double files, each fastened by a handcuff and a short chain to a longer chain which passed through the whole group from front to rear. The women walked in the same fashion but unchained, while mothers of infants and the little children brought up the rear, huddled in a cart. This was the coffle-gang, the sight of which inspired Lincoln when a representative in Congress to offer his bill for gradual emancipation in the District of Columbia. . . .
>
> Besides being a distributing center for the slave trade, Washington was an excellent point from which to make a dash for freedom. The city therefore developed in addition to L'Enfants's orderly plan of streets, another that bore the same relation to the first which shadows bear to light. Secret lanes and friendly cellars led toward the water-front, where small vessels poked their noses among the ill-kept wharves to discharge wood or garden-truck. Sometimes they waited until slaves came to them singly or in frightened groups down these secret runways, and departed with hidden cargoes.

In that period free blacks outnumbered slaves in the District of Columbia. "Free persons of color" were estimated at eight thousand. The slave population was about two thousand.

Free blacks, however, did not enjoy first-class citizenship. Each free black who took up residence in the District, or slave who got his freedom while there, had to pay to the District a fifty-dollar registration fee for each member of his family. He then had to provide a thousand-dollar bond signed by five white citizens, guaranteeing "good and orderly conduct" for himself and each member of his family. The bond had to be renewed annually. Any black found within the District who could not establish his title to freedom was jailed, and could be sold for nonpayment of jail fees. The Mayor could not grant a license for any purpose whatever to a black or mulatto. They were also subject to arrest and a ten-dollar fine if found playing cards, dice, or "any other game of an immoral tendency," or if found present where such a game was being played. They could be arrested if found on the street after 10:00 P.M., "except such as had a pass from a Justice of the Peace or was engaged in driving a cart or carriage."

The District was one of the busiest transfer points for slaves. They were often bought, sold, and delivered there, but still more often the District served as a depot for the transfer of slaves sold elsewhere. The public jails quartered slaves in transit, supplementing the privately owned "slave pens." A few years before Lincoln came to Washington, a Pennsylvania Congressman stated that over a five-year period 742 blacks had been incarcerated in the District— "not one of whom had been accused or convicted of a crime." Most were lodged in jail just for safekeeping prior to shipment. Others were imprisoned on suspicion of being fugitives.

These abusive practices continued until Lincoln became President. On January 6, 1862, Congressman Grimes of Iowa told the House of Representatives:

> When I visited the jail the other day I had hardly entered the threshold before a colored boy stepped up to me and tapped me on the shoulder. He happened to know who I was. Said he, "I have been here a year and four days." I asked him for what offence. He said he was confined as a runaway. I asked him if anyone claimed him. "No." "Are you a free boy?" "Yes." Turning around to the jailer I asked him if that was so. He said it was. I asked him: "How do you know it to be so?" I found that the boy had been confined, not twelve months only, but for more than fourteen, and that simply on the suspicion of being a runaway.

As President, Lincoln sent an order to the marshal of the jail that instructed him not to receive into custody any persons claimed to be held to service or labor within the District or elsewhere unless charged with a crime or misdemeanor, and that those arrested were not to be detained more than thirty days unless by special order of competent civil authority.

But as Congressman, Lincoln reacted to slavery with restraint. He was never identified with the ardent abolitionist Members of the 30th Congress.

In order to assess Congressman Lincoln's feelings toward slavery it would be unfair to use as a gauge his later presidential actions. His relationship to slavery in the 1840s must be measured in its own context.

Slavery loomed large as an issue in the 30th Congress. The Wilmot Proviso was sure to resurface; slavery in the District of Columbia was certain to be debated; and the strident abolitionism of Joshua Giddings, John Palfrey, and other antislavery Members ensured that if the slavery issue could be injected into a debate, it would be. The establishment of territorial government in Oregon would doubtless be linked to slavery as the prospect of acquiring land from Mexico increased. Captured by the narcotic of "Manifest Destiny," the nation eagerly expanded its territory. The future of slavery hung in the balance. Should it be allowed in newly acquired territory? In the past, carefully wrought compromises had provided for the addition of one new slave state for each new free state admitted to the Union. A delicate balance between slave and free state power was maintained in Congress, although that balance did favor the South. Surely there would be a clamor for a slave state to balance Oregon. In facing these issues, Lincoln adhered to the principles he had expressed in his 1837

Men in chains—"A slave-driver . . . might march his captives straight past the Capitol, actually in the shadow of the dome." (Kiplinger Washington Collection)

200 Dollars Reward.

RANAWAY from the Subscriber, on Sunday last, the 30th ultimo,

TWO SLAVES,

OF THE FOLLOWING DESCRIPTION, TO WIT:

DAVY, who calls himself DAVID HERBERT,
Is a Mulatto Man, about 47 or 48 years of age, 5 feet 9 or 10 inches high; strong, and well-made; of good countenance, and good manners, generally, when spoken to, especially by his superiors. His hair is very grizzly, but his eye-brows are large and dark, and nearly meet. He has been brought up on a farm, and is a good hand at all work.

JOHN HERBERT, (his Brother,)

Also a Mulatto, about 36 years of age, is upwards of 6 feet high; strong and powerful in his frame, and of good appearance. He has a scar on one of his lips, in consequence of being bitten in a contest with a fellow servant some years ago; and, I believe, another scar on his thigh, the effect of a sore on that part a few years since. He has also lost one, or perhaps two, of his front teeth, which injures the expression of his face, when he talks or laughs. Both these men took with them a variety of CLOTHING, some of which was of excellent quality. Although the features of these men are different, yet, there is something in the expression of their faces, by which they can be easily recognized as brothers. I have no doubt they have forged passes, and perhaps free papers.

Davy and John are nephews to Robert Henson, who is the Steward of one of the Steamboats running between Philadelphia and Trenton; and, although I do not believe, from his very respectable character, that he would aid or assist these men to escape from my service, yet, it is highly probable that they may try to get into his neighborhood and under his protection.

, I will give ONE HUNDRED DOLLARS for each of them, no matter where taken, provided they are lodged in jail, and information given to BENJAMIN ODEN, Esq., or myself, so that they are recovered.

R'D. W. WEST,
Wood-Yard, near Upper Marlborough, Prince George's County,
MARYLAND.

JUNE, 1830.

Slave runaway notice posted in the Washington vicinity. *(Library of Congress)*

JOURNAL
OF THE
HOUSE OF REPRESENTATIVES
DECEMBER 5, 1836.
VANDALIA, ILL.

The following protest was presented to the House, which was read and ordered to be spread on the journals, to wit:

"Resolutions upon the subject of domestic slavery having passed both branches of the General Assembly at its present session, the undersigned hereby protest against the passage of the same.

They believe that the institution of slavery is founded on both injustice and bad policy; but that the promulgation of abolition doctrines tends rather to increase than to abate its evils.

They believe that the Congress of the United States has no power, under the constitution, to interfere with the institution of slavery in the different States.

They believe that the Congress of the United States has the power, under the constitution, to abolish slavery in the District of Columbia; but that that power ought not to be exercised unless at the request of the people of said District.

The difference between these opinions and those contained in the said resolutions, is their reason for entering this protest."
DAN STONE,
A. LINCOLN,
Representatives from the county of Sangamon.

(Library of Congress)

protest to the Illinois state legislature. He believed that while slavery was morally wrong, radical abolition doctrines only increased the evils of slavery.

Lincoln's first votes in Congress relating to slavery came on questions of tabling petitions. On December 30, 1847, Amos Tuck of New Hampshire presented a petition of citizens of Philadelphia seeking the use of public lands for the extinction of slavery. They thought the proceeds from the sale of public lands could be used to compensate slave owners for their slaves. Lincoln voted with the minority against tabling the petition and for referring it to a committee for consideration. Similarly, on December 21 and again on December 28, 1847, Lincoln voted against tabling petitions presented respectively by Joshua R. Giddings and Caleb B. Smith seeking the abolition of slavery and the slave trade in the District of Columbia. Again, the motion to table carried.

In assessing Lincoln's votes on these petitions, it is necessary to keep in mind a dilemma with which he wrestled. On one hand he believed that promulgation of abolition doctrines "tended to increase rather than abate evil." On the other he had firm convictions regarding the Constitution. The 1st Amendment clearly set forth the right of the people to "petition the government for a redress of grievances." Lincoln's votes on these antislavery petitions may have reflected more his respect for the constitutional right of petition than an ardent antislavery attitude.

Lincoln and his messmates also discussed slavery at Sprigg's boardinghouse, where by the end of December the Lincolns were firmly established. Several of their fellow residents were in the congressional group of abolitionists. Their presence undoubtedly made slavery regular fare at the dinner table. Dr. Samuel Busey, a member of Mrs. Sprigg's mess, recalled Lincoln's role when slavery conversations became heated:

> When such conversation would threaten angry or even unpleasant conten-
> tion, he would interrupt it by interposing some anecdote, thus diverting it
> into a hearty and general laugh, and so completely disarrange the tenor of
> the discussion that the parties engaged would either separate in good humor
> or continue conversation free from discord. This amicable disposition made
> him very popular with the household.

On Friday, January 14, 1848, slavery became more than a topic of table conversation. That evening three armed men burst into the boardinghouse. Flashing revolvers, they sought out one of the waiters, a slave. They struck him, cursed him, and put irons on his wrists. They dragged him away while his wife and the boarders, including the Lincolns, looked on helplessly.

The hapless waiter had been working there for some time. Under an agreement with his owner, he had gradually been purchasing his freedom. When he had paid off all but sixty dollars of the price, the owner changed his mind, reneged on the agreement, and took custody of the slave.

A copy of the Declaration of Independence was located in the House chamber, and Lincoln said he never had a political thought not inspired by it. *(Mickey Senko)*

Joshua Giddings—*"the legality of slavery in the District of Columbia was of paramount importance." (Library of Congress)*

Abolitionist Joshua Giddings in particular was livid. He introduced a resolution in the House reciting the facts and concluded:

> Whereas outrages like the foregoing have been of common occurrence in this District, and are sanctioned by the laws of Congress, and are extremely painful to many of the Members of this House, as well as in themselves inhuman:
> Therefore,
> *Resolved,* that a select committee of five members be appointed to inquire into and report upon the facts aforesaid; also as to the propriety of repealing such acts of Congress as sustain or authorize the slave trade in this district, or to remove the seat of government to some free state.

John Gayle of Alabama offered a routine motion to table, but the House surprisingly voted it down 87 to 85. Lincoln voted against tabling. Parliamentary maneuvering by southern representatives produced some modifications in the resolution, and once more a motion to table was made. Lincoln again voted nay, but enough additional proslavery Members had hurried to the floor to reverse the earlier decision. The measure was tabled by a 94 to 88 vote. Two weeks later, on

January 31, 1848, Giddings revived the issue, calling for the appointment of a select committee of five "to inquire into and report to this House whether the slave trade is carried on within the District of Columbia; if so by what legal authority it is sustained; and whether any modification . . . is expedient at the present time." On this motion too Lincoln opposed tabling. The House nevertheless laid over the resolution, and it was never approved.

These votes can be viewed as somewhat inconsistent with his belief that the spread of abolition doctrine was potentially dangerous. They perhaps reflected the outrage he must have felt at the vicious treatment of the slave waiter. But the votes on these motions were the sum total of Lincoln's protest. Lincoln did not take up the antislavery cause just yet.

The question Giddings wanted to raise—the legality of slavery in the District of Columbia—was of paramount importance to the antislavery movement. To be sure, the District held only a minute portion of the slave population, but the symbolic nature of a victory over slavery there was enormous. As one modern historian has stated, "Slavery in the District was the Achilles' heel of the entire institution." The strategic importance of the District of Columbia in the antislavery crusade derived from the peculiar role of Congress in the District government. Argument could rage over the authority of Congress to take any steps regarding slavery in territories or in states where it already existed, but there could be no argument over Congress's power to act in the District. If slavery in the District were abolished, it would sound the death knell for the institution elsewhere.

The District of Columbia had become increasingly important to the slave trade in the years just before Lincoln's congressional term. By 1835 Washington was the center for slave transactions for most of Maryland and Virginia. The largest firm, Franklin & Armfield, was based in Alexandria, now in Virginia, but then a part of the District of Columbia. Alexandria was still a part of the District when Franklin & Armfield became the nation's largest slave dealer. It was retroceded to Virginia in 1846.

By the time Lincoln ran for Congress, the District of Columbia had become "the very seat and center" of the slave trade in the United States. Thus, it is hardly surprising that the situation in the nation's capital inspired heated debate on the slavery issue.

Three months after the affair at the boardinghouse, another event occurred in Washington that fanned antislavery fires in Congress. On Sunday morning, April 16, 1848, Washingtonians awakened to find empty tables, cold stoves, and abandoned slave quarters. Slave owners soon determined that approximately eighty slaves from Maryland, Alexandria, and parts of the District were missing. They also learned that the slaves had left on the schooner *Pearl*, commanded by Daniel Drayton and Edward Sayres. They formed a pursuit party and overtook the *Pearl* in Cornfield Harbor, Maryland. On April 18 the escaped slaves and Drayton and Sayres were brought back to Washington and thrown in the

Daniel Drayton captured the imagination of the abolitionist movement by his effort to free eighty slaves in the District of Columbia. *(Greenwood Press, Inc.)*

John G. Palfrey—his *"strident abolitionism . . . ensured that if the slavery issue could be injected into a debate, it would be."* *(Library of Congress)*

District jail. Belligerent mobs threatened Drayton and Sayres and later in the evening attacked the building that housed the new abolitionist paper in Washington, the *National Era.*

Learning of the capture of Drayton and Sayres and the slaves, Joshua R. Giddings visited the D.C. jail and took E. S. Hamlin, a former Ohio Congressman, with him. Hamlin had agreed to serve as counsel for Drayton and Sayres. When Giddings and Hamlin visited the jail, mobs were still gathered around the building. Largely quiet, many in the crowd recognized Giddings and threatened him. They suspected him of complicity in the affair. Upon his return to the House of Representatives, Giddings rose on the floor and asked for unanimous consent to introduce a resolution. The resolution called for the appointment of a select committee to investigate the legality of using the Washington jail to confine persons who had attempted to escape from slavery. Giddings felt that such a use of the jail was "derogatory to our National Character, incompatible with the duty of a civilized and Christian people, and unworthy of being sustained by an American Congress." Not unexpectedly, Giddings did not receive unanimous consent and could not introduce the resolution.

Two days after the first legislative skirmish, Congress became deeply embroiled in a heated debate on the *Pearl* affair. In the House of Representatives the discussion began when John Gorham Palfrey introduced a resolution raising a privileged question. Such a resolution did not require unanimous consent to be considered. Giddings told Palfrey of the personal risk he had endured when he had visited Drayton and Sayres in jail. Since the life of a Member of the House had been threatened by the mob, Palfrey's resolution inquired into the adequacy of present legislation protecting members. He used this subterfuge to bring the issue of slavery in the District of Columbia to the House floor. The debate began.

For several days southern Members harangued against abolitionists in general and against Giddings in particular. Robert Rhett of South Carolina, in a summary of the southern position, stated that "they had no right to say that they would protect a man, because he was a Member of Congress, in aggressions upon the rights of the citizen in acts no way connected with his duties as a Member." It was abundantly clear that many of the southern Members viewed Giddings's visit to the jail and his efforts to secure lawyers for Drayton and Sayres as "aggressions upon the rights of the citizen" if not an outright violation of the law.

The highlight of the House debate occurred several days later, on April 25, when Giddings rose to deliver a speech on the question of privilege. For two days he had quietly sat at his desk while abuse was heaped upon him. Now he addressed the House with barely controlled fury. He personally impugned the character of the slaveholding Members of Congress:

> I have too often witnessed the spirit of slave-holding violence on this floor to ask protection of the Members of this House. . . . If I ever had cause to ask protection from human violence, it was from the violence of Members of this floor. . . . What is slavery, and what are its effects? Why, Sir, a gentleman [Mr. Clay] once a Member in the other end of the Capitol, and a slaveholder, of accurate information, some years since stated that the average life of slaves, after entering upon the sugar plantations, was only five years, and upon the cotton plantations only seven years. . . . Now, Sir, is it not as much as murder to destroy the life of our fellow man, by a torture of five or seven years, as it would be to strike him down at one blow? Yea, is not this prolonged torture a refinement in cruelty? I have no time to refer to the licentiousness, or indeed to the almost total obliteration of moral sentiment, to be found not only among slaves, but among all slaveholding communities.

In closing, Giddings reminded the Members of the House of Thomas Jefferson's words: "I tremble for my country when I reflect that God is just and that his justice cannot sleep forever." Once again, the future Emancipator remained silent. He uttered not a word on the record.

After the debate ended Giddings exulted. He declared publicly that the debate had been "the most profitable to the nation that had ever occurred in Congress." In a letter to his son, he reaffirmed this view, although he expressed some dissatisfaction with his own speech.

> There was never a lot of fellows more anxious to be rid of any matter than the slaveholders and Doughfaces were to get rid of Palfrey's resolution. The object of introducing it was fully attained. Public attention was called to the facts and Northern men had a chance to show themselves. I got the floor yesterday and spoke my brief here. I was led off from the train of remarks which I had introduced, but my attention was called to other matters. I can't say how they report me. I do not think my speech was very creditable to me, yet my friends insist that they are satisfied. . . . I was perhaps more cruel upon our slaveholding gentry than at any other time.

Washington's mayor, Joseph Gales, asked President Polk to use federal troops to quell the rioting after the *Pearl* incident. *(National Portrait Gallery)*

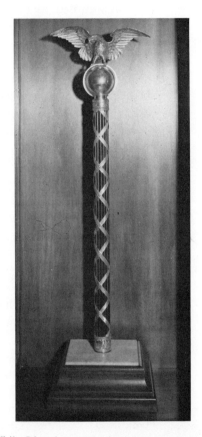

While Lincoln watched, the mace of the House was used one of the few times in history to quell a near riot on the floor of the House, which occurred when Mr. Duer of New York called Mr. Meade of Virginia a liar for disavowing that he was a "disunionist" during a debate on slavery. *(Architect of the Capitol)*

John P. Hale—Calhoun would "just as soon argue with a maniac from bedlam as with the Senator from New Hampshire." *(Library of Congress)*

Slaveholders, on the other hand, were not pleased. One anonymous slaveholder wrote to Giddings and informed him that the evil he wanted to eradicate was an imaginary one; that the social system welcomed slavery. The slaveholder signed his letter, ironically, "yours in the bonds of Liberty—equality—fraternity, Joseph J. Slavedealer."

The debate in the House of Representatives finally ended when the resolution was tabled. Lincoln voted yes.

When he introduced the resolution to table, Congressman Albert G. Brown of Mississippi noted that he wanted to prevent the subject from going "to the country to a greater extent than it had already gone out." By voting for it, Lincoln returned to his belief that "the promulgation of abolition doctrines tends rather to increase than to abate its evils." In addition, the Palfrey resolution had little to do with the slavery issue other than to provide a means for Palfrey and Giddings to get the slavery issue before the House.

On the other side of the Capitol, a debate as heated as that in the House, though lasting for only a day, raged between John C. Calhoun of South Carolina and John P. Hale of New Hampshire. Hale precipitated the debate when he moved to introduce a bill designed to protect the property of District citizens. Hale, of course, had editor Bailey and the *National Era* in mind rather than Washington slave owners. Hale quickly pointed out that his bill was similar to measures that had been enacted in Maryland and several other states. Colleagues attempted unsuccessfully to prevent the reading of the bill. The discussion began. Calhoun, of course, was completely opposed to Hale's bill, even though he had insisted that it be read. If any bill were introduced, he said, it should be one that would "prevent these atrocities, these piratical attempts, these wholesale captures, these robberies of seventy odd of our slaves at a single gasp." As Calhoun ended his oration, several other southern Senators joined in a verbal assault on Hale. Hale fought back single-handedly.

Henry S. Foote of Mississippi, one of the angry southern Members, undertook to denounce Hale. He substituted personalities for issues, and the debate degenerated into a name-calling cat fight. It reached a low point when Foote invited Hale to Mississippi—to be lynched. The decorum of the Senate fell apart. Even the courtly Calhoun forgot himself and stated that he would "just as soon argue with a maniac from bedlam as with the Senator from New Hampshire." Senator Hannegan of Indiana finally restored order and the Senate soon adjourned.

The vindictiveness of the debates over the *Pearl* brought greater attention to the affair than might otherwise have been the case. The publicity served, as Charles Sumner noted, "to bring this hypocritical sin before the country." Occurring as they did while Congress celebrated the overthrow of tyranny in France, the discussion brought the hypocrisy of those who supported slavery into even clearer focus. The bitter sectional rivalry between North and South became even harsher, and congressional forces polarized.

Later in the session, on May 29, 1848, Amos Tuck of New Hampshire introduced a resolution on slavery in the District of Columbia. Tuck noted the numerous petitions and memorials relating to slavery and the slave trade in the District of Columbia that had been presented, and asked that committees to which such petitions and memorials had been referred be directed to consider them and issue a report "at the earliest practicable period." The House failed to grant unanimous consent, so Tuck moved that the rules of the House be suspended so he could introduce the resolution. The motion was defeated 90 to 54. Lincoln voted with the majority in this instance. At first glance, this seems a curiously contradictory vote, particularly in light of his vote on the Giddings resolution in January. However, pending was a bill to establish a territorial government in Oregon—which would have had a far greater impact on more substantive questions regarding the extension of slavery. In addition to Lincoln, nine other antislavery Members of the House voted against Tuck's motion. Twenty-four Members failed to vote on it, but did vote when the rules were suspended to consider the Oregon question. Many of those not voting were antislavery Whigs who doubtless "skulked" the vote rather than appear opposed to an antislavery measure.

As the months passed, Lincoln sought ways to express more adequately his own view of slavery in the District of Columbia. He must have been uncomfortable with some of his votes. On December 13, 1848, John Palfrey wanted to introduce, without previous mention, a bill repealing all acts relating to slavery and the slave trade in the District of Columbia. Lincoln voted against the introduction of the bill, and this privilege was denied, 68 to 89. On December 18 Joshua Giddings introduced a bill calling for a referendum by the people of the District of Columbia (including free Negroes) on the issue of slavery. Lincoln voted to table the bill, and the resolution to table passed, 106 to 79.

And before the month ended, in a surprise move, the House approved a resolution by New York's Daniel Gott, which directed the House Committee on the District of Columbia to report out a bill to abolish slavery in the District. Lincoln voted no.

Proslavery interests immediately made efforts to reconsider the vote. One such effort occurred on January 10. If successful, it would have enabled the House Members to reverse the favorable vote of December and rescind the instruction to the committee.

Lincoln's Illinois colleague, Democrat John Wentworth, got the floor to offer a motion that would table the motion to reconsider. He wanted the Gott resolution to stand. Nevertheless, before forcing a vote on the motion to table, as a courtesy, he yielded time to Lincoln.

This gave Lincoln the opportunity to take the House floor to discuss a proposal of his own concerning slavery in the District, a topic that had absorbed his interest for years. His views had been expressed as early as 1837 as a representative in the Illinois General Assembly. He stated then, and still believed, that Congress could abolish slavery in the District, but it could do so only with the consent of the voters of the District. Two days earlier, January 8, 1849, Giddings's diary noted that "Mr. Dicky of Pa. and Mr. Lincoln of Illinois were busy preparing resolutions to abolish slavery in the D C this morning. I had a conversation with them and advised them that they [ought to] draw up a bill for that purpose and push it through. They hesitated and finally accepted my proposition. . . . Mr. Lincoln called on me this evening, read his bill and asked my opinion which I freely gave."

Lincoln consulted the next day with William W. Seaton, Mayor of Washington, reporting back to Giddings. The Mayor had expressed the opinion that Giddings would oppose the bill, and Giddings recorded in his diary, "Thinking that such an idea may be useful, [Lincoln] did not undeceive him."

The next day Lincoln entered debate in the House. Accepting the time yielded by Wentworth, he announced that he had an amendment he would seek to offer if the House elected to reconsider the Gott resolution. Actually, he explained, it was a substitute for Gott's language. It would strike everything after the word "resolved," and insert, after a suitable preamble, the following:

SEC. 1. No person within the District shall ever be held in slavery within it.
SEC. 2. No person now within the District, or anyone owned by anyone in it, or hereafter born within it, shall be held in slavery; except that officers of the Government who are citizens of slaveholding States may bring their personal slaves there temporarily while the owners are on Government service.
SEC. 3. All children born of slave mothers now within the District shall be free after January 1, 1850. They shall be maintained and educated by their mothers' owners until they shall have reached ---- years of age. The municipal authorities of Washington and Georgetown shall make provision for the enforcement of this Section.
SEC. 4. Owners of present slaves may emancipate their slaves with compensation, after which such slaves shall be forever free. The President, Secretary of State, the Secretary of the Treasury shall be a board to determine the value of such slaves to be freed. They shall hold a meeting on the first Monday of each month to discharge these duties.
SEC. 5. The municipal authorities of Washington and Georgetown are required to provide active and efficient means to arrest and deliver up to their owners all fugitive slaves escaping into the District.
SEC. 6. The foregoing provisions are to be placed before the free white male citizens of the District over 21 years of age for a referendum vote; if a majority votes to adopt this Act it shall be placed into effect by proclamation of the President.
SEC. 7. Involuntary servitude in punishment of crime shall not be affected by this Act.
SEC. 8. For the purposes of this Act, the jurisdiction of Washington is extended to all parts of the District except Georgetown.

Lincoln's bill would free the slaves in the District. It also would make illegal the reenslavement of a District of Columbia black in a different state, but it made a careful distinction between slaves residing in the District and slaves in the District on a transitory basis (such as the personal slaves of slave-state Congressmen). It provided compensation to slave owners. A fugitive slave provision would prevent the District from becoming a haven for runaways. Finally, his bill provided it would be effective only if approved by a referendum of free white male citizens over twenty-one in the District.

Lincoln spoke briefly. He said about fifteen leading citizens of the District had examined his bill and had authorized him to say that all approved. He was interrupted with the question, "Who are they?" Another colleague demanded, "Give us their names."

According to the *Congressional Globe* Lincoln made no response. Debate time returned to Wentworth, whose motion to table was accepted, and Lincoln's brief and ineffective venture into antislavery debate on the House floor ended. He had observed the rising controversy over the Gott resolution, the effective organization against it by southerners, and the reluctance of northern Whigs to support it. On one motion two prominent northern Whigs, Caleb Smith and Truman Smith, were seated in the House chamber when the vote was taken but did not answer. When their silence was called to the attention of the chair, Speaker Winthrop said the rules required every Member present to vote but provided no means of enforcement.

While Lincoln's draft bill never got to the hopper (the wooden box near the Speaker's desk in which all new bills and resolutions are placed before printing and referral to committee), it nevertheless was the topic of discussion and reference even after his January 10 speech.

On January 11 Giddings wrote, "This evening our whole mess [at Mrs. Sprigg's] remained in the dining room after tea and conversed upon the subject of Mr. Lincoln's bill to abolish slavery. It was approved by all. I believed it as good a bill as we could get at this time and was willing to pay for slaves in order to save them from the southern market as I suppose nearly every man . . . would sell his slaves if he saw that slavery was to be abolished."

On January 12 Lincoln gave notice to the House of Representatives that he would introduce the bill, but he never did. Years later he explained his failure to act in a letter to James Quay Howard: "Finding that I was abandoned by my former backers and having little personal influence, I dropped the matter knowing that it was useless to prosecute the business at that time."

Shortly thereafter the conference of southern Senators and Representatives, led by Senator John C. Calhoun and inspired in part by the consideration of the Gott resolution, issued the "Address of Southern Delegates in Congress, to their Constituents." In reality Calhoun's personal declaration took note, ominously, of bills presented in Congress, including the Gott resolution and others such as that of "a Member from Illinois."

On motion of Mr. WHITE, the same leave was granted to William Fuller.

Mr. LINCOLN gave notice of a motion for leave to introduce a bill to abolish slavery in the District of Columbia, by consent of the free white people of said District, and with compensation to owners.

Mr. KING, of Georgia, asked that the committees be called for reports.

The SPEAKER said it could be done only by general consent.

Mr. KING hoped that consent would be given.

ARREST OF DAVID TAYLOR.

Lincoln's bill—subject to a referendum, it would have freed the slaves in the District and compensated their owners. *(Library of Congress)*

Joshua Giddings's diary—*"Mr. Dicky . . . and Mr. Lincoln . . . were busy preparing resolutions to abolish slavery in the D C this morning." (Ohio State Historical Society)*

By Mr. Horace Mann: The memorial of citizens of the State of North Carolina, praying for the passage of a law excluding slavery from the territories of New Mexico and California; which was referred to the Committee on Territories.

By Mr. Rose: The petition of citizens of Ontario county, in the State of New York, praying for such modification of the patent laws as shall more effectually protect inventors and others engaged in the useful arts; which was referred to the Committee on Patents.

By Mr. Lincoln: The petition of citizens of Morgan county, in the State of Illinois, praying Congress to take such measures as shall abolish slavery and the slave traffic in the District of Columbia.

Ordered, That the said petitions be referred to the Committee for the District of Columbia.

A petition by Morgan County citizens—*Lincoln actually introduced only one antislavery petition. (House of Representatives Library)*

Lincoln also got some attention in Illinois. The *Journal* in Springfield printed the bill and a report on it on January 31.

This intervention constituted the sum total of Lincoln's utterances in Congress concerning slavery. Never before, nor after, as a Congressman did he speak of it. He cast many votes on slavery questions but spoke not one additional word, for or against.

Not all Congressmen kept silent. Many speeches on slavery were made in the first session, and with the surprise approval of the Gott resolution, the pace quickened. The second session rang with thirty-six major addresses—two by Illinoisans, Thomas J. Turner and Orlando B. Ficklin, none by the future Emancipator.

Lincoln actually introduced only one antislavery petition during the entire Congress, a "petition of J. M. Sturtevant [president of Illinois College, Jacksonville, Illinois] and others, citizens of Morgan County, praying for the abolition of the slave trade in the District of Columbia."

The larger issue of the extension of slavery into the territories came up several times in the 30th Congress. Members voiced their opinion largely by their votes on the Wilmot Proviso, which appeared under several guises. In 1854 in his famous campaign speech in Peoria, Illinois, Lincoln asserted that:

> In December, 1847, the new Congress assembled. I was in the lower House that term. The "Wilmot Proviso" or the principle of it, was constantly coming up in some shape or other, and I think I voted for it at least forty times.

The Wilmot Proviso, which Lincoln so ardently supported, (his claim of forty times, however, must be viewed charitably as campaign exaggeration), originated in the Congress that preceded Lincoln's. Antislavery Congressmen—both Whigs and Democrats—nurtured a suspicion that the Mexican War had been provoked by President Polk in an effort to increase territory into which slavery could spread. Congressman David Wilmot, an antislavery Pennsylvania Democrat, tacked a rider onto a bill authorizing negotiations with Mexico stating "that in territory thus acquired, there shall never be slavery." The bill, proviso and all, passed the House, but the Senate failed to act prior to adjournment.

In the 30th Congress, as Lincoln stated, the measure reappeared in a number of forms. Lincoln's opposition to the extension of slavery had been clearly enunciated in his letter to Williamson Durley in 1845. He felt that Congress could not affect slavery where it already existed (except in the District of Columbia) but he said he would never support a measure that would add to slaveholding territory.

The principle of the Wilmot Proviso came up in the 30th Congress on February 28, 1848, in a resolution introduced by Congressman Harvey Putnam of New York. Putnam's resolution was tabled. Lincoln opposed the motion to table, thus supporting the Wilmot Proviso. On August 2, 1848, Lincoln again supported the proviso, albeit indirectly. During debate on a bill to establish a territorial government in Oregon, a motion was made to strike from the bill a provision extending the Ordinance of 1787. Since the Ordinance of 1787 provided that slavery should not exist north of the Ohio River, Lincoln voted no, supporting the principle of the Wilmot Proviso.

PROHIBITION OF SLAVERY.

Mr. PUTNAM moved the following preamble and resolution:

Whereas, in the settlement of the difficulties pending between this country and Mexico, territory may be acquired in which slavery does not now exist; and whereas Congress, in the organization of a Territorial Government at an early period of our political history, established a principle worthy of imitation in all future time, forbidding the existence of slavery in free territory: Therefore,

Resolved, That in any territory which may be acquired from Mexico, over which shall be established Territorial Governments, slavery or involuntary servitude, except as a punishment for crime, whereof the party shall have been duly convicted, should be forever prohibited; and that, in any act or resolution establishing such Governments, a fundamental provision ought to be inserted to that effect.

Mr. P. moved the previous question.

Mr. BRODHEAD moved to lay the resolution on the table.

Wilmot Proviso. *(House of Representatives Library)*

HON. DAVID WILMOT.

David Wilmot—author of a provision to abolish slavery in newly created territories. *(Library of Congress)*

A number of other votes vaguely relating to slavery also arose during the 30th Congress. These dealt with compensation to slave owners who had slaves that had been lost or killed, and on whose behalf bills "for relief" were introduced. On May 19, 1848, Lincoln voted to compensate the estate of one Cornelius Manning $280 for a slave carried away by the British fleet in 1814. Most antislavery Members opposed the measure, but it should be recalled that Lincoln accepted the legality of slavery where it existed; in such circumstances slaves represented property to be protected. Lincoln obviously felt that if compensation were provided for property seized by the British, that included compensation for slave property.

In a different and somewhat more complicated case, Andrew Pacheco claimed compensation for a slave who had run away and joined the Florida Indians. In 1835 the United States army captured and sent west a number of Indians— including Pacheco's slave. Pacheco wanted a thousand dollars in compensation. The committee that considered the bill reported favorably and a long bitter debate followed. It was moved that an independent board for the adjudication of such claims be established, and this motion came to a vote on January 6, 1849. The expectation was apparently that an independent board would vote favorably on such claims. A vote of nay would be considered an antislavery vote; Lincoln voted nay.

Lincoln's actions and votes during the 30th Congress were admirably consistent with his publicly stated views. Not believing in "the promulgation of abolition doctrines," he refrained from participating in the bitter debates over slavery that occupied so much time on the House floor. At the same time he supported his belief that Congress had the power to outlaw slavery in the District of Columbia with the consent of its citizens by proposing a measure that would abolish slavery, but only after a referendum. He confirmed his view that slavery should not be allowed to spread by his consistent support for the Wilmot Proviso.

It appears that during the 30th Congress, Lincoln also embraced a new doctrine as a method of dealing with the institution of slavery in the United States. Lincoln's ideal, Henry Clay, had long espoused the concept of colonization—the removal of blacks to Africa or elsewhere—and had been a longtime member of the American Colonization Society. Throughout his service in Congress, Lincoln voiced no support for colonization. On January 18, 1848, however, Henry Clay presided over a mass meeting of the American Colonization Society in the House chamber. Lincoln surely attended and by then had probably adopted the colonization idea as the long-range solution to the slavery problem, as well as the larger problem represented by the presence of blacks in American society. After leaving Congress, on July 6, 1852, Lincoln delivered a eulogy on Henry Clay in Springfield. Touching on colonization, Lincoln concluded:

> This suggestion of the possible redemption of the African race and the African continent was made twenty five years ago. Every succeeding year has added to the hope of its realization. May it indeed be realized!

For many years to come, colonization was a mainstay of Lincoln's racial thought. He expressed his belief in it frequently during his political campaigns, including the Lincoln-Douglas debates. As President, Lincoln proposed a plan calling for compensated emancipation and subsequent colonization in a State of the Union message; he attempted to establish a Negro colony in the Chiriqui (now Panama) in Central America. He even signed a contract to colonize blacks in Haiti, as a result of which several hundred sailed to Ilé a Vache, Haiti. The contract was signed December 31, 1862, the eve of the day the Emancipation Proclamation became effective. Certainly the proclamation did not deter him from the colonization concept. Only in the last year of his Presidency did Lincoln swerve from it as an objective.

Looking back on Lincoln's congressional career, it is evident that while he remained remarkably silent on slavery the events surrounding him had deep effect. Stirred by the turbulence provoked by slavery in the District of Columbia, and a thoughtful listener to the slavery debates that swirled around his seat in the House chamber, he began slowly to shift his position. The transformation in Lincoln's view of slavery was gradual and moderate, never radical. He was never identified with the ardent abolitionists in the 30th Congress. He would be shocked if one of his colleagues had predicted that most slaves would be freed by executive order in less than twenty years and appalled at the thought that he might give the order.

9

"A war . . . unconstitutionally begun."

MARCH 8, 1846. The sun streamed through the Texas sky. The soldiers welcomed the change in weather after months of chill, cold, and rain. They were about to set out, under presidential orders, for the Rio Grande River. Zachary Taylor, a seasoned veteran of the War of 1812 and the Seminole Indian campaigns, commanded the troops. He stressed to his men—and to the citizens of Texas—that the movement was a peaceful one. Taylor and his troops did not want to provoke war. So they said.

Seven hundred miles to the northeast, Abraham Lincoln paced nervously around the clapboard residence at the corner of 8th and Jackson in Springfield, Illinois. He was already a candidate for Congress, assured of nomination and confident of election. The day before he had cast his vote in a justice of the peace election in Springfield.

The military events unfolding that day in Texas were to make Lincoln a war protester. Less than two years later, as a United States Congressman, he vigorously assailed the President for America's involvement in the war. He censured only the manner of involvement, not the war's prosecution. He sought to prove that hostilities began on Mexican, not United States, soil and had been unnecessarily and unconstitutionally provoked by the President himself.

But today Lincoln's thoughts centered on home and family. His wife, Mary, was about to give birth to their second son. Little Eddy was to make his appearance on March 10.

More than a thousand miles from Taylor and eight hundred miles from Springfield, James K. Polk sat in the White House. His orders had been issued more than a month before. He knew that Taylor's move might provoke war. He knew too that his own party was sharply divided on his course of action. Southern Democrats, seeking expansion of slave territory, favored war. They dominated the administration. Northern Democrats, many of whom opposed war, grumbled at the southern domination that had guided the party for years.

Polk's marching orders were the culmination of years of bickering among Mexico, Texas, and the United States. In 1836, when Texas won its independence, it proclaimed the Rio Grande River as its boundary. An agreement signed by Mexican General Santa Anna contained a provision to that effect. Mexico insisted that the agreement had been signed under duress, and the Mexican Congress immediately repudiated the provision. Nevertheless, Texas continued to claim the Rio Grande. When the United States annexed

Santa Anna provoked the Mexican War by attacking American troops in disputed territory. *(Library of Congress)*

EL ESCMO S G DE DIVISION D. ANTONIO LOPEZ DE SANTA ANNA

Presidente de la Republica Mexicana.

Zachary Taylor in camp—*didn't want to provoke war. So they said.* *(National Portrait Gallery)*

Texas in 1844, President Polk also assumed the Rio Grande as the boundary.

The United States engaged in ongoing negotiations on other matters with Mexico. During the struggle for Texas independence, a great deal of American property had been destroyed by the Mexican government. A claims review board had established a figure for remuneration, but the Mexican government had defaulted.

In order to discuss the claim difficulties, the boundary dispute, and several

145

other matters of concern, President Polk sent John Slidell as American Minister to Mexico. When he arrived, the Mexican government refused to receive him. A revolution was brewing, and the government feared that any appearance of conciliation toward the United States—particularly on the boundary issue— would ignite the smoldering discontent. Polk, however, saw the refusal to receive Slidell as an insult. He insisted he could neither dismiss nor ignore it. Consequently, he ordered Taylor to take position on the east bank of the Rio Grande River.

General Taylor's encampment on the riverbank, which began March 10, 1846, did indeed provoke the Mexicans. On April 24 General Mariano Arista issued orders for Mexican troops to cross the Rio Grande River. A small skirmish followed. On May 9 President Polk learned of the bloodshed. He sent a message to Congress a few days later, and both Houses of Congress overwhelmingly approved a declaration of war on May 13, 1846. The war began in earnest.

The political forces that led the United States to war with Mexico were much the same that twenty years later led to fratricidal conflict. The expansion of the United States in the years between the adoption of the Constitution and the 1840s stirred a belief that it was the "destiny" of the United States to expand and fill the continental boundaries of North America.

The Lousiana Purchase and the annexation of Texas pushed our national boundaries westward; increasing clamor for the conquest of Canada looked for northward expansion as well. Few people disputed the belief that the United States was preordained to be bound only by the Atlantic and Pacific oceans. A divisive issue arose, though, over the question of whether or not to permit slavery in new territories.

The 1830s saw a wave of antislavery sentiment sweep eastward from its western origins. Moral revulsion seized reformers and liberals. Initially at least the movement demanded that slavery not be expanded to the new territories and, hopefully, eliminated in the District of Columbia. Thus, southern expansionists who viewed the acquisition of territory as a means to extend slavery and eventually to gain greater control of the national legislature were in direct conflict with antislavery advocates who believed in manifest destiny but did not want slavery to spread. The Mexican War became a focal point of that conflict.

The overwhelming approval of the declaration of war against Mexico by both the House and Senate belies the questions, qualms, and reservations held by many Members—mostly Whigs. Passion and stampede took over when the legislation was considered. Both Houses severely limited time for debate; Members were not given time to study the documents that had accompanied the war message. Most Members voted for the declaration rather than appear to be abandoning the United States Army. On May 13, 1846, a Kentucky Whig in the House of Representatives wrote to a friend that he had voted for the declaration even though he believed there was no actual war, and that any

John Slidell—*Polk . . . saw the refusal to receive Slidell as an insult. (Library of Congress)*

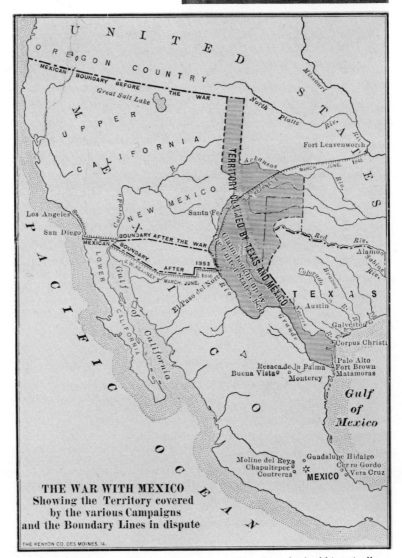

THE WAR WITH MEXICO
Showing the Territory covered
by the various Campaigns
and the Boundary Lines in dispute

THE KENYON CO. DES MOINES, IA.

Whigs pointed out that the Nueces, not the Rio Grande, had historically been the dividing point . . . Sending troops . . . was clearly an act of provocation. (Library of Congress) hostilities had been deliberately provoked by President Polk's actions in ordering troops to the Rio Grande.

In the wake of the congressional action, a tide of prowar sentiment swept the country. Recruiting rallies had the unique problem of having too many recruits. In Illinois John Hardin was the first man in the state to volunteer. E. D. Baker, serving in Congress, appeared in the House chamber in full dress uniform and gave a stirring speech resigning his seat in order to serve in the Army.

On May 30, 1846, congressional candidate Abraham Lincoln addressed a crowd in Springfield and urged prompt and unified efforts to support the prosecution of the war. In the year and a half that passed between the time Lincoln addressed the people of Springfield that day and the time he took his seat in the House of Representatives, he uttered not a single word on the Mexican War. When the words finally came, they thundered. In his second speech as a Congressman, Lincoln sounded a biblical trumpet: "The blood of this war, like the blood of Abel, is crying to heaven against President Polk."

But as Congressman-elect he kept his silence.

As the 29th Congress progressed, the Whig position became increasingly clear and unified. Whigs pointed out that the Nueces, not the Rio Grande, had historically been the dividing point; the questionable provision in the agreement signed by Santa Anna provided the only sanction for the Rio Grande as a boundary. Sending troops to a disputed area was clearly an act of provocation at best, and of aggression at worst. One Whig characterized Polk's order as being the same as pointing a loaded pistol at someone's breast.

Still, Whigs (including Lincoln) were largely unfailing in their support of the troops in the field through military appropriations. The feeling seemed to be that by their vote on the war bill, they had committed troops and thus had an obligation to support them. The Whigs were in a somewhat paradoxical position; they denounced the origin of the war and put the blame on Polk, making no mention of the Whig votes in Congress that helped to pass the war declaration. At the same time they loudly proclaimed pride in the victorious military forces.

The great majority of dissidents in Congress were Whigs, but there were a few Democrats who were troubled over the war, its origins, and its implications for the future of slavery.

David Wilmot, the antislavery Pennsylvania Congressman, became the best known.

While Congress debated, the United States Army fought. The outcome was never in doubt. Mexico could not match the resources of the United States. Inexorably, the United States forces moved to defeat the Mexican Army. The only setback to the progress of United States arms came on a delicately ironic note. General Santa Anna, an exile in Cuba, returned to Mexico with the covert help of President Polk. He had assured Polk that he would negotiate for peace on terms favorable to the United States. Instead, he reorganized the Mexican forces and spurred his troops to more vigorous action.

Lincoln's political idol, Henry Clay, suffered the death of a son at the Battle of Buena Vista. Lincoln and his constituents suffered the death of John Hardin, who had volunteered to serve in the popular war. *(Library of Congress)*

Whig generals led the armies on the field—General Zachary Taylor turned his heroism in the Mexican War into a distinct campaign advantage, frequently using his famous exhortation, "A little more grape Capt. Bragg," as a campaign slogan calling attention to his military record. *(Library of Congress)*

The outcome was never in doubt—these previously unpublished photographs are of heavy artillery captured from the Mexicans and brought to West Point. *(Library of Congress)*

Capitol Hill as President Polk saw it—as criticism of the Mexican War mounted, and persistent promises of a peace settlement failed to materialize, popular support for the war and for Polk waned. *(Kiplinger Washington Collection)*

Resolved by the House of Representatives, That the President of the United States be respectfully requested to inform this House—

1st. Whether the spot on which the blood of our citizens was shed, as in his messages declared, was or was not within the territory of Spain, at least after the treaty of 1819, until the Mexican revolution.

2d. Whether that spot is or is not within the territory which was wrested from Spain by the revolutionary Government of Mexico.

3d. Whether that spot is or is not within a settlement of people, which settlement has existed ever since long before the Texas revolution, and until its inhabitants fled before the approach of the United States army.

Lincoln's "spot" resolution. *(House of Representatives Library)*

As with any war, this one had its share of heroes and martyrs. John Hardin, Lincoln's opponent for the congressional nomination, died gallantly in battle and subsequently received a hero's funeral in his hometown of Jacksonville, Illinois. Plaudits poured in from all over the country. It is ironic that although the war began during a Democratic administration, Whig generals led the armies on the field. Whig partisans made political hay of Whig-led military exploits and succeeded in sending a Whig majority to Congress in the election of 1846. Lincoln was one of the majority. By the time Lincoln took his seat in December 1847, military victory had been virtually achieved, but a peace treaty had not been negotiated.

Whig criticism of Polk's role in provoking war continued. It loomed as a likely major issue for the presidential campaign of 1848. Persistent promises of a peace settlement failed to materialize, and popular support for the war and for Polk waned considerably. Polk had announced shortly after his inauguration that he would serve only one term, but his record provided grim forebodings for the Democratic candidate in 1848. Unrelenting Whig harping on Polk's role continued, and Lincoln played a prominent role in the anti-Polk chorus early in the first session of the 30th Congress.

On December 22, 1847—barely two weeks after the Congress had convened—Lincoln introduced in the House a resolution consisting of a set of questions to President Polk. These have come to be known as the "spot" resolutions. The text:

> *Whereas*, The President of the United States, in his message of May 11, 1846, has declared that "the Mexican Government not only refused to receive him [the envoy of the United States], or to listen to his propositions, but after a long-continued series of menaces, has at last invaded our territory and shed the blood of our fellow citizens on our own soil."
>
> And again, in his message of December 8, 1846, that "we had ample cause of war with Mexico long before the breaking out of hostilities; but even then we forebore to take redress into our own hands until Mexico herself became the aggressor by invading our soil in hostile array, and shedding the blood of our citizens."
>
> And yet again, in his message of December 7, 1847, that "the Mexican Government refused even to hear the terms of adjustment which he [our minister of peace] was authorized to propose, and finally, under wholly unjustifiable pretexts, involved the two countries in war, by invading the territory of the State of Texas, striking the first blow, and shedding the blood of our citizens on our own soil."
>
> *And Whereas*, this House is desirous to obtain a full knowledge of all the facts which go to establish whether the particular spot on which the blood of our citizens was shed was or was not at that time our own soil: therefore,
>
> *Resolved by the House of Representatives*, That the President of the United States be respectfully requested to inform this House—
>
> 1st. Whether the spot on which the blood of our citizens was shed, as in

151

his messages declared, was or was not within the territory of Spain, at least after the treaty of 1819, until the Mexican revolution.

2d. Whether that spot is or is not within the territory which was wrested from Spain by the revolutionary Government of Mexico.

3d. Whether that spot is or is not within a settlement of people, which settlement has existed ever since long before the Texas revolution, and until its inhabitants fled before the approach of the United States army.

4th. Whether that settlement is or is not isolated from any and all other settlements by the Gulf and the Rio Grande on the south and west, and by wide uninhabited regions on the north and east.

5th. Whether the people of that settlement, or a majority of them, or any of them, have ever submitted themselves to the government or laws of Texas or of the United States, by consent or by compulsion, either by accepting office, or voting at elections, or paying tax, or serving on juries, or having process served upon them, or in any other way.

6th. Whether the people of that settlement did or did not flee from the approach of the United States army, leaving unprotected their homes and their growing crops, *before* the blood was shed, as in the messages stated; and whether the first blood, so shed, was or was not shed within the enclosure of one of the people who had thus fled from it.

7th. Whether our *citizens,* whose blood was shed, as in the messages declared, were or were not, at that time, armed officers and soldiers, sent into that settlement by the military order of the President, through the Secretary of War.

8th. Whether the military force of the United States was or was not so sent into that settlement after General Taylor had more than once intimated to the War Department that, in his opinion, no such movement was necessary to the defence or protection of Texas.

Shortly after introducing the "spot" resolutions, Lincoln again registered his opposition to the war, or, rather, his displeasure with the means by which the war began by a vote on an amendment offered by Congressman George Ashmun, a Whig of Massachusetts. The amendment added to a vote of thanks to General Zachary Taylor the phrase "in a war unnecessarily and unconstitutionally begun by the President of the United States." Lincoln voted in favor of the amendment.

On January 12 Lincoln made his second major speech in the House of Representatives. It was a well-organized castigation of Polk and the administration actions that had precipitated the war. The speech was derived largely from arguments advanced by Henry Clay in a speech Lincoln may have heard in Lexington, Kentucky, and from an editorial that had appeared in the *National Intelligencer,* a Whig newspaper published in Washington.

Lincoln expounded the Whig view at some length; he deplored "party wantonness" but said his own honest reflections were responsible for his conclusion that Polk had provoked war with Mexico. He reviewed the history of the boundary, going back to the sale of Texas to Spain by the United States in

1819. He spoke movingly of the Texas uprising, and staunchly defended the right of a people to rise up in revolution. (Somewhat to his chagrin, he had this portion of his speech thrown back at him by southern partisans who argued for the right of rebellion during the Civil War.) He surveyed the actions of the Polk administration and the failure of the Mexican government to receive Minister Slidell. He could not draw any conclusion except that Polk had deliberately created a situation in which war became inevitable. The speech lasted for three-quarters of an hour and had its emotional high points. Lincoln castigated Polk for "the continual effort of the President to argue every silent vote given for supplies into an indorsement of the justice and wisdom of his conduct." He cited his "spot" resolution and piqued Polk:

> Let the President answer the interrogatories I proposed, as before mentioned, or some other similar ones. Let him answer fully, fairly, and candidly. Let him answer with facts and not with arguments. Let him remember he sits where Washington sat, and so remembering, let him answer as Washington would answer. As a nation should not, and the Almighty will not, be evaded, so let him attempt no evasion—no equivocation.

Referring to Polk's various attempts to justify the war, Lincoln closed with a bit of psychoanalysis of the President.

> His mind, taxed beyond its power, is running hither and thither, like some tortured creature on a burning surface, finding no position on which it can settle down and be at ease. . . . He knows not where he is. He is a bewildered, confounded, and miserably perplexed man.

By and large, however, the rest of Lincoln's speech is as dull as most congressional speeches. It is almost like a lawyer's brief—factual and tedious.

The views Lincoln expressed reflected a partisan orthodoxy. He had, indeed, followed the Whig "party line." A perplexing problem for some historians over the years has been reconciling the perception of Lincoln as a towering moral force with the pedestrian partisan who, to them, emerged from the bitter debates on the Mexican War. Some historians resolve this dilemma by contending that Lincoln was a petty party politician whose movement toward a politics of morality constituted a shrewdly calculated and well-executed maneuver. Others maintain that after his experience in the 1840s and the increased attention he gave to the slavery issue, Lincoln genuinely moved to a greater awareness of the profound moral and legal dilemmas posed by antebellum society. A third possibility is that Lincoln was both a man of deep moral convictions and an adept political practitioner. This is my view.

A politician who articulates the sentiments of the party to which he belongs frequently acquires the label "party hack." A cynicism toward partisan politics prompts this response, and it is often unjustified. Surely there are occasions when party consensus honestly reflects deeply held convictions of individual

153

George Ashmun's amendment labeled it *"a war unnecessarily and unconstitutionally begun by the President of the United States."(Library of Congress)*

William H. Herndon—"[his] *view . . . places our President where kings have always stood." (Illinois State Historical Library)*

party members. Indeed, I would hope everyone joins the political party that most nearly reflects his own political views. I believe Lincoln spoke from conviction in questioning Polk's role in the Mexican War. Evidence of this can be found in two letters Lincoln wrote to William H. Herndon.

Herndon was Lincoln's friend and law partner. There was no need to posture, no incentive for Lincoln to be less than candid with him. On February 1, 1848, Lincoln wrote to Herndon defending his vote on the Ashmun amendment:

Dear William,

Your letter of the 19th ultimo was received last night, and for which I am much obliged. The only thing in it that I wish to talk to you about at once is that because of my vote for Mr. Ashmun's amendment you fear that you and I disagree about the war. I regret this, not because of any fear we shall remain disagreed after you have read this letter, but because if you misunderstand I fear other good friends may also. That vote affirms that the war was unnecessarily and unconstitutionally commenced by the President; and I will stake my life that if you had been in my place you would have voted just as I did. Would you have voted what you felt and knew to be a lie? I know you would not. Would you have gone out of the House, skulked the vote? I expect not. If you had skulked one vote you would have had to skulk many more before the end of the session. Richardson's resolutions, introduced before I made any move or gave any vote upon the subject, make the direct question of the justice of the war; so that no man can be silent if he would. You are compelled to speak; and your only alternative is to tell the truth or a lie. I cannot doubt which you would do. . . .

I do not mean this letter for the public, but for you. Before it reaches you, you will have seen and read my pamphlet speech, and perhaps been scared anew by it. After you get over your scare, read it over again, sentence by sentence, and tell me honestly what you think of it. I condensed all I could for fear of being cut off by the hour rule, and when I got through I had spoken but forty-five minutes.

Herndon did read Lincoln's January speech denouncing Polk and was "scared anew by it." He wrote to Lincoln and advanced constitutional arguments dealing with the power of the President to engage in war. Lincoln addressed the constitutional issues Herndon raised:

Washington, Feb. 15, 1848

Dear William,

Your letter of the 29th of January was received last night. Being exclusively a constitutional argument, I wish to submit some reflections upon it in the same spirit of kindness that I know actuates it. Let me first state what I understand to be your position. It is that if it shall become necessary to repel invasion, the President may, without violation of the Constitution, cross the line and invade the territory of another country, and that whether such necessity exists in any given case the President is the sole judge.

Before going further consider well whether this is or is not your position. If it is, it is a position that neither the President himself, nor any friend of his, so far as I know, has ever taken. Their only positions are—first, that the soil was ours when the hostilities commenced; and second that whether it was rightfully ours or not, Congress had annexed it, and the President for that reason was bound to defend it; both of which are clearly false in fact as you can prove that your house is mine. The soil was not ours, and Congress did not annex or attempt to annex it. But to return to your position. Allow the President to invade a neighboring nation whenever he shall deem it necessary to repel an invasion, and you allow him to do so whenever he may choose to say he deems it necessary for such purpose, and you allow him to make war at pleasure. Study to see if you can fix any limit to his power in this respect, after you have given him so much as you propose. If, today, he should choose to say he thinks it necessary to invade Canada, to prevent the British from invading us, how could you stop him? You may say to him, "I see no probability of the British invading us" but he will say to you "be silent; I see it, if you don't."

The provision of the Constitution giving the war making power to Congress was dictated, as I understand it, by the following reasons: Kings had always been involving and impoverishing their people in wars, pretending generally, if not always, that the good of the people was the object. This our Convention understood to be the most oppressive of all Kingly oppressions, and they resolved to so frame the Constitution that no one man would hold the power of bringing this oppression upon us. But your view destroys the whole matter, and places our President where kings have always stood.

155

The significance of Lincoln's letters to Herndon as an expression of his honest beliefs lies in Herndon's relationship to Lincoln. Herndon and Lincoln were very close. An active Whig in the 7th District, he served as a political adviser to Lincoln. If Lincoln were merely supporting the Whig cause, he could just as easily have told Herndon that the necessity of presenting a united front demanded an antiwar posture. It is sometimes argued that Lincoln had an eye on the patronage that would follow Whig victory in the presidential election of 1848. In view of the single-term tradition, it is said, Lincoln knowingly ignored the sentiment of his constituency to pluck a ripe plum in the patronage wars. He could easily have confided this to Herndon if it were the case. Instead, he gave Herndon a consistently moral and legal argument for opposing the war, or, more specifically, the circumstances of its origin. In view of his past relationship with the Whig party—often sacrificing immediate personal advancement for the good of the party and his own long-range gain—the cynical interpretation of Lincoln's motivation should be rejected. Surely he would not have jeopardized Whig strength in his district by deliberately taking a position in which he lacked conviction and which offended his constituents.

Press coverage of Lincoln's January speech supports this view. In the past historians have cited numerous newspaper accounts condemning Lincoln—stating that he had "spotted" fever, or calling him "spotty"—yet all such accounts were published in Democratic newspapers. Whig newspapers generally approved of Lincoln's stand. Given the bitter partisan tone of most nineteenth-century newspapers, the press reacted as one would expect.

The evidence shows that Lincoln's opposition to the war reflected a conviction that President Polk had usurped congressional power and flouted the constitutional requirements for war-making.

The question became an academic one, however, shortly after Lincoln's speech. In February 1848, Ambassador Nicholas P. Trist completed negotiations for a peace treaty with Mexico. The Senate quickly and overwhelmingly approved the treaty and the Mexican War passed into history.

A decade later, in the tumultuous campaigns of 1858 and 1860, political opponents tried to revive the Mexican War issue and make it a liability for Lincoln. In the Lincoln-Douglas debate at Ottawa, Senator Stephen A. Douglas charged that Lincoln had opposed the war and failed to support American troops. Lincoln replied:

> I think my friend, the judge is . . . at fault when he charges me at the time when I was in Congress of having opposed our soldiers who were fighting in the Mexican war. The judge did not make his charges very distinctly, but I can tell you what he can prove, by referring to the record. You remember I was an old Whig, and whenever the Democratic party tried to get me to vote that the war had been righteously begun by the President I would not do it. But whenever they asked for money, or land-warrants, or anything to pay the soldiers there, during all that time, I gave the same vote as Judge Douglas.

Democrats gained glory at the Battle of Cerro Gordo, particularly Thomas L. Harris, who used his newly gained popularity as a war hero to wrest control of the 7th Congressional District in Illinois from the Whigs in 1848. This embarrassment contributed greatly to the theory that Lincoln committed political suicide with his Mexican War stand. *(Library of Congress)*

James K. Polk—*usurped congressional power and flouted the constitutional requirements for war-making.* (Library of Congress)

Ambassador Nicholas P. Trist—the Senate overwhelmingly approved the treaty he had negotiated. *(Library of Congress)*

Stephen A. Douglas—*"to pay the soldiers . . . I gave the same vote as Judge Douglas." (Library of Congress)*

As a leader of the newly formed Republican party in Illinois, Lincoln had little to lose and much to gain by repudiating his earlier stance had it not been a sincerely held personal conviction. Instead, he never denied the assertion of the Ashmun amendment that President Polk had begun the war "unconstitutionally and illegally." The issue arose again during the presidential campaign of 1860, but Lincoln never backed down. The whole record over the Mexican War origin put Lincoln not in the position of party hack, but a man whose ambition was, according to Lincoln scholar Don E. Fehrenbacher, "notably free of pettiness, malice and overindulgence. It was, moreover, an ambition leavened by moral conviction and a deep faith in the principles upon which the republic had been built."

Lincoln in the 1840s was as thoroughly principled in his opposition to the Mexican War as he was in the 1860s in opposition to slavery.

10

"I shall try again tomorrow."

THE MEXICAN WAR AND the divisive slavery issue occupied a great deal of time in the 30th Congress, yet there were lesser issues to be debated, committee work to be done, and constituent requests to be filled.

While remaining largely silent on slavery, Lincoln was hardly a quiet first-termer. He ignored the tradition that freshmen Congressmen should be seen and not heard—because of the probability that this first term would also be his last. He had to make his mark in his first—and only—term.

The *Congressional Globe*, predecessor of the *Congressional Record*, contains over fifty Lincoln "interventions." These included extensive reporting of his major speeches.

Seven complete pages of the large and closely printed *Globe* were devoted to his three major addresses of the first session. The attack he made on the Mexican War and his discussion of internal improvements each occupied two pages. The third speech, dealing with the territories ceded to the United States by Mexico, took three pages.

Historians have rightly judged that the debates on slavery—its future in the District of Columbia and its extension into territories—and the nature of the war-making power were the most significant in the House of Representatives in 1847–1849. But these topics took only a fraction of the work time of Congressmen.

Life for Lincoln had its drudgery, disappointment, triumph, and at least one major embarrassment.

His failure to get a river and harbor bill through the House deeply disappointed him. President Polk's veto of a massive bill on this subject enacted by the 29th Congress created a storm of protest, particularly in the West, of which Illinois was a part. Polk contended that such expenditures worked to the benefit of one section of the country at the expense of the rest of the country. As a Congressman from Illinois with a well-deserved reputation as a chief mover for internal improvements when he served in the Illinois state legislature, Lincoln wanted to revive the internal improvements issue. He had much of the wind taken out of his sails by Polk's veto, but the issue did not die.

On December 21, 1847, the House took a vote on a resolution declaring that the federal government had the right to construct harbors and improve rivers for commerce and defense. It was approved overwhelmingly by a margin of 134 to 54. Lincoln voted aye.

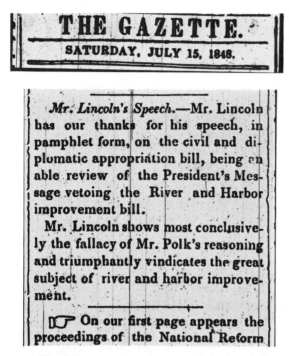

His failure to get a river and harbor bill through the House deeply disappointed him. (Illinois State Historical Society)

John Wentworth—"Wentworth and Lincoln are both men of mighty stature, and their intellectual endowments correspond with their physical." (Library of Congress)

Six months later, in June 1848, Lincoln brought up the subject of internal improvements and spoke at length during a debate on the Civil and Diplomatic Appropriations bill. In an editorial comment several days later, Horace Greeley's New York *Tribune* noted:

> The Civil and Diplomatic Bill being before the House in the Committee of the whole, sundry speeches were let off, having of course no relation to the subject. Mr. Lincoln of Ill. made a very sensible speech upon the question of Internal Improvements. He evidently understood the subject, and, better still, succeeded in making the House understand it. Tall men come from Illinois. John Wentworth and Lincoln are both men of mighty stature, and their intellectual endowments correspond with their physical.

For the rest of the session, though, the internal improvements issue remained in the background.

A year later Lincoln made the New York *Tribune* news columns again but this time the mention was not the kind he would clip and save. It was in connection with an unsavory bit of scandal.

By then the *Tribune* editor, Horace Greeley, had been elected to Congress, filling a vacancy in the New York delegation. He continued to write for the *Tribune*, and quickly combined his skill as an investigative reporter and his newly acquired resources as a Congressman to produce an exposé of what may have been the first—but certainly not the last—congressional pay scandal.

Greeley's newspaper published a detailed report that listed by name and amount the mileage stipend paid to each Congressman, along with the number of miles between the Congressman's home and the Capitol as computed by Post Road figures. It appeared that many Members were using their mileage allowance to fill their wallets. Among them was Congressman Lincoln.

The mileage allowance was fixed at $8 for each 20 miles traveled—40¢ a mile. For both sessions Lincoln received a mileage allowance of $2,601—almost as much as his grand total per diem. That meant he received $1,300.50 for each round trip and therefore was reimbursed for 3,252 miles each time. The round-trip mileage from Springfield recognized now by the Clerk of the House is 1,800 miles.

It appears that Lincoln collected almost twice what he should have, but there was a catch in the law. Greeley's exposé relied on Post Road figures—and the law governing mileage specified "the most usual route." This distinction was eagerly seized on by the Committee on Mileage when it issued a report on a resolution offered in the wake of Greeley's exposé. No individual Member could be charged with wrongdoing, the report concluded, because the responsibility for determining "the most usual route" lay with the Committee on Mileage; and while the committee did receive information from some of the Members, it still had the final responsibility.

So much for Horace Greeley's effort at investigative reporting. In fairness to Lincoln, however, it should be added that he followed the practice of most of his colleagues and predecessors. (For example, Congressman Edward D. Baker claimed $1,264 for mileage for the first session of the 29th Congress. Baker resigned to serve in the Mexican War and his successor, "Mileage Congressman" John Henry, received $1,292 for the second session round trip.)

It may be noted that pay and perquisites of a Congressman were modest indeed in 1848. In that era, Congressmen received $4 for each legislative day. For the two sessions of the 30th Congress, this per diem allowance for Lincoln came to a total of $2,728. The contingent fund of the House of Representatives paid for his stationery, newspaper subscriptions, and a few other expenditures. That was all. The paucity of allowance and pay doubtless accounted for the imagination with which Lincoln and his colleagues constructed their mileage claims. But these facts were little consolation as Honest Abe pondered his bad press.

Press—bad or good—was one reason Lincoln kept a close ear to political sentiment back home. He felt deeply obligated to the views of his constituency. He took seriously the title of his office: Representative in Congress. That is how his office was described on the ballots that elected him, and that is how he identified his office in correspondence. Moreover, he generally believed a legislator to be obligated to vote the will of his constituency, even when his own preference was otherwise.

NEW-YORK TRIBUNE.

NEW-YORK, FRIDAY DEC. 22.

In the following tables, we have copied from the records the name of each Member of Congress at the last Session, the number of Miles charged by him as the distance traveled in coming to Congress, with the amount of Mileage therefor, (the amount charged for coming and going inclusive,) to which we have appended the number of miles which each Member respectively actually lives from Washington by the nearest post-route, as set down in the last Official list of Post-Offices with their several distances from Washington; and the last column of figures gives the amount which each Member has received for Mileage more than he would have received had he traveled by the nearest post-route, and charged accordingly.

Let no man jump at the conclusion that this excess has been charged and received contrary to law: The fact is otherwise. The members are all honorable men—if any irreverent infidel should doubt it, we can silence him by referring to the prefix to their names in the newspapers—

HOUSE OF REPRESENTATIVES.

Names.	Actual No. of Miles by Post Route.*	Miles charged.	Mileage charged.	Excess of Mileage charged.
Lewis C. Levin, Pa...	138	137	109 60*	
Thos. W. Ligon, Md...	45	45	36 00	
Abraham Lincoln, Ill..	780	1626	1300 80	676 80
Frederick W.Lord,N.Y	326	326	260 80	
John H. Lumpkin, Ga.	672	923	738 40	200 80

It appeared that many Members [of Congress] were using their mileage allowance to fill their wallets. (Library of Congress)

Clerk's report of checks paid to Lincoln, who was above average in the amount of padding he applied to his claim. *(National Archives)*

Perquisites were paltry. (House of Representatives Library)

No. 526.—R. B. MOORE:

For boxes furnished the following members:

Hon. W. Hunt, 1 - - -		$1 50
P. W. Tompkins, 2, lock and hinges, - - -		4 00
S. W. Harris, 1 - -		1 50
A. Lincoln, 1, lock and hinges,		2 50
J. R. Ingersoll, 1, do -		2 50
R. Toombs, 1, do -		2 50

Charged to stationery account.
J. M. JOHNSON, *P. M. Ho. of Reps.*

No. 414.—J. V. N. THROOP:

For stationery furnished the following member

Hon. W. S. Featherston - -	$0 7
S. A. Bridges - - -	
A. Stewart - - -	
G. Petrie - - -	1
H. A. Haralson - -	2
A. Lincoln - - -	1 0
J. S. Wiley - - -	
E. La Sere - - -	
George Ashmun - -	
Alex. Evans - - -	
R. M. McLane - -	
L. B. Peck - - -	1 2
H. S. Conger - -	1 5
N. Evans - - -	5
A. Birdsall - - -	3 0
R. S. Donnell - -	
J. A. Woodward - -	

Charged to stationery account.
J. M. JOHNSON, *P. M. Ho. of Rep*

Every Congressman surely encounters moments when he ponders the question: Should he vote his own convictions or the will of his district? This question has been put to me many times, especially by students. My answer: I vote my own convictions, but I do not believe this policy puts me at variance with the will of my district. I reason that the majority of my constituents would vote the way I do if they occupied my position and had before them the same information I have.

Lincoln must have confronted similar queries. A political view known as the "doctrine of instruction" was widely discussed in his day, which required a legislator to vote the will of his district when so instructed by his constituents. Lincoln did not reject the doctrine. On one occasion in 1848 Lincoln called instruction "the primary, the cardinal, the one great living principle of all democratic representative government—the principle, that the representative is bound to carry out the known will of his constituents."

In a statement he prepared for use by Richard Yates, undated but probably made late in 1850, Lincoln gave a fuller explanation of his philosophy of legislative representation. He wrote: "If elected [to Congress], and, on taking my seat, this question shall still be open, and the wish of my district upon it shall be known to me, that wish shall govern me." Later in the text, referring to Henry Clay's attempted 1850 compromise that had lost in the Senate, he wrote: "Had it passed the Senate, and I been a member of the lower House I think I should have voted for it, unless my district otherwise directed me."

Still, there were exceptions. In the same document, Lincoln wrote:

> There are, however, some things upon which I feel I am, and shall remain, inflexible. One of them is my opposition to the extension of slavery into territories now free. In accordance with this, I have been for the Wilmot Proviso; and I should adhere to it in Congress, so long as I should suppose such adherence, the best mode of preventing such extension of slavery; and, at the same time as not endangering, any dearer object. In this I mean to say I can conceive a case in which a dogged adherence to the Proviso by a few, might aid the extension of slavery—that is, might fail in its direct object, defeat other restraining measures, and allow slavery to be pushed wherever nature would allow and in such a case, should I believe it to exist, I would at once abandon the Proviso. Again, of all political objects the preservation of the Union stands number one with me; and whenever I should believe my adherence to the Proviso tended to endanger the Union, I would at once abandon it.

In short, Lincoln accepted the doctrine of instruction except when fundamental principle was at stake. Then, inflexible adherence to his own convictions was the proper course.

In practice, the doctrine of instruction has little interest beyond academic discussion for the simple reason that a legislator can rarely be absolutely certain of the "wish" of his district upon any particular question. In my service in

Report No. 325.

[To accompany bill H. R. No. 301.]

HOUSE OF REPRESENTATIVES.

NEWSPAPER SUBSCRIPTIONS.

MARCH 9, 1848.

Mr. LINCOLN, from the Committee on the Post Office and Post Roads, made the following

REPORT:

The Committee on the Post Office and Post Roads, to whom was referred the resolution of the House of Representatives, entitled "An act authorizing post masters at county seats of justice to receive subscriptions for newspapers and periodicals, to be paid through the agency of the Post Office Department, and for other purposes," beg leave to submit the following report:

The committee have reason to believe that a general wish pervades the community at large, that some such facility as the proposed measure should be granted by express law, for subscribing, through the agency of the Post Office Department, to newspapers and periodicals which diffuse daily, weekly, or monthly, intelligence of passing events. Compliance with this general wish is deemed to be in accordance with the principles of our republican institutions, which can be best sustained by the diffusion of knowledge and the due encouragement of a universal national spirit of inquiry and discussion of public events through the medium of the public press. The committee, however, has not been insensible to its duty of guarding the Post Office Department against injurious sacrifices for the accomplishment of this object, whereby its ordinary efficacy might be impaired or embarrassed. It has therefore been a subject of much consideration; but it is now confidently hoped that the bill herewith submitted effectually obviates all objections which might exist with regard to a less matured proposition.

The committee learned, upon inquiry, that the Post Office Department, in view of meeting the general wish on this subject,

The former New Salem Postmaster now served as a knowledgeable member of the Committee on Post Offices and Post Roads. *(Library of Congress)*

Congress I have always sent out questionnaires and invited constituents to public discussions with me regularly in order to provoke the expression of home-district viewpoints. But I have never felt bound by the outcome of these surveys. I solicit the views of all half million of those I represent but usually receive a response of only about 20,000 individuals. This is less than 5 percent of the total population, and many views are expressed on the basis of sketchy information. I regard them as valuable but not binding.

Lincoln did not send out questionnaires to his constituents. There is no record suggesting that he ever invited constituents to shoot questions at him during a public meeting. The volume of his mail from constituents was but a tiny fraction of that flowing into my office. Few constituents ever got to Washington. None had a telephone. In short, he could voice his limited support of the doctrine of instruction without the least fear that it would inhibit him from voting his own conscience on each proposition that came before Congress. He could be comforted by the knowledge that his constituency would have no way clearly to make its wish known to him.

The same knowledge has comforted me, especially in those circumstances when I have had a strong suspicion that the "wish" of my constituency did not at the moment square with my votes in Congress. I always voted for civil rights bills, and during the earliest days I suspect that many of my constituents would not. The "wish" of every Congressman's constituency, of course, is effectively registered every two years on election day, and it reflects a general appraisal of a Congressman's voting record—not just a singe issue. What causes a Congressman to act in a truly representative fashion is the knowledge of certain retirement at the next election if his voting departs too often and too fundamentally from the "wish" of the folks back home.

In addition to slavery and the war, some of the issues that could make or break political careers during the 30th Congress were measures to improve the military services, increase veterans' pensions, and increase war bounty lands. John Parker Hale, although best known for his antislavery views, fought strenuously for more humane treatment of sailors in the United States Navy. He found the practice of flogging particularly repugnant.

Growing recognition of the problem of juvenile delinquency also cropped up in the debates of the 30th Congress, and was frequently juxtaposed with Horace Mann's educational efforts. Then as now floor debates on such issues were rarely decisive. Such debate will improve receptivity for legislation on particular issues, or result in the modification of a piece of legislation, but the foundation of the legislative process is the committee system.

When the first session of the 30th Congress convened, Lincoln received appointment by Speaker Winthrop, also a Whig, to serve on two committees, the Committee on Post Offices and Post Roads and the Committee on the Expenditures of the War Department. Since Lincoln had been a Postmaster at New Salem, his first appointment was singularly appropriate. The Committee on War Department Expenditures proved politically useful, and Lincoln conscientiously did his committee work.

Committees operated in difficult circumstances. They met and conducted business in corners of the House chamber—and in one or two small rooms in the basement of the House wing of the Capitol—as contrasted to the various committee rooms and subcommittee rooms now provided in the House office buildings. Committee records were modest. There were no transcripts of testimony, no statements from various witnesses on different issues. Records consisted mainly of letters, copies of petitions, reports, and bills.

The Committee on Post Offices and Post Roads was one of the busiest in the House. It received scores of petitions, memorials, and bills. Every community in the country, it seemed, wanted new mail routes or post offices established and postage rates reduced. Postmasters wanted increases in their remuneration and more reimbursement for sums of money spent out of pocket.

On December 20, 1847, just a week after completing its election of officers, the House of Representatives on voice vote instructed the Committee on Post Offices and Post Roads to "inquire" into a controversial section of a law passed by the 29th Congress—a provision that denied a long-standing practice under which newspapers were mailed free of postage to subscribers living within thirty miles of the place of publication.

The entry brought memories of my own early days in Congress. Supported by two other former publishers of country weekly newspapers, Congressmen John Ashbrook and Charles Mosher of Ohio, I sponsored a change in the postal law that terminated the free mailing practice. Not all our colleagues in the newspaper business approved, but we convinced a majority of the Congress that this substantial subsidy to the newspaper business should be discontinued. The subsidy had merit, no doubt, in the early frontier days of the Republic as an incentive to the spread of useful information. But that justification had long since vanished by the time we arrived in Congress in 1961 and by the end of the next year free mailing of newspapers was ended.

Despite the antisubsidy initiative the three of us led, Congressmen usually are highly solicitous of the feelings and concerns of newspaper editors and publishers. At the top of my checklist when I visit a home-district community is the local newspaper editor as well as other news media. I read every editorial published in the district and sometimes place the text in the *Congressional Record.*

Lincoln's newspaper ties were strong, and he responded to postal rate proposals that affected newspapers. On February 7, 1848, he introduced a petition of citizens from Tazewell County asking for reduced postage on newspapers containing less than five hundred square inches, as well as publications intended for juveniles. On February 18 he did the same on a petition of citizens from Edgar County. The petitions got nowhere and just as well. Just one page of a modern newspaper contains almost four hundred square inches, so the sought reduction in postage would affect only the smallest newsletter-size publications.

The first committee report prepared by Lincoln came on a petition by William Fuller and Orlando Saltmarsh. The petition had been presented on January 19, 1848. Fuller and Saltmarsh had acquired two Georgia mail routes in 1835, but through a clerical error the change in contractors was never properly recorded in the records of the Post Office Department. Saltmarsh and Fuller provided service on the routes for almost three years without payment from the Post Office Department. Now they were petitioning for relief. Lincoln's report briefly summarized the facts, and concluded that the petitioners deserved payment for their services, to be adjusted by the Post Office Department. A bill for that purpose was introduced and passed on June 2, 1848.

On March 9, 1848, Lincoln presented two reports from his committee. One reported on a petition of H. M. Barney, a storekeeper and Postmaster at Brimfield, Illinois. Barney's store caught fire one day, and the receipts and records of the Post Office were destroyed by the flames along with the merchandise Barney had for sale. He felt that in view of the personal loss he had sustained, he should not also be responsible for reimbursing the Post Office Department for cash and currency lost in the fire. The committee agreed and presented a joint resolution absolving Barney from any responsibility.

Lincoln also won House approval for a bill reinstating subscription service at post offices. He drafted the report accompanying "an Act authorizing post master at county seats of Justice to receive subscriptions for newspapers and periodicals, to be paid through the agency of the Post Office Department." The public clamored for this measure. Under it, postmasters would take subscription money for various periodicals and order the requisite number of the periodical to be delivered to the Post Office where customers could pick them up. For two years, from 1845 to 1847, the Post Office Department had permitted this practice, but then dropped it. Postmasters complained that they lacked oversight of the money collected, and that it required a great deal of extra and unnecessary work.

Lincoln's report is a model of compromise. Lincoln and the committee proposed that the system be reestablished but only in post offices in county seats. It established better control over the money collected and defined the legal responsibility for the deposits. Lincoln concluded:

> The Committee, conceiving that in this report all the difficulties of the subject have been fully and fairly stated, and that these difficulties are obviated by the plan proposed in the accompanying bill; and believing that the measure will satisfactorily meet the wants and wishes of a very large portion of the community beg leave to recommend its adoption.

The House approved the measure but doubtless left a great deal of grumbling behind. Some citizens who wanted to use this service probably complained of the extra distance they might have to travel to reach a county seat; postmasters at county seats probably resented the extra work thus imposed on them.

Lincoln's other committee assignment proved useful to him during his work in the 1848 presidential campaign. Zachary Taylor's backers charged that his opponent, Lewis Cass, had misused government funds. As a member of the Committee on Expenditures of the War Department, Lincoln had access to documents detailing payments to Cass. Undoubtedly he made these available to Whig partisans during the campaign. Indeed, he even attempted to have these figures published by the Congress. On August 14, 1848, as the first session of the 30th Congress drew to a close and campaigning began in earnest, Lincoln announced that the Committee on Expenditures of the War Department had prepared a report on extra compensation paid to Cass and Taylor, and asked the House to suspend the rules so he could move printing the documents supporting the report. It smacked of partisanship and the House rejected the motion in the final decision before adjournment.

The scarce references that survive suggest that throughout the sessions of the 30th Congress Lincoln was diligent in his attention to committee work—a measure of the importance he attached to legislative responsibility.

He also established a record on voting and attendance remarkable for the 30th Congress—or for any of those before or since. Of the 456 record votes—those in which Members are recorded for or against a proposition—Lincoln missed only 13. He failed to vote seven times in the first session and six in the second. He missed only one quorum call in the entire Congress.

His percentage of participation in record votes for the Congress: an admirable 97. This contrasts with 74 percent by all other Members in his Congress, and with 88.5 percent by all those in the 95th Congress.

Close examination of the questions Lincoln missed suggests that only twice did he deliberately duck voting, and both times the question was on the minor issue of adjournment.

Six of Lincoln's missed votes were on procedural matters and had no direct bearing on questions of substance. He missed four votes related to adjournment and two on the motion for the House to resolve itself into the Committee of the Whole, a routine step that speeds up the amendment process.

A record vote on such questions is rarely demanded. When the demand occurs, it is always a dilatory tactic. In my experience, a record vote has occurred when a disgruntled group of Members has used it to call attention of the House leadership to a grievance.

Lincoln made a dazzling start. He had an unblemished attendance record for his first five months in office. Not until May 11 did he miss a vote on a motion to consider a bill admitting Wisconsin to the Union. It failed 94 to 46, so Lincoln's absence was not crucial to the outcome. He was one of ninety-two not voting. The absenteeism was great enough to suggest the record vote occurred unexpectedly. In any event, Lincoln was not absent for the entire day. Later in the afternoon he cast a vote that helped to keep alive a bill dealing with the congressional franking privilege.

Called "skulking" in Lincoln's day, vote ducking was an infrequent practice then and even less popular today. After all, people elected to Congress are expected to help decide questions, not duck them. A remote constituency in central Illinois might not be fully up to date on activities of its Representative in 1848. No Illinois newspaper had a full-time or even part-time correspondent watching over the work of the Illinois House delegation. The electronic media, of course, did not exist. In contrast, four full-time Washington correspondents covered my activities with those of a few other Members in the 95th Congress. In addition, my activities were covered on a less intensive basis by dozens of other correspondents. Teletype, radio, and television speed the news back home.

Even in Lincoln's day the news eventually got to his constituents. He could not hope to keep secret a bad voting record. The *Congressional Globe* and the House *Journal* printed names of all Members present for record votes and quorum calls. Excessive absenteeism could become a political issue in the next campaign whether Lincoln himself was a candidate or not. And, on the political hustings, not voting is usually more difficult to explain than voting yes or no.

In this instance, with a perfect voting record at stake, it is unlikely that

Lincoln deliberately sat out the Wisconsin statehood vote. More likely, he was occupied elsewhere in Washington and simply did not get to the floor in time. In my experience, Members often keep appointments elsewhere in the city, handle mail in their offices—yes, play handball in the House gym—while the House is in session. They have missed votes because they did not hear warning bells, were fogged in at an airport, trapped in a stalled elevator or a downtown traffic jam, or engrossed in a luncheon conversation or telephone call. Most of us have rushed to the House floor at least a few times to find the voting process ended.

Lincoln did not contend with elevators, airports, telephones, or automobile traffic jams. He had no private office where constituents might detain him long enough to miss a vote. There was no House gym. The committees on which he served usually met in a corner of the House chamber and only when the House was not in session.

But Lincoln's day had complications of its own which could thwart his attendance and voting. Travel was by foot and horseback. The distance from most government offices to the House chamber was too great to be covered in the ten to fifteen minutes consumed by each record vote or quorum call. A poorly timed lunch in the restaurant downstairs could put a not-voting entry in the House journal. Lincoln was fond of bowling. Did legislative business ever get so dull that he slipped across the plaza to roll a few balls?

Most Members who miss votes are not trying to duck; they sometimes face difficult choices. I have missed votes in order to keep what I considered to be important appointments: with the President or a Cabinet officer, or to participate in other conferences or events I believed to be more important than the legislative issue being decided. Members of Congress are more than just evaluators of legislative questions. They are formulators of immensely diverse and complicated policy who often do their best work away from the House chamber building public understanding for a position or persuading the executive branch to a certain policy. I have missed votes because of opportunities to take part in conferences in another city, or another country. Weighing an opportunity of this sort against the legislator's responsibility to vote is not always easy. Sometimes I have resolved the dilemma by getting an opinion from the leadership on whether the upcoming vote will be close.

On Lincoln's first miss—the vote to bring up a bill providing statehood for Wisconsin—the motion lost by more than 2 to 1. Perhaps Lincoln checked with his party leadership in advance and, advised that the motion would go down heavily, decided his vote could be spared.

Within a month Lincoln had missed four votes. Three related to adjournment questions and the fourth was a vote to table a New York proposal to build a railroad.

The first was a motion to adjourn. The motion failed 73 to 50. Lincoln and 108 other Congressmen did not vote. They had probably left the Capitol confident the day's work was done. And with good reason, for a record vote on adjournment seldom occurs. Adjournment is the last event of the day's business and rarely controversial. As soon as legislative business is completed, Members usually scurry for the exits, certain that adjournment will be perfunctory and nonrecord.

The other two propositions on which Lincoln failed to vote during the month were efforts by Congressman Ashmun to settle the question of the final adjournment of the first session of the 30th Congress. On May 29 and again on June 10 he asked that the rules be suspended to fix adjournment for July 17. The first motion came midway in a busy legislative day during which four other record votes occurred. Lincoln was recorded on the other four votes but missed the adjournment question.

The vote was close, 113 to 69, falling just short of the two-thirds necessary to suspend the rules. Ashmun tried again on June 12 and this time won, 119 to 40. Again, Lincoln did not vote, although he was recorded on questions both earlier and later the same day.

Was Lincoln out to lunch or elsewhere occupied both times? Unlikely. The circumstances suggest strongly that Lincoln "skulked." He probably wanted to cooperate with those opposed to the July 17 adjournment date but did not want to vote no. He cooperated in the next best way by simply not voting at all.

The vote to table the New York railroad proposal was light but close. A bare quorum was present, and the proposition went down 66 to 60. Lincoln and 105 others did not vote. Little evidence of "skulking" here, more likely an unexpected vote that caught Lincoln and others away from the House chamber.

Despite Ashmun's efforts, Congress did not adjourn July 17. In fact, it did not wrap up the year's work until August 14. The last two months of the session, Lincoln missed only two record votes—a close 84 to 76 rejection of an amendment to a bill on the Supreme Court, a bill Lincoln later in the day opposed, and a vote on transporting mails between Charleston and Havana by way of Key West. The latter came from one of Lincoln's committees and was handily approved, 82 to 51, the only recorded vote of the day.

The day Lincoln missed the Supreme Court amendment the vote came near the end of legislative business. It was the eleventh of twelve recorded votes. On the tenth Lincoln helped to kill a motion that would have tabled the bill, but on the final vote of the day he helped to defeat the bill itself. Perhaps Lincoln, weary with the day's proceedings and convinced the bill would be rejected, opted for a bowl of soup in the House restaurant downstairs instead of waiting to vote on the amendment.

Shortly after the second session of the 30th Congress began, Lincoln missed a record vote on a procedural question—whether the House should resolve itself into the Committee of the Whole—and one that established a quorum. Both misses occurred the same day, December 22, 1848. It was the only quorum call Lincoln missed during the entire Congress.

During the balance of the Congress, Lincoln missed only five other record votes. The first was another of those late-in-the-day surprise demands for a record vote on adjournment and the second a procedural vote on resolving the House into the Committee of the Whole. The other three missed votes were on matters of substance, but none momentous: to reclaim swampland in Louisiana, pay employees of the Capitol, and agree to a Senate amendment to a treaty with Mexico.

Business elsewhere seems the best explanation for Lincoln's absence on the treaty question. It was the third of seven votes of the day. It produced the lightest vote of the seven. The bill to agree with the Senate amendment was defeated by only eight votes, but it was a day of close votes. Other propositions that day were decided by margins of only one, two, four, and seven votes. The resolution to pay Capitol employees passed 69 to 56 and the bill to reclaim swampland went down 100 to 45.

By any standard, Congressman Lincoln deserved high marks for diligence in attention to voting duties.

The 30th Congress was highly partisan at times. Democrats controlled the White House, Whigs the House of Representatives. Passions were intensified by the controversy over the Mexican War. Several eruptions of partisanship resulted, and on two occasions Lincoln started with the partisans, then abandoned them.

On January 13, 1849, Lincoln voted with the majority to insult the President by tabling a resolution that would have halted debate in the House at 2:00 P.M. in order to receive a presidential message. Later the same day on a similar proposal Lincoln reversed himself and helped to approve the 2:00 P.M. debate termination. The vote to table was 89 to 75. The vote to approve was 100 to 95. Clearly the Democrats used the intervening time to bring a few missing Members to the floor and in the process Lincoln shifted his vote to a position respectful of the Presidency.

On January 26 three successive votes occurred before a majority approved a resolution to receive at 2:00 P.M. the annual message from the President. Lincoln helped to defeat the resolution the first two tries, then along with a tiny band of Whigs, reversed himself on the third vote. The first vote was 119 to 71 against, the second 100 to 98 against, the third 102 to 96 for.

On August 7 Lincoln helped to table a message from the President. The vote was 76 to 64.

It was a presidential election year, to be sure, but never in my experience, not even in the darkest days of the Richard Nixon administration, did the House ever respond so discourteously to messages from the White House.

Another function served by Congressmen—growing since Lincoln's day—is that of personal representative of constituents. When Lincoln took his seat in the 30th Congress, he represented approximately 55,000 people. Today, the typical congressional district includes nearly half a million people. In that distant era the federal government did not touch the lives of citizens in the pervasive way that it now does. There was no income tax, no social security program, no selective service system, nor any of the multitudinous social welfare programs that now exist. And yet, although government was far simpler, at least one element has remained constant. A Congressman had to court his constituents.

In the 30th Congress each Congressman had a desk assigned to him on the House floor. There he did most of his work. Lincoln's desk was No. 188, located on the back row on the Whig side. On a typical day his desk would be cluttered with letters from constituents (his predecessor, Hardin, received three or four hundred during his term), communications from various federal departments, bills and reports being considered, and so forth. If Lincoln did not finish his work on the floor he usually took it to the boardinghouse. There were no House office buildings, no personal staffs, little congressional staff at all, and little preferential treatment from government agencies.

Today a Congressman has secretaries and other staff members—in both Washington and his home district—to handle many of the problems that constituents bring to him; problems that range from delays in receiving social security checks to help in finding employment. In 1848 Lincoln had to deal personally with every constituent's complaint—such as those relating to bounty land claims, pension claims, military appointments, patent applications, reimbursement from the government, and poor postal service.

Lincoln arrived in Washington on December 3, 1847. In less than a week, on December 8, he began writing officials on behalf of his constituents. Franklin L. Rhoads of Pekin and Thomas Graham, Jr., of Beardstown wanted commissions in the Army. Lincoln wrote to President Polk on their behalf, recommending that they be appointed lieutenants in the Army. A few days later, he wrote again on Rhoads's behalf and forwarded an additional recommendation by E. D. Baker. No record of any commission for these two men has been found.

Two Sangamon County constituents came to Lincoln with another problem that month. John Huckleberry and Thomas Collins were Mexican War veterans and entitled to land warrants for their services. A long-standing practice in the United States rewarded volunteer soldiers with land. (Lincoln received such bounty land for his service in the Black Hawk War.) This was one of several means used by the government to encourage the settlement of the frontier. Apparently Huckleberry and Collins had a problem in obtaining their land, and accordingly contacted their Congressman. Lincoln wrote to the Pension Commissioner on December 26, 1847, and inquired about the status of their claims. The Commissioner's response is not known nor is the ultimate fate of the claims.

W. H. Hodge of Bloomington referred another Mexican War claim to Lincoln. Andrew Hodge, his son, had been killed in the Mexican War, and the father was entitled to the pay and bounty land his son had earned by his service. The Treasury Department dragged its feet in responding to his claim, so

Lincoln's desk and chair—*cluttered with letters from constituents . . . bills and reports . . . and so forth. (Smithsonian)*

Congressman Lincoln wrote to the second auditor of the Treasury Department.

Lincoln handled several other Mexican War bounty and pension claims for his constituents. In February he assured William H. Young of Mount Pulaski that he would attend to Young's bounty land claim. In April he certified to the Pension Commissioner facts regarding the Mexican War service of Lieutenant Thomas Davis in order to help his brother, Walter Davis, receive his pension and bounty land. In January 1849, Lincoln and Oliver Diefendorf presented an affidavit to the War Department verifying the service of Joseph Newman, another Illinois war casualty.

Illustrating the personalized service that Lincoln gave his constituents is his letter to William Brown and Richard Yates regarding claims by Mrs. Eliza Pearson:

> Your letter, enclosing the papers for bounty land and extra pay for Mrs. Eliza Pearson, was received Saturday night. This [Monday] morning I went to the pension office, filed the Bounty land papers; went to the Pay master, and had the claim for extra pay rejected, because of two witnesses that Mrs. Pearson, is the widow of the soldier–which proof, they say, is indispensable. I went back to the pension office to see if the papers left there might not supply the proof, but the office was so full, I could get no chance. I shall try again tomorrow morning.

In one instance, Lincoln sought to assist Joseph Ball secure payment promised for his labors in 1846 to help construct boats for the Army. The letter to Quartermaster General Thomas Sidney Jesup is not in Lincoln's handwriting, although it bears his signature, suggesting that Congressmen nevertheless found ways of lightening their workload in the absence of personal secretaries. What disposition was made of the request is unknown.

There is, I think, a gentle irony in the fact that Lincoln, the only Member of the Illinois delegation to speak out against the Mexican War, handled so many Mexican War pension and land claims.

The wide publicity Lincoln's "spot" resolutions and Mexican War speech received may have led to correspondence with two other Lincolns about genealogy. Less than two months after the war speech, Solomon Lincoln of Hingham, Massachusetts, wrote his Congressman, Artemas Hale, asking him to find out from Congressman Lincoln information concerning Lincoln's ancestry.

On March 6 the Congressman wrote to Solomon Lincoln:

> My father's name is Thomas; my grandfather's was Abraham, the same as my own. My grandfather went from Rockingham county in Virginia to Kentucky about the year 1782; and, two years afterwards, was killed by the indians. We have a vague tradition that my great-grandfather went from Pennsylvania to Virginia; and that he was a Quaker. Further back than this, I have never heard anything. It may do no harm to say that "Abraham" and "Mordecai" are common names in our family; while the name "Levi" so common among the Lincolns of New England, I have not known in any instance among us.
>
> Owing to my father being left an orphan at the age of six years, in poverty, and in a new country, he became a wholly uneducated man; which I suppose is the reason why I know so little of our family history. I can say nothing more that would at all interest you. If you shall be able to trace my connection between yourself and me, or in fact, whether you shall or not, I should be pleased to have a line from you at any time.

Actually, Lincoln's ancestors had come from Solomon's hometown and Abraham and Solomon were distantly related. The letter from Solomon quickened Congressman Lincoln's interest and through his colleague James McDowell he learned of the existence of David Lincoln in Rockingham, Virginia. On March 24 he wrote to both David and Solomon.

To David he wrote: "I shall be much obliged, if you will write me, telling whether you in any way know anything of my grandfather, what relation you are to him, and so on. Also, if you know, where your family came from, when they settled in Virginia, tracing them back as far as your knowledge extends."

To Solomon he wrote of David: "That he is of our family I have no doubt."

On April 2 he pursued the genealogical trail with enthusiasm. He wrote to David:

Last evening I was much gratified by receiving and reading your letter of the 30th of March. There is no longer any doubt that your uncle Abraham and my grandfather was the same man. . . .

I think my father has told me that grandfather had four brothers, Isaac, Jacob, John and Thomas. Is that correct? and which of them was your father? Are any of them alive? . . . What was your grandfather's christian name? Was he or not a Quaker? About what time did he emigrate from Berks county, Pa. to Virginia? Do you know anything of your family (or rather I may now say, our family) farther back than your grandfather?

What new information he learned about his ancestry cannot be discovered.

Lincoln also received several other types of requests from constituents while he was a Congressman. In January 1848, J. R. Diller, the Postmaster of Springfield, complained to Congressman (and former Postmaster) Lincoln that postal fees and his allowances were simply not adequate. On January 19 Lincoln wrote and promised that he would do what he could to have Diller's allowances for clerk hire and other expenses increased. Since Lincoln was a member of the appropriate committee, presumably he would have some influence over postal matters. No correspondence between Lincoln and the Postmaster General concerning Diller's request exists, but he may have taken the matter up with the Postmaster General personally. Whatever Lincoln tried to do for Diller, in 1849, Lincoln recommended a replacement and Diller lost his job as Postmaster. In making his recommendation to the Postmaster General, Lincoln wrote:

> J. R. Diller, the present incumbent, I can not say has failed in the proper discharge of any of the duties of the office. He, however, has been an active partisan in opposition to us.

In response to a Mr. Merriman, Lincoln wrote: "Your letter, asking me to procure passports, has just been received. I have just been to Mr. Buchanan, who turned me over to an understrapper. . . . He gave me a printed circular showing exactly what is to be done, which I transmit to you." The Mr. Buchanan to whom Lincoln refers was James Buchanan, then Secretary of State, but destined to precede Lincoln as President.

Another government agency Lincoln visited was the Patent Office. On April 19, 1848, he inquired there about Jesse Lynch's application for a patent. On April 20 he went again to obtain information for Benjamin Kellogg. On December 8, 1848, he offered to file a patent application for Amos Williams.

> Your letter of Novr. 27, was here for me when I arrived on yesterday. I also received the one addressed to me at Springfield; but seeing I could do nothing in the matter *then and there*, and being very busy with the Presidential election, I threw it by, and forgot it. I shall do better now. Herewith I send you a document of "information &c" which you can examine: and then if you think fit to file a caveat, you can send me a description or drawing of your "invention" or "improvement" together with

James Buchanan—destined to precede Lincoln as President, turned him over to an "understrapper" to help his constituent secure a passport. *(Library of Congress)*

$20.00 in money, and I will file it for you. Nothing can be done, by caveat; or by examining the models here, as you request without a *description* of your invention. You perceive the reason of this.

The knowledge Lincoln picked up about proper handling of matters at the Patent Office he later put to good use in behalf of his own patent interests.

Lincoln had another reason for visiting the Patent Office. The original Declaration of Independence was displayed there at that time along with other historical memorabilia. Lincoln, who later claimed that he never had a political thought not inspired by the Declaration, probably derived a large measure of personal delight at the opportunity to gaze at the original document.

Another constituent-related service still performed by Congressmen is the recommendation of young men (and today, of course, young women) to the military service academies. On April 20, 1848, Lincoln recommended to Secretary of War William L. Marcy that Hezekiah Garber of Petersburg, Illinois, be appointed to the Military Academy at West Point. Garber was the beneficiary of bipartisan support. In addition to Lincoln, Garber received the recommendation of Thomas L. Harris, a Mexican War hero and Democrat who succeeded Lincoln as Congressman. Harris said of Garber:

> Physically, mentally and morally, he is one I believe, whom Illinoisans (and they ought not to be careless in such matters) can safely trust, and should his application be successful, neither the Sec'y nor the country would regret it.

Garber received the appointment, and on July 1, 1848, he entered the academy. The four years he spent there were completely undistinguished. He graduated in 1852, forty-third out of a class of forty-three.

In addition to individual constituent service, Congressmen—then as now—served as a conduit for problems shared by constituents of a particular area. Often citizens would send their Congressmen a petition or memorial in the

176

expectation that it would be introduced in the House and referred to a committee for action. Lincoln received several petitions from time to time. Most of the petitions and memorials that Lincoln presented to the House were requests for grants of public land for railway or road use and requests for the establishment of mail routes. On December 22, 1847, for example, Lincoln presented a "memorial of citizens of the State of Illinois, on behalf of the Great Western Railway . . . praying for aid by the right of pre-emption to the lands through which the said road may pass." On January 25, 1848, he presented a petition from the citizens of Scott County, Illinois, who wanted a mail route established between St. Louis and Jacksonville, Illinois. All such petitions and memorials were referred to committees, but none was reported out.

Petitions and memorials were also a way to respond to individual problems after administrative appeals had failed. One of Lincoln's closest friends, Dr. Anson G. Henry, had provided supplies to some members of E. D. Baker's volunteer regiment, which went on to distinguished service in the Mexican War. Dr. Henry had never been reimbursed for these supplies, and the War Department ignored his claims. Shortly after he arrived in Washington, Lincoln helped Dr. Henry draft a petition, and presented it on December 20, 1847. The petition was referred to the Committee on Claims. In due course the committee made its report, recommending passage of a bill for Dr. Henry's relief but

Patent Office: Where Lincoln transacted important business on behalf of his constituents, and also saw the original copy of the Declaration of Independence. (*Library of Congress and Kiplinger Washington Collection*)

Secretary of War William L. Marcy accepted Lincoln's request to appoint his Petersburg constituent to the Military Academy at West Point. *(Library of Congress and National Archives)*

stipulating that the amount to be paid him would be determined by "the proper accounting officers of the government." The bill passed quickly, but Dr. Henry's troubles continued. Treasury Department officials doubted the legitimacy of some of Dr. Henry's claims. Once again Lincoln intervened on Henry's behalf. On July 17, 1848, the Congressman wrote to Secretary of War William L. Marcy. He explained that Dr. Henry's claim had been partially disallowed, but asked that the Secretary direct a "re-examination of the claim" on the basis of recent statutes expanding the authorization for such claims. Eventually, Dr. Henry received full reimbursement.

A different case is that of Uriah Brown. On January 21, 1848, Lincoln presented Brown's petition, "praying for a further testing of his discovery of 'liquid fire' to be used in national defenses." On February 29 the committee reported the petition. In contrast to today's bulky committee reports, the report on this petition was short and to the point:

> The Committee on Naval Affairs, to whom was referred the memorial of Uriah Brown, respectfully report: That they can see nothing in the results of the experiments already made by the memorialist justifying any further action on the part of the government. They, therefore, report adversely to the prayer of the memorialist, and beg to be discharged from the further consideration of the subject.

At least Mr. Brown had the benefit of a report on his petition. Two other of Lincoln's constituents had not even that small consolation. On January 24, 1848, Lincoln presented a petition for John Dawson who sought remuneration for acting as pension agent for Illinois during President Tyler's administration. Dawson's petition never even reached a committee. On April 29, 1848, Lincoln presented a memorial by the heirs of Abraham Tipton. Tipton was a deceased Revolutionary War veteran and his heirs were trying to obtain his pension. They

Dr. Anson Henry, a crony from Springfield, on whose behalf Lincoln sought reimbursement for medical expenses incurred during the Mexican War. *(Illinois State Historical Library)*

had started their efforts in 1835. Their memorial died in the Committee on Revolutionary Pensions.

Lincoln was not the only Congressman whose quests in behalf of constituents sometimes came to naught. Disappointment in outcome is frequent, not just occasional.

In fact, it would be surprising if there were not times when Lincoln knew the quest to be utterly futile before he set out on a particular mission. There are times when Congressman and constituents alike suspect that nothing will change things. But even then the quest has value. It comforts the constituent to know that his Congressman thought enough of his problem to give it personal attention. Even though the memorial Lincoln handled in 1848 died in committee, the Tipton heirs must have felt reassured that all that could be done was done.

Congressman Lincoln viewed constituent service as a vital part of his job. In the intervening years it has changed only in variety and quantity. A Congressman, in addition to fulfilling his law-making responsibility, must still serve as a personal representative of his constituents. To be sure, Congressmen today have many more resources for this task than did Lincoln. We have long-distance telephones, a staff to research cases and examine basic laws and regulations, secretaries to type letters, and home district offices. These extra resources are useful. For every constituent request Congressman Lincoln handled, today's Congressman handles at least a hundred. And despite these extra resources we often find it essential, as did Lincoln, to handle the problem personally—to walk the corridors of the federal agencies, seeking out and talking directly with the officials in question. Sometimes we find, as did Lincoln in the Patent Office, "the room too full." In pursuing a quest we must often deal with what Lincoln would call an "understrapper" rather than the head of a department or agency. And now, as then, despite the best efforts to provide fast service to a pleading constituent, the interim response must often be, simply, "I shall try again tomorrow."

11

"We can win with Taylor."

Debate, committee work, and constituent service occupied much of Lincoln's time as a Congressman, but he remained a politician as much as a budding statesman. The often brusque world of political adventure provided many of the most exciting moments of Lincoln's congressional career.

Lincoln had been elected to Congress as a result of a rotation in office practice based on the contention that "turn about is fair play." He himself had engineered the practice, and therefore he could hardly run for reelection in good conscience unless no other Whig wanted the nomination. While clearly presenting himself as a noncandidate for reelection, he nevertheless had in mind the prospect he might in a later election seek another term. He therefore had a personal reason to keep a close watch on political developments in Illinois' 7th Congressional District. At the same time, he paid considerable attention to the presidential contest that was emerging.

On January 1, 1848, Lincoln wrote to Richard S. Thomas, "There is a good deal of diversity among the Whigs here as to who shall be their candidate for the Presidency; but I think it will result in favor of General Taylor." Thereby Lincoln, who for years had idolized Henry Clay, intimated that in 1848 he would desert his hero. The Whig national convention was still six months away, but as Lincoln put it, "We can win with Taylor." The presidential campaign that year developed into one of the most colorful and exciting in which Lincoln participated.

The military victories of General Zachary Taylor during the Mexican War provided the impetus for Whig leaders to sound him out on his availability for the presidential nomination. Taylor had never before been involved in politics (to the point of never even having voted), but he decided to accept the nomination if it came his way.

To gain support for Taylor, several Whig members of Congress formed an informal group known as the "Young Indians." The members of the group included Truman Smith of Connecticut, Alexander H. Stephens and Robert Toombs of Georgia, Thomas Flournoy, William B. Preston, and John Pendleton, all of Virginia and, of course, the lone Illinois Whig, Abraham Lincoln. This group coordinated its efforts with those of Senator John Crittenden. From the time the 30th Congress convened until the Whig national convention in June, this group unceasingly urged Taylor for President over Henry Clay, John McLean, and every other potential nominee.

Robert Toombs of Georgia and William B. Preston of Virginia—members of the "Young Indians." *(Library of Congress)*

Senator John Crittenden joined forces with Lincoln's "Young Indians" group in pushing for General Taylor's nomination for President. *(Library of Congress)*

Lincoln opposed Whig presidential hopeful John McLean, Justice of the Supreme Court. *(U.S. Supreme Court)*

Lincoln first publicly expressed his support for Taylor on February 9, 1848. In response to an invitation to attend a pro-Taylor meeting in Philadelphia on February 22, Lincoln wrote:

> It will not be convenient for me to attend, yet I take the occasion to say, I am decidedly in favor of General Taylor as the Whig candidate for the next Presidency. I am the only Whig member of Congress from Illinois, so that the meeting will probably hear nothing from that State, unless it be from me through the medium of this letter.

Lincoln went on to note that a constitutional convention had been held in Illinois the previous summer, and that the Whigs there had almost unanimously indicated their preference for Taylor as the presidential nominee. In a letter of February 17, 1848, Lincoln expressed his reasons for supporting Taylor to Thomas Flournoy, a fellow "Young Indian":

> I am in favor of General Taylor as the Whig candidate for the Presidency because I am satisfied we can elect him, that he would give us a Whig administration, and that we can not elect any other Whig.

With his choice made, Lincoln set about the task of promoting Taylor's candidacy in Illinois and elsewhere. He wrote broadly to his Whig friends and urged them to send delegates committed to Taylor to the national convention. On February 20, 1848, he wrote his friend and fellow Whig Usher F. Linder, a former legislative colleague and Illinois Attorney General, a short letter urging that "you should simply go for General Taylor; because by this, you can take some Democrats and lose no Whigs; but if you go also for Mr. Polk on the origin and mode of prosecuting the war, you will still take some Democrats, but you will lose more Whigs." Lincoln's letter did not entirely convince Linder, however, and on March 22, 1848, Lincoln wrote him a lengthy letter defending Whig opposition to the Mexican War, and denying that the Whig party was falling into abolitionism. The vigor of Lincoln's second letter presumably did the job.

In April 1848, Lincoln wrote to Jesse Lynch, Elihu B. Washburne, and Archibald Williams. All three letters discussed Henry Clay's efforts to obtain the nomination. To Lynch, Lincoln stated, "Our only chance is with Taylor. I go for him, not because I think he would make a better President then Clay, but because I think he would make a better one than Polk, or Cass, or Buchanan, or any such creatures, one of whom is sure to be elected if he is not."

Lincoln confided to Elihu Washburne, "My hope of Taylor's nomination is as high, a little higher than it was when you left. . . . Send us a good Taylor delegate from your circuit." He bluntly assessed Clay's chances for the nomination in his letter to Archibald Williams: "Mr. Clay's chance for an election, is just no chance at all. . . . In my judgment we can elect nobody but Gen. Taylor; and we can not elect him without a nomination. Therefore, don't fail to send a delegate." Busily trying to convert men devoted to Clay, as he

Zachary Taylor: *"we can elect him . . . and . . . we can not elect any other Whig." (Library of Congress)*

Lincoln exhorted Elihu Washburne, a prominent lawyer from northern Illinois, to "send us a good Taylor delegate from your circuit." *(Library of Congress)*

himself had been for many years, Lincoln spared no energy to unite Illinois Whiggery behind Taylor.

On June 9, 1848, the Whig national convention meeting in Philadelphia nominated Zachary Taylor for President on the fourth ballot. Millard Fillmore, a longtime party regular, received the nomination for Vice-President. Lincoln attended the convention, although not as a delegate, and his elation at Taylor's nomination may well be imagined. He began active campaigning for the nominee immediately. The day following the nomination, on his way back to Washington, Lincoln made his first campaign speech. In Wilmington, Delaware, he and three congressional colleagues spoke to a meeting. The local press characterized Lincoln's speech as "eloquent and patriotic" and Lincoln called himself the "lone star of Illinois."

Lincoln surveyed the political scene as spring changed to summer and his hopes for Taylor's election grew. By early June Lincoln was certain of Taylor's election. The elements that made up Taylor's popularity—his record as a war hero, a long and distinguished career in military service, and the lack of political enemies—could transcend much of the fragmentation that was beginning to weaken the major parties. On June 12 Lincoln wrote to Herndon with an optimistic prediction:

> By many and often, it had been said they would not abide the nomination of Taylor; but since the deed has been done, they are fast falling in, and in my opinion we shall have a most overwhelming, glorious triumph. One unmistakable sign is, that all the odds and ends are with us—Barnburners, Native Americans, Tyler men, disappointed office seeking locofocos, and the Lord knows what . . . Taylor's nomination takes the locos on the blind side. It turns the war thunder against them. The war is now to them, the

gallows of Haman, which they build for us, and on which they are doomed to be hanged themselves.

Lincoln asked Herndon if something could not be done for the Whig cause even in Illinois, where a national Whig candidate had never carried the state and where no Whig candidate had ever won a statewide office. He indicated the extent to which he was involved in campaigning for Taylor by excusing himself for the shortness of his letter: "I have so many to write that I cannot devote much time to any one."

Throughout the month of June he both sought and dispensed political advice. Only a few letters still exist, but they provide some measure of his activity. On June 19, 1848, he wrote to Richard S. Thomas asking if he knew of any Democrats who would vote for Taylor, or any Whigs who would not vote for him. He wanted their names and a quick response. He probably intended to try to persuade disaffected Whigs to rejoin the ranks, and cultivate Taylor-inclined Democrats. On June 26 Lincoln advised Walter Davis that he would not be "alarmed by the accounts of Whig defection. . . . Barnburnerism, among the locos, will more than match it."

He exhorted Billy Herndon,

> You young men get together and form a "Rough and Ready Club," and have regular meetings and speeches. Take in everybody you can get . . . gather up all the shrewd, wild boys about town . . . let every one play the part he can best.

The Whig defections Lincoln mentioned to Davis loomed as the only serious obstacle to Taylor's campaign. The Whig party contained a faction called the "conscience Whigs," composed of vehemently antislavery Whigs from New England. They were particularly incensed by the nomination of Taylor, a slaveholder. To these conscience Whigs, the Liberty and Free-Soil parties became attractive alternatives in the wake of Taylor's nomination. As Lincoln told Davis, however, there were more Barnburners in the Democratic party who would probably go Whig than there were conscience Whigs who would desert the party because of Taylor. It seemed ironic. The Barnburners—the antislavery element of the Democratic party—turned to the Whigs in the election of 1848, while the antislavery element of the Whig party turned to yet a third party.

As the summer wore on, the campaign became more heated. Lincoln intensified his efforts for the Whig cause. On July 10 he wrote to Stephen A. Hurlbut on a form soliciting subscribers to the *Battery*, the Whig campaign newspaper. He added a short personal note offering to pay the subscription price himself if Hurlbut did not want to. Lincoln's involvement with the campaign newspaper indicates that he worked directly with the Whig Central Committee, the national party organization. On July 14, in a note to John Hogan, Lincoln noted that "Taylorism seems to be going right, for which, I am very glad. Keep the ball rolling."

KNOCK'D INTO A COCK'D HAT.

Taylor's nomination knocked Lewis Cass "into a cock'd hat." *(Library of Congress)*

Campaign banner for the election of 1848. *(Library of Congress)*

Northerners and southerners alike wanted to know where Zachary Taylor stood on the Wilmot Proviso and the question of extending slavery. But as the Negro slave in this 1848 cartoon says, "He dam cunning. he wants to get in fust. he keep dark on de Wilmot Proviso till de beery last. de dam ole Fox." *(Library of Congress)*

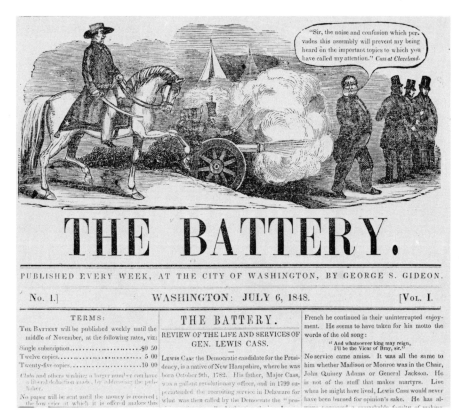

(Library of Congress)

The politically charged atmosphere of the summer months invaded the House of Representatives, and several members seemed to take every opportunity to make partisan speeches as the first session drew toward a close. On July 27 Lincoln indulged in partisan politicking on the floor.

The *Congressional Globe* reporter dryly summarized Lincoln's speech: "Mr. Lincoln spoke on politics in general and on the merits of the candidates for the Presidential office." This did not do justice to Lincoln's speech. He apparently used the same text on several occasions during the campaign. In this speech Lincoln presented a lengthy discussion of the Mexican War, the excesses of the Democratic party, and the abuses of the purse allegedly committed by Lewis Cass as Governor of Michigan. He then concluded with his famous passage ridiculing the efforts of the Democrats to portray Cass as a military hero:

> By the way, Mr. Speaker, did you know I am a military hero? Yes, sir; in the days of the Black Hawk war I fought, bled and came away. Speaking of General Cass's career reminds me of my own. I was not at Stillman's defeat, but I was about as near it as Cass was to Hull's surrender; and like him, I saw the place very soon afterward. It is quite certain that I did not break my sword, for I had none to break; but I bent a musket pretty badly on one occasion. If Cass broke his sword, the idea is he broke it in desperation; I bent the musket by accident. If General Cass went in advance of me in picking huckleberries, I guess I surpassed him in charges upon the wild onions. If he saw any live, fighting Indians, it was more than I did; but I had a good many bloody struggles with mosquitoes, and although I never fainted from the loss of blood, I can truly say I was often very hungry. Mr. Speaker, if I should ever conclude to doff whatever our Democratic friends may suppose there is of black-cockade federalism about me, and therefore they shall take me up as their candidate for the Presidency, I protest they shall not make fun of me, as they have of General Cass, by attempting to write me into a military hero.

For the first time Lincoln cast himself in a presidential role.

Lincoln's speech amused his colleagues and attracted some favorable attention from the press. The Baltimore *American* wrote:

> He is a very able, acute, uncouth, honest, upright man, and a tremendous wag, withal. . . . Mr. Lincoln's manner was so good natured, and his style so peculiar, that he kept the House in a continuous roar of merriment for the last half hour of his speech. He would commence a point in his speech far up one of the aisles, and keep on talking, gesticulating, and walking until he would find himself, at the end of a paragraph, down in the centre of the area in front of the Clerk's desk. He would then go back and take another head, and work again, and so on, through his capital speech.

But if the speech pleased the Baltimore *American*, it enraged President Polk. On August 7, 1848, the President wrote petulantly in his diary: "The House of Representatives . . . have been engaged . . . in making violent party speeches

A WAR
PRESIDENT.

Manifest Destiny

New Mexico,
California,Chihuahua,
Zacatecas, MEXICO, Peru,
Yucatan, Cuba.

PROGRESSIVE DEMOCRACY.

"If Cass broke his sword, the idea is he broke it in desperation,"
as this 1848 cartoon chides the Democratic candidate. *(Library
of Congress)*

Lewis Cass—*"went in advance of me in
picking huckleberries." (Library of Congress)*

on the Presidential election. . . . This is a great outrage and they should be held
to a strict account . . . for their wanton waste of the public time."

Lincoln continued his correspondence for the Whig cause, now branching out
beyond the borders of Illinois. On August 8 he wrote to William Schouler,
editor of the Boston *Atlas,* "Now that the Presidential candidates are all set, I
will thank you for your undisguised opinion as to what New England generally,
and Massachusetts particularly will do." On September 3 he wrote similarly to
Thaddeus Stevens: "I desire the undisguised opinion of some experienced and
sagacious Pennsylvania politician, as to how the vote of that state, for governor
and president, is likely to go." Lincoln clearly enjoyed his role in the national
political arena.

After Congress adjourned August 14, Lincoln joined a group of his Whig
colleagues in a project that took nearly three weeks—franking out documents
useful in the campaign for Taylor. The group mailed out as many as 20,000 items
a day. Lincoln enthusiastically used the congressional frank permitting him to
mail documents and letters free; he had voted against a bill on February 1, 1848,
which would have abolished the franking privilege.

His personal expenditure for documents—most of them speech reprints that were mailed out under the frank—was among the highest in Congress.

In the first session he sent out 7,080 copies of his own speeches and 5,560 copies of speeches by others. The total printing bill was $136.40. His own cost him $76.80; speeches of others cost the balance, $59.60. All this printing and mailing occurred before the elections of 1848. In the second—post-election—session, Lincoln spent only $4 for speech reprints.

When the mailing chores were done—shortly after the adjournment of the House of Representatives—Lincoln began to take to the stump for Taylor. The Whig Central Committee probably felt that his House speech would please and amuse audiences. On August 24, 1848, Lincoln spoke to a crowd in Seneca, Maryland. The *Republican Citizen*, a Frederick, Maryland, newspaper, reported that roughly six hundred people were there and that "Mr. Lincoln . . . a high protective tariffite, *free soil-Wilmot Proviso*-abolition Whig supported the cause of Taylor." Two days later, Lincoln spoke in Rockville, Maryland. According to the *National Intelligencer*, "The Whig convention of Montgomery County met at Rockville . . . on the night of the same day the *Rough and Ready Club* held a meeting in the courthouse and was addressed in a most interesting speech by the Hon. Mr. Lincoln of Illinois." On September 2 the Baltimore *Clipper* reported that "the *Rough and Ready Club* held a meeting last night . . . Messrs. Brady and Lincoln, of the House of Representatives, delivered addresses." The pithy humor that characterized the speech Lincoln first made in the House of Representatives undoubtedly entertained his listeners and bolstered support for Taylor.

While Lincoln delivered his speeches in the Maryland suburbs, the Whig Central Committee viewed with growing alarm the defections of conscience Whigs, particularly in Massachusetts where antislavery sentiment was quite strong. Many Massachusetts Whigs shared their concern. One of these was Junius Hall, a Boston attorney who had been associated with Lincoln in several

Thaddeus Stevens—an *"experienced and sagacious Pennsylvania politician." (Library of Congress)*

Illinois cases. It appears that he had a high regard for Lincoln's abilities, for on August 31, 1848, he wrote to Lincoln and asked him if he would be willing to speak in Boston and perhaps in Worcester. Lincoln replied on September 3:

> Your letter of the 31st ult. was received yesterday, and you may be sure I am a good deal flattered by it. I expect to leave here on Tuesday morning and to leave New York for Boston on Saturday morning. If anything happens to break in upon this, I will write you again. As to speechmaking, I have the elements of one speech in mind, which I should like to deliver to a community politically affected as I understand yours to be, *provided* always a tolerable proportion of the community should intimate a willingness to hear me. About going to Worcester I cannot say. I am somewhat impatient to go home now, although it is not very probable Illinois will go for Taylor. Please accept my thanks for your kindness.

Between the time Lincoln wrote to Hall and the time he arrived in Massachusetts, he decided to include Worcester on his itinerary, as well as several other towns between Worcester and Boston.

In Worcester Lincoln proved that he did not need much advance notice as a speaker. The chairman of a Whig meeting scheduled for September 12—the eve of the Whig state convention—could not get a speaker. The frantic chairman, learning that Lincoln had arrived in town, hurried to his hotel late in the afternoon and quickly got his agreement to speak that very night. The speech went well. At the end there were three cheers for Illinois, and three for Lincoln.

The next day, in an impromptu speech at the railway station, Lincoln's remarks were cut short by the arrival of a special train bringing Speaker Robert Winthrop and other prominent Whigs.

The Boston *Daily Advertiser* reported on September 14 that:

> Mr. Lincoln has a very tall and thin figure, with an intellectual face, showing a searching mind and a cool judgment. He spoke in a clear and cool and very eloquent manner for an hour and a half, carrying the audience with him in his able arguments and brilliant illustrations.

He defended Taylor against oft-proffered charges that "he had no principles." He discussed slavery, and added with a touch of humor that "the people of Illinois agreed entirely with the people of Massachusetts on this subject, except perhaps that they did not keep so constantly thinking about it."

The main purpose of his speech, however, was to unite the Whigs. He told them, much as he had told Williamson Durley in 1845, that votes for Free-Soil or Liberty candidates were actually votes for the Democratic party. He pointed out that the danger of the extension of slavery was far greater in the event of Cass's election than Taylor's, and that by taking votes from Taylor, the antislavery forces actually did their own cause greater real damage. He rebuked the Free-Soilers for their failure to deal with the Mexican War. In pointing out that many former Whigs turned Free-Soilers had opposed the war, he noted that

A Boston political meeting like the one Lincoln addressed. *(Library of Congress)*

Van Burenites (Barnburners) had supported the war. In view of that, he declared "of all the parties asking the confidence of the Country, this new one had less of principle than any other."

The next morning, before the opening of the Whig state convention, Lincoln and several other speakers briefly addressed a group of delegates. When the convention got under way, Lincoln listened to the Whig leadership plead for party unity in the state. That evening the "Lone Star Whig of Illinois" attended a dinner given by former Massachusetts Governor Levi Lincoln. The dinner was one of Lincoln's most vivid memories of his trip to Massachusetts. He quipped to Governor Lincoln, "I *hope* we belong, as the Scotch say, to the same clan; but I *know* one thing, and that is, we are both good Whigs."

The Governor's dinner may have made a deep impression on Lincoln, but he too made an impression on the Bay Staters. More accustomed to high-flown oratory, his Massachusetts audiences seemed to have enjoyed the homespun quality and humor of the western stump speaker. On September 14 he spoke in New Bedford and on the fifteenth he urged party unity in a speech before the Boston Whig Club. The Boston *Atlas* reported:

> They were addressed by the Hon. Abraham Lincoln, of Illinois, in a speech . . . which for sound reasoning, cogent argument and keen satire, we have seldom heard equalled. . . . His remarks were frequently interrupted by rounds of applause. As soon as he had concluded, the audience gave three cheers for Taylor and Fillmore, and three more for Mr. Lincoln. . . . It was a glorious meeting.

The next day Lincoln spoke at Lowell and on the eighteenth in Dorchester. On the nineteenth he spoke at a meeting in Chelsea. The papers there reported that "the Honorable Abraham Lincoln made a speech, which for aptness of illustration, solidity of argument and genuine eloquence, is hard to beat." On the twentieth he attended a Whig meeting in Dedham, and spoke to a group in Cambridge that evening.

Lincoln's speeches impressed even the opposition. The Bristol *County Democrat* reported a speech Lincoln gave at Union Hall in Taunton:

> The Taylor men were well entertained by an address from the Hon. Abraham Lincoln of Illinois. The address as well as the speaker was such as to give unlimited satisfaction to the disheartened Taylorites. . . . It was relieving to hear a man speak as if he believed what he was saying and had a grain or two of feeling mixed up with it; one who could not only speak highly of Taylor, but could occasionally swell with indignation or burst in hatred on the Free Soilers.

Such praise from an opposing newspaper was rare in that era of blatant journalistic vituperation and partisanship.

Lincoln gave his last Massachusetts campaign speech at Tremont House in Boston. William H. Seward shared the platform with Lincoln as the principal speaker that day. Lincoln followed and "spoke about an hour and made a powerful and convincing speech." Seward's speech had been a vigorous antislavery appeal, and apparently had considerable impact on Lincoln. Seward recalled Lincoln's reaction in his memoirs, "I have been thinking about what you said in your speech. I reckon you are right. We have got to deal with this slavery question, and got to give much more attention to it hereafter than we have been doing," said the man who became the Great Emancipator.

At any rate, the trip had been a good experience for Lincoln. He had met many party leaders, had been well received by the people to whom he spoke, and cordially reported in the local Whig press. Perhaps the first vague aspirations to the Presidency began to stir in him as a result of his successful tour of the Bay State.

Shortly after his departure from Massachusetts, the Boston *Atlas* published the following short notice:

> In answer to the many applications which we daily receive from different parts of the State for this gentleman to speak, we have to say that he left Boston on Saturday morning on his way home to Illinois.

While Lincoln had been drumming up enthusiasm for Taylor in Maryland and Massachusetts, at home the Whigs were suffering their first loss since the 7th Congressional District had been established. Democratic nominee Thomas L. Harris scored a victory over the Whig candidate and former Lincoln law partner Stephen T. Logan on August 6. The presidential vote did not occur until November 7.

Levi Lincoln—*"I hope we belong . . . to the same clan; but I know one thing . . . we are both good Whigs." (Library of Congress)*

William H. Seward—*"I reckon you are right." (Library of Congress)*

Tremont House—*aspirations to the Presidency began to stir. (Library of Congress)*

Lincoln returned to Illinois to stump for Taylor. In light of the Whig defeat for his own congressional seat, Lincoln could easily have been disheartened, but he maintained a cheerful optimism. Many Whigs had written prior to the congressional election and told him that they were unable to support Logan. He realized full well the value of Harris's war service as a vote-getter and hoped that Taylor's war record could put him over the top in Illinois. He stoutly maintained his Whig optimism in a letter to William Schouler late in August, "That there is any political change against us in the District I cannot believe."

On October 5 Lincoln reached Chicago and registered at the Sherman House. A month earlier he had been chosen as an assistant presidential elector and set eagerly to work. The Whigs held a rally at the courthouse in Chicago on the evening of October 6, but the crowd grew so large that the meeting had to be moved to the public square. There Lincoln spoke for two hours. A contemporary account reported:

> Which time he [Lincoln] devoted to a most earnest, candid and logical examination of the great questions involved in the present Presidential canvass. He clearly and conclusively showed that the defeat of Gen. Taylor would be a verdict of the American people, against any restriction or restraint to the extension or perpetuation of slavery in newly acquired territory. In this he resorted to no special pleading but with well arranged and pertinent facts, and sincere arguments he fully demonstrated it. During his speech he introduced several humorous, but very appropriate illustrations.

The Chicago *Journal* further observed that Lincoln's speech was "one of the very best we have heard or read since the opening of the campaign."

From Chicago, Lincoln traveled to Peoria, and along with J. Y. Scammon addressed a crowd the evening of October 9. The partisan *Democratic Free Press* predictably reported Lincoln's speech unfavorably: "Mr. L. blew his nose, bobbed his head, threw up his coattail, and in the course of two hours was delivered of an immense amount of sound and fury." Lincoln more than likely repeated his Chicago speech in Peoria, and the contrasting reports in the newspapers reflect the intense partisanship practiced by journalists of that era.

On October 10 Lincoln returned home to Springfield. The Democratic Illinois *State Register* noted humorously on the thirteenth:

> Hon. Abraham Lincoln . . . arrived at home on Tuesday last. . . . We are pleased to observe that his arduous duties since the adjournment of Congress in franking and loading down the mails with Whig electioneering documents, have not impaired his health. He looks remarkably well.

If he looked well, he apparently felt the need of a short respite from his arduous campaigning. He did not take to the stump again until October 19. Then he visited Beardstown and delivered a speech urging the voters to support the Whig ticket.

194

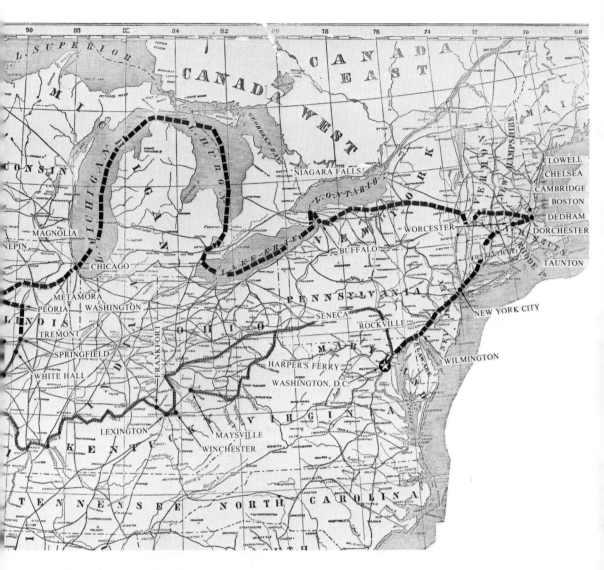

Map of Lincoln's travels on the stump.

On October 21 Lincoln traveled to Jacksonville to plead the same cause. Here he engaged in a debate, foreshadowing the tactics of his famous campaign against Stephen A. Douglas for the Senate seat in 1858. His opponent in 1848 was Murray McConnell, a prominent Morgan County Democrat. The only known report of the debate was carried in the unfriendly Illinois *State Register* on October 27. The *Register* account made it appear that Lincoln was completely overwhelmed by McConnell's arguments.

McConnell asked, according to the *Register*, "if Mr. Lincoln did not know
. . . that he was misrepresenting the wishes of the patriotic people of this
District" by voting "Yes" on the Ashmun amendment, which declared that the
Mexican War had been "unconstitutionally" begun. Lincoln responded, "No, I
did not know it, and don't believe it yet."

The *Register* concluded its report by stating that "Lincoln has made nothing
by coming to this part of the country to make speeches. He had better have
stayed away."

On November 3 the *Register* reported a speech Lincoln made in Petersburg on
October 23. "Lincoln attempted to make a defence of his course in Congress
when he was most signally 'used up' by Ferguson. Lincoln beat a retreat to
Springfield swearing that Billy's home thrusts were 'unconstitutional and
unnecessary.'" The last remark was a humorous jibe at Lincoln's vote on the
Ashmun amendment. The Democrats clearly felt they could make political hay
of Lincoln's antiwar stand. Only the election would tell how successful they
were.

After the Petersburg speech, Lincoln took another week off, plainly resting up
for the all-out campaigning of the last week before the election. On October 30
he resumed his heavy schedule, this time in company with his friend Dr. Anson
G. Henry. He spent the entire week giving speeches. On the thirtieth Lincoln
and Henry spoke together in Metamora in the afternoon. Next, they journeyed
to Magnolia, Hennepin, Lacon, Washington, Tremont, Pekin, and Peoria.
Lincoln hammered away at the need for party unity. The Lacon, Illinois, *Gazette*
reported that on November 1:

> Dr. Henry and Hon. A. Lincoln addressed a numerous assemblage of our
> citizens from all parts of the country. Mr. Lincoln followed [Dr. Henry] with
> one of his most brilliant efforts. His main purpose was to show that the peace
> and prosperity of the country, and the limitation of slavery depended upon
> the election of a Whig congress and Gen. Taylor. . . . He declared that the
> contest was between Taylor and Cass and admonished all Liberty and Van
> Buren men to cast their votes for Gen. Taylor, and not indirectly for Gen.
> Cass. . . . He scored with the most scathing language, that "*consistency*" of
> the abolitionists which, while they professed great horror of the proposed
> extension of slave territory, they aided in the election of Mr. Polk; for
> which, and its disastrous consequences they were responsible.

The campaign ended on November 7. Lincoln cast his ballot in Springfield,
voting for Whig presidential electors. As he had said earlier to Junius Hall,
however, "It is not likely Illinois will go for Taylor." He proved to be a sound
prophet. Taylor lost Illinois, but by a margin of only 3,523. The nation went for
him; his popular vote was 1,360,099. Cass polled 1,220,544. Van Buren
received 291,263. Lincoln's efforts had contributed to Taylor's victory and to his
strong showing in Illinois. In 1844 Polk, the Democratic presidential candidate,
had carried Illinois by a majority nearly four times as large—12,392. In Lincoln's

The inauguration of Zachary Taylor. *(Library of Congress)*

own 7th Congressional District, the results were even more satisfying. Taylor had received a majority there of about 1,300 votes—nearly as large as Lincoln's margin in the congressional election of 1846. Clearly the Whig party had made large gains in Illinois.

With a Whig headed to the White House, Lincoln prepared to return for the second and shorter session of Congress. The new administration would have a great deal of patronage to hand out, and Lincoln expected to have a role in dispensing whatever plums went to Illinois. He also hoped to receive his own just reward from the patronage mill for helping Taylor become President.

12

"Is the center nothing?"

THE SECOND SESSION OF the House of Representatives had only just begun when Lincoln received a flood of letters. In the wake of Zachary Taylor's election, Whig office seekers from throughout the state of Illinois, as well as many outside the state, importuned Lincoln to put in a good word for them with the powers that be in Washington. It is some measure of Lincoln's reputation that they expected that a word spoken by him in the right places would have great weight.

Lincoln, however, did not want to make promises he could not keep. He always assured job hunters of his personal regard for them, but noted that he might not have the responsibility or authority to dispense patronage positions. Lincoln viewed patronage as a highly important means of political control, and he pursued his own role in it with great care. He zealously sought to live up to the promises he made. He was accurate in his appraisals and fair in his recommendations.

His efforts had only limited effect on the distribution of patronage of the Taylor administration, but the experience helped prepare him for the future. When Lincoln assumed the Presidency, he made patronage a tool of policy.

Before returning for the second session, while still in Springfield, Lincoln had told Walter Davis, a young stalwart Whig, that he would try to get him a patronage job. Upon his return to Washington, he found a reminder letter from Davis. His reply demonstrated his own uncertainty as to whether he would be able to affect the distribution of any jobs.

> Your letter is received. When I last saw you I said, that if the distribution of office should fall into my hands, you should have *something;* and I now say as much, but can say no more. I know no more than I knew when you saw me, as to whether the present officers will be removed, or, if they shall, whether *I* shall be allowed to name the persons to fill them.

No doubt one of the major uncertainties was whether Lincoln or E. D. Baker would have the major role in deciding who should receive which jobs. Baker had just been elected Whig Representative to the 31st Congress, this time serving Illinois' 6th Congressional District in the northwest corner of the state where he had recently moved. Lincoln would be leaving Washington at the end of the session and the district he represented—the 7th—would be served in the 31st Congress by a Democrat.

The applicant . . . got the job because . . . he was poor, out of health, and had a large family.
(Library of Congress)

Letter from Lincoln to Meredith. *(Library of Congress)*

After a short time, Baker and Lincoln worked out an understanding, clearly spelled out in a letter to Treasury Secretary William M. Meredith:

Dear Sir:

Col. E. D. Baker and myself are the only Whig members of Congress from Illinois—I, of the 30th & he of the 31st. We have reason to think the Whigs of that state hold us responsible, to some extent, for the appointments which may be made of our citizens. We do not know you personally; and our efforts to see you have, so far, been unavailing. I therefore hope I am not obtrusive in saying, in this way, for him and myself, that when a citizen of Illinois is to be appointed in your Department to an office either in or out of the state, we most respectfully ask to be heard.

Your obt. Servt.
A. Lincoln.

As a consequence of their understanding, most of the recommendations for appointments of Illinoisans carried the signatures of both Lincoln and Baker. For example, on March 8, 1849, Secretary of State John M. Clayton received the following letter:

Dear Sir:

We recommend that Archibald Williams [former colleague of Lincoln and Baker in the Illinois General Assembly], of Quincy, Illinois, be appointed U.S. District Attorney for the District of Illinois, when that office shall become vacant.

Your Obt. Servts.
A. Lincoln

I beg leave to urge this particularly.

E. D. Baker.

Lincoln and Baker wrote similar letters on behalf of Matthew Gillespie, Anson G. Henry, Nathaniel G. Wilcox, Benjamin Bond, and several other Illinois Whigs.

At the same time, if an appointment were completely within the congressional district to be represented by Baker, or the district represented by Lincoln, the recommendation came solely from the Congressman concerned. Thus, when Lincoln recommended Abner Y. Ellis as Postmaster for Springfield, he noted at the end of the recommendation that "this office, with its delivery, is entirely within my district; so that Col. Baker, the other Whig representative, claims no voice in the appointment."

Many of Lincoln's recommendations, either singly or with Baker, received favorable action. Abner Ellis received his appointment as Postmaster of Springfield. Archibald Williams became U.S. District Attorney for the District of Illinois. Matthew Gillespie soon occupied a position in the Land Office in Edwardsville, Illinois.

It is uncertain whether a distant relative of Lincoln's ever received a job, or for that matter a recommendation from Lincoln. Ann E. Campbell, who wrote

Treasury Secretary William M. Meredith—"our efforts to see you alone have, so far, been unavailing . . . when a citizen of Illinois is to be appointed in your Department . . . we most respectfully ask to be heard." (Library of Congress)

Jacob Collamer, the new Postmaster General, to whom Lincoln wrote recommending Abner Ellis to be Postmaster of Springfield. (Library of Congress)

Thomas Ewing—Lincoln could have had the position . . . for the asking. (Library of Congress)

on behalf of her husband seeking a patronage position, added this postscript: "Should you have forgotten, ask Mary who I am." There is no record that Lincoln acted upon the request.

Many patronage jobs under Taylor were not parceled out by high—or even relevant—standards. The applicant for the postmastership at Pekin got the job because—according to Lincoln's recommendation—he was poor, out of health, and had a large family. His rival labored under the handicap of wealth. Similarly, Haza Parsons was old, poor, and lame so that he could not work at labor. He had a large family—and Lincoln's recommendation. He got the postmastership at Bloomington.

Others sought Lincoln's intercession but were unsuccessful in securing a position. In fact, Lincoln first saw the enormous obligations consequent upon a victorious election campaign in the wake of Zachary Taylor's election. When he became President twelve years later he found himself on the other side of the table, being importuned by dozens of Congressmen who had just the right candidate for each and every position in his administration.

Lincoln's most notable failure in securing a patronage appointment was, without doubt, the one he wanted the most—for himself.

According to Thomas Ewing, Secretary of the newly established Department of the Interior, Lincoln could have had the position of Commissioner of the General Land Office for the asking. The job was one of the most important available for a western state, and certainly would have given Lincoln a golden opportunity to further internal improvements, something he felt the Land Office had not done in the past. A largely autonomous sub-Cabinet post, the position had originally been under the Department of the Treasury, but Congress moved it to the Department of the Interior in 1849. This shift reflected a change in public land policies created by the Distribution and Pre-emption Act of 1841. Prior to the act, public lands were sold and distributed by the Land Office primarily to generate revenue for the federal government. After the act, the disposition of public lands encouraged increased settlement in the west. In addition, through judicious sales to state governments, transportation and other internal improvement projects were furthered. Transportation facilities induced settlers to move west just as much as the cheap land price of $1.25 per acre.

The position as Commissioner had political attractiveness as well. Surveys and sales of land for the right projects could earn the Commissioner gratitude from state officials, who might be expected to show their appreciation in some future political contest. Too, the $3,000 annual salary rivaled Lincoln's earnings as a Congressman.

At the same time, Lincoln had promised that he would try to get it for his old friend Cyrus Edwards, a former Whig candidate for Governor. Even though he wanted the job for himself, Lincoln felt honor bound to keep his pledge to Edwards. Still, he made every effort possible to further his own interests while remaining faithful to his pledge. In a letter to William Warren and several other

CYRUS EDWARDS

Cyrus Edwards—*"used as a cat's paw to promote the success of one on whom I relied."* *(Illinois State Historical Library)*

Justin Butterfield—*"of the quite one hundred Illinoisans, equally well qualified, I do not know of one with less claims to* [the General Land Office]." *(Chicago Historical Society)*

Lincoln requested letters of recommendation from many political supporters. *(Illinois State Historical Library)*

Illinois Whigs, Lincoln explained his position:

> In answer to your note concerning the General Land Office, I have to say
> that, if the Office can be secured to Illinois by my consent to accept it, and
> not otherwise, I give that consent. Some months since I gave my word to
> secure the appointment to that office of Mr. Cyrus Edwards, if in my power,
> in case of a vacancy; and more recently I stipulated with Col. Baker that if
> Mr. Edwards and Col. J.L.D. Morrison could arrange with each other for
> one of them to withdraw, we would jointly recommend the other. In
> relation to these pledges, I must not only be chaste but above suspicion. If
> the office shall be tendered to me, I must be permitted to say "give it to Mr.
> Edwards, or, if so agreed by them, to Col. Morrison, and I decline it; if not,
> I accept. With this understanding, you are at liberty to procure me the offer
> of the appointment if you can; and I shall feel complimented by your effort,
> and still more by its success. It should not be overlooked that Col. Baker's
> position entitled him to a large share of control in this matter; however, one
> of your number, Col. Warren, knows that Baker has at all times been ready
> to recommend me, if I would consent. It must also be understood that if at
> any time, previous to an appointment being made, I shall learn that Mr.
> Edwards and Col. Morrison have agreed, I shall at once carry out my
> stipulation with Col. Baker, as above stated.

Within a few weeks, however, the complexion of the situation changed. A
new applicant for the post appeared on the scene—Justin Butterfield. A native
of New Hampshire, Butterfield emigrated to Chicago in 1835. A highly
successful lawyer, he claimed friendship with the distinguished Whig Senator
Daniel Webster, and had been active in New Hampshire Whig politics. In
1840, after the election of William Henry Harrison, he had been appointed
U.S. District Attorney for the district of Illinois. An active exponent of internal
improvements (like Lincoln), he had played a major role in the development of
the Illinois Canal.

When he learned that some Whigs were urging Butterfield for the Commissioner's position, Lincoln replied to his informant, Josiah Lucas:

> Your letter of the 15th is just received. Like you, I fear the land office is not
> going as it should; but I know nothing I can do. In my letter written three
> days ago, I told you the Department understands my wish. As to Butterfield,
> he is my personal friend, and is qualified to do the duties of the office; but of
> the quite one hundred Illinoisans, equally well qualified, I do not know of
> one with less claims to it. . . . He fought for Mr. Clay against Gen. Taylor
> to the bitter end as I understand; and I do not believe I misunderstand. . . .
> It will now mortify me deeply if Gen. Taylor's administration shall trample
> all my wishes in the dust merely to gratify these men.

Lincoln then mounted a letter-writing campaign in order to head Butterfield off.
He wrote to several of his Whig friends in Illinois urging them to write to
officials in Washington discouraging the appointment of Butterfield as Commis-

204

sioner of the Land Office. He did not advance any claims for himself, but simply noted that Butterfield had not actively supported Taylor during the campaign. He also wrote to several Cabinet officers, Whig Congressmen, and unofficial advisers to General Taylor urging against Butterfield's appointment. For example, on May 25, 1849, Lincoln wrote this letter to Elisha Embree:

CONFIDENTIAL

Hon E. Embree   Springfield, Ills.
Dear Sir: May 25, 1849
    I am about to ask a favor of you—one which, I hope will not cost you much. I understand the General Land Office is about to be given to Illinois; and that Mr. Ewing desires Justin Butterfield, of Chicago, to be the man. I give you my word, the appointment of Mr. B. will be an egregious political blunder. It will give offence to the whole whig party here, and be worse than a dead loss to the administration, of so much of its patronage. Now, if you can conscientiously do so, I wish you to write General Taylor at once, saying that either *I, or the man I recommend,* should, in your opinion, be appointed to that office, if any one from Illinois shall be. I restrict my request to Ills. because you may have a man of your own, in your own state, and I do not ask to interfere with that. Your friend as ever

                                                                A. Lincoln

Cyrus Edwards, recognizing that Interior Secretary Ewing would appoint Butterfield before himself, offered to withdraw as a candidate for the office, but Lincoln advised him not to. On June 2, 1849, however, Lincoln learned that it had come down to a choice between Butterfield and himself. The next day he began writing to every influential Whig he knew to ask for endorsements and recommendations. An example of his form letter is the following to Duff Green:

Dear Sir: Springfield Ills. June 5. '49
    Would you as soon I should have the Genl. Land Office as any other Illinoisan? If you would, write me to that effect at Washington where I shall be soon. No time to lose. Yours in haste

                                                                A. Lincoln

Butterfield did not stay idle during this time either. He obtained a recommendation from Henry Clay, and busily sought endorsements from Whigs in Illinois. His friendship with Daniel Webster also placed him in a good position. Webster had served in the Senate with Secretary Ewing and, even though a friend of Lincoln, is believed to have recommended Butterfield. Correspondence suggests that most who wrote stated that the appointment of either Butterfield or Lincoln would be satisfactory to the Whigs of Illinois. Butterfield even secured such a letter from Benjamin Bond, whose appointment to a patronage job had been helped along by a strong recommendation by Lincoln.

In the second week of June, both Lincoln and Butterfield hurried to

John M. Clayton, Secretary of State, who Lincoln felt withheld from the President letters recommending him for the Land Office. *(Library of Congress)*

Washington to lobby for the appointment. Butterfield had written to Lincoln on June 9, offering to stay away from Washington if Lincoln would do so. Lincoln replied through Levi Davis that while he personally would "cheerfully" refrain from going to Washington, he "had so far committed himself to his friends" that he felt he must go. Thus, Lincoln once again traveled to the capital, his last trip there until he went in 1861 as President-elect.

In order to push his case, Lincoln prepared the following memorandum for President Taylor:

> Nothing in my papers questions Mr. B's competency or honesty, and, I presume, nothing in his questions mine. Being equal so far, if it does not appear I am preferred by the Whigs of Illinois, I lay no claim to the office.
>
> But if it does appear I am preferred, it will be argued that the whole northwest, and not Illinois alone, should be heard. I answer I am as strongly recommended by Ohio and Indiana, as well as Illinois; and further, that when the many appointments were made for Ohio, as for the Northwest, Illinois was not consulted. When an Indianan was nominated for Governor of Minnesota, and another appointed for Commissioner of Mexican Claims, as for the Northwest, Illinois was not consulted. Of none of these have I ever complained. In each of them, the State whose citizen was appointed was allowed to control, and I think rightly. I only ask that Illinois be not cut off with less deference.
>
> It will be argued that all the Illinois appointments, so far have been South, and that therefore this should go North. I answer, that of the local appointments every part has had its share, and Chicago far the best share of any. Of the transitory, the Marshall and Attorney are all; and neither of these is within a hundred miles of me, the former being South and latter North of West. I am in the center. Is the center nothing?—that center which alone has ever given you a Whig representative? On the score of locality, I admit the claim of the North is no worse, and I deny that it is any better than the center.

Simeon Francis—*"principal editor of . . . the leading Whig paper of the state." (Illinois* State Journal-Register)

This memorandum failed to help, however. On June 21, 1849, Justin Butterfield received the appointment as Commissioner of the General Land Office. Lincoln's chagrin must have been great, for he not only lost the position but severely strained his relationship with Cyrus Edwards. Edwards felt he had been used "as a cat's paw to promote the success of one on whom I relied to procure the appointment for myself."

After the appointment had been made, Lincoln immediately wrote to Ewing asking for the letters that had been written on his behalf. He did this, he said, in order to prevent embarrassment to anyone who had supported his efforts.

On August 10 Secretary of State John M. Clayton wrote to Lincoln to advise him that he had been appointed Secretary of the Oregon Territory. Lincoln, however, preferred that the appointment be given to his old friend Simeon Francis, editor of the Springfield *Journal.* Accordingly, he wrote to Clayton on August 25:

> Your letter of the 10th Inst., notifying me of my appointment as Secretary of the Territory of Oregon, and accompanied by a Commission, has been duly received. I respectfully decline the offer.
>
> I shall be greatly obliged if the place be offered to Simeon Francis, of this place. He will accept it, is capable, and would be faithful in the discharge of its duties. He is the principal editor of the oldest, and what I think may be fairly called, the leading Whig paper of the state,—the Illinois Journal. His good business habits are proved by the facts, that the paper has existed eighteen years, all the time weekly, and part of it tri-weekly, and daily, and has not failed to issue regularly in a single instance.
>
> Some time in May last, I think, Mr. Francis addressed a letter to Mr. Ewing, which, I was informed while at Washington in June, had been seen by the cabinet and very highly approved. You possibly may remember it. He has, for a long time desired to go to Oregon; and I think his appointment would give general satisfaction.

Simeon Francis never did receive the appointment, despite the fact that Lincoln made a greater effort on Francis's behalf than he did for anyone else (even greater than that for Cyrus Edwards).

Secretary Clayton apparently heard that Lincoln felt demeaned by the low-level appointment as Oregon Territory Secretary and subsequently offered him the position as Governor of the Territory. But this post too Lincoln declined.

On the surface it may seem odd that Lincoln would reject the governorship, certainly a prestigious position. Yet there were compelling reasons. He had undoubtedly been deeply hurt by his failure to win the position as Commissioner of the General Land Office. In addition, there were several political considerations. While it was traditional for a territorial Governor to become the first Senator when the territory became a state, Oregon was a heavily Democratic territory. As a Whig, Lincoln would face political uncertainty in Oregon. He had worked hard to develop his Illinois constituency. The property he owned and all his financial interests were in Springfield. Indeed, some historians believe that the prime factor in Lincoln's decision not to accept the governorship was not a political one but a personal one. Mrs. Lincoln put her foot down. A family move to an unsettled wilderness did not appeal to her. Their three-year-old son, Eddy, was ailing and getting worse. Whatever the reasons, Lincoln declined. Instead, he continued to play an active role in Whig politics in Illinois and gave special attention to the dispensation of patronage.

13

"Politically dead and buried . . ."?

WHILE PRIMARILY CONCERNED with dispensing patronage during the second and final session of Congress, Lincoln kept pondering his own political future. With Hardin dead and Baker representing a different congressional district he wondered whether a way might open for him to run for reelection.

Lincoln's desire to continue in Congress had been evident even during the first session. He had hardly taken his seat in Congress when his attention turned to the possibility, remote though it was, of running again in 1848. A month later the thought remained in his mind. On January 8, 1848, he replied to a letter from Billy Herndon:

> It is very pleasant to learn that there are some who desire that I should be re-elected. . . . I made the declaration that I would not be a candidate again, more from a wish to deal fairly with others . . . and to keep the district from going to the enemy . . . so that . . . if . . . nobody else wishes to be elected, I could not refuse the people the right of sending me again.

Lincoln obviously would not have minded being returned to Congress, but he could hardly actively seek the nomination. Since he had secured election on the basis of the principle that "turn about is fair play," he would look awkward indeed rejecting the same principle to suit his own convenience. And someone else did wish to be elected—his former law partner, Stephen T. Logan of Springfield. And not just Logan.

Between January and April, the Whigs in the 7th District suffered internal strife. The Whigs in Morgan County felt that Sangamon County's Whigs had dominated the district long enough. William B. Warren of Morgan County announced that he would seek the congressional seat, contesting the ambitions of Springfield's Logan. Alarmed at the potential divisiveness, Billy Herndon dashed off a note to Richard Yates in Jacksonville:

> Judge Logan . . . wishes to go but one term and Lincoln not wishing to run at all, I think it would be the better policy of the people of Morgan to help us for this term and after this is over I think the field will be clear to all men who have any idea of running for that seat.

The Lacon *Gazette* editorially suggested another alternative on April 15, 1848:

> Still, it is a question . . . whether a change of representative for every congress is expedient and productive of the greatest good. It is seldom that a

new member wields extensive influence in congress. This is the work of time—comprehending certainly more than two years. So far as we are informed, Mr. Lincoln, our present representative, has ably and faithfully discharged his duties; and if he has at no time intimated a willingness or desire to retire at the expiration of the term for which he was elected, we are not sure but that the interests of the district would be quite as well promoted by his re-nomination and re-election for another term.

Lincoln nevertheless put the temptation behind him. He declined to follow the example of Hardin who had tried unsuccessfully in 1846 to thwart the "turn about" principle. He concluded he should not attempt to take advantage of party problems for his personal advantage if it required him to break a pledge. He also decided not to attempt the role of peacemaker in the political affairs of the 7th Congressional District. He left to others the healing of the badly bruised morale of district Whigs and concentrated his own efforts on the national political scene. Besides, if Logan became the Whig candidate for Congress, his prospects for winning were not the best, and Lincoln could do little to improve them.

The Democrats had as their candidate Thomas L. Harris—a native of Norwich, Connecticut, thirty-two years old, a graduate of Washington College in Hartford, Connecticut, and a lawyer. In 1842 he began to practice law in Petersburg, Illinois. When the Mexican War broke out, Harris raised and commanded a company in the 4th Illinois Regiment, reaching the rank of Major. Harris distinguished himself at the Battle of Cerro Gordo and for his gallantry the state of Illinois presented him with a sword. His popularity as a war hero made him a formidable candidate and in 1846 he was elected to the State Senate, though in absentia.

On April 5, Harris had written to Charles Lanphier, editor of the Democratic Illinois *State Register*, advising him of his decision to run for Congress:

> After I left Springfield last Wed. I went to Jacksonville, where I was urged on all hands to become a candidate for Congress, I was assured of a majority there, and by some as high as 200—Even whigs—Maj Warren for one came out boldly in the streets & desired me to run and expressed a strong desire for my election—I was satisfied from all I saw that I could do well there and concluded to try my hand and fortune in the fight—At Virginia and Beardstown also I had even encouragement—and I came home with the full determination to give battle—I intended to have written you yesterday but the mail was off in the morning (instead of evening) before I knew it—
>
> But lo! down comes word today that Baker is off and Logan on the track— I know not which is the stronger of the two and care as little—But Col. Dunlap said to me he felt sure I can beat Logan badly in Morgan, and beat him in the District—I am after him, let us give him thunder and lightning— I will meet him anywhere and upon any thing, let us force the issues upon them—Rouse up the *young men*—The gallant heroes of the 1st & 4th who have done themselves so much honor and drowned the state with imperishable glory—Review the Congressional courses of Henry, Baker &

Richard Yates reestablished Whig control of the 7th Congressional District in 1850. *(Library of Congress)*

Thomas L. Harris—*"a trumpet of fury."* *(Library of Congress)*

THE GAZETTE.

named above. Still, it is a question (which, it will be conceded the Northern portion of the district have a right to ask) whether a change of representative for every congress is expedient and productive of the greatest good. It is seldom that a new member wields extensive influence in congress. This is the work of time—comprehending certainly more than two years. So far as we are informed, Mr. Lincoln, our present representative, has ably and faithfully discharged his duties; and if he has at no time intimated a willingness or desire to retire at the expiration of the term for which he was elected, we are not sure but that the interests of the district would be quite as well promoted by his re-nomination and re-election for another term.

(Library of Congress)

Stephen T. Logan—*"a failure, and a fizzle."* *(Illinois State Historical Library)*

Lincoln, votes, pay and all and the people will exclaim with Lady Macbeth "Out damned spot—" I think we may as well *light up* the district in a blaze at once and if "Hell is murky" let us know it—Roberts and Delahay will cooperate with you & it might be well to have an understanding with each other fully—Logan ought to be attacked in every vulnerable point—his whole career criticized severely—his identity with the Mexican party shown and let a trumpet of fury for political sins

> "Beat upon his naked soul
> in one eternal storm"

With the encouragement which I receive from all sides I believe I can beat him—I shall try with that determination—Let us know of no such thing as fail—commence with confidence and fight with victory in view—if the fight shall not be succcessful, let us at least show that we are entitled to justice from the next districting legislature.

The Whig district convention did indeed select Logan to oppose the young, vigorous, aroused war hero. While Logan had served the Whig party loyally, as a candidate for Congress he had problems. Approaching fifty years of age, he was unimpressive in his appearance— "utterly careless in his dress," as one Lincoln supporter noted. In addition, he had a thin, shrill voice. His elective experience consisted of three terms in the state legislature.

Logan had been eager for the seat in Congress since 1846. William H. Herndon had remarked on that year's nomination:

> The struggle among Whig aspirants narrowed down to Logan and Lincoln. The latter's claim seemed to find such favorable lodgment with the party workers, and his popularity seemed so apparent, that Logan soon realized his own want of strength and abandoned the field to his late law partner.

Contemporary newspaper accounts indicate that as a result of making known his aspiration in 1846, Logan felt he should be included two years later in the "rotation of office" policy adopted by the Pekin convention. Whether he deserved to be in the rotation sequence or not, he did receive the nomination in 1848.

Logan could not, however, even count on wholehearted support from his own party. His nomination occurred only after squabbling so intense that some effort was made to field a second Whig candidate. This did not occur but Logan's nomination severely damaged party morale.

He waged a lackluster campaign. One event in particular illustrates ineptness if not stupidity. *The Ticket*, a campaign paper issued by the Democrats, charged that Logan had contributed only fifty cents to a fund for bringing home the body of a soldier killed in Mexico. Logan angrily retorted that the charge was untrue—that he had actually given three dollars. Logan, well known as a man of wealth, failed to see the unholy glee with which Democrats would greet this response. He obviously did not know enough to leave certain campaign charges unanswered.

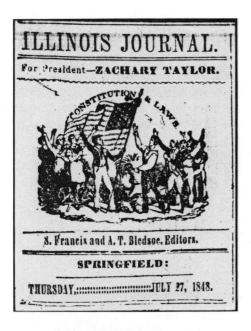

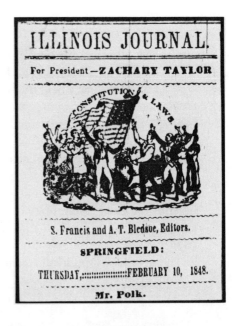

ILLINOIS JOURNAL.

For President—ZACHARY TAYLOR.

CONSTITUTION & LAWS

S. Francis and A. T. Bledsoe, Editors.

SPRINGFIELD:

THURSDAY,:::::::::::::::::::::::JULY 27, 1848.

ILLINOIS JOURNAL.

For President—ZACHARY TAYLOR

CONSTITUTION & LAWS

S. Francis and A. T. Bledsoe, Editors.

SPRINGFIELD:

THURSDAY,::::::::::::::::::FEBRUARY 10, 1848.

Mr. Polk.

"The Ticket" in regard to

THE MEXICAN WAR.

It is said on the third page of the Ticket of July 15, that Logan endorsed the course of Lincoln
in Congress in voting that the war was *unjust* and
unconstitutional, and brought on by the act of the
President. This charge contains two palpable *lies.*

In the first place Mr. Lincoln never gave such a
vote in Congress ; he did not vote that the war was
unjust--and the man who penned the charge knew
it was a lie when he penned it ; he substituted the
word "unjust," knowing it not to be so, because,
only on it could he hope to hang his charges with
effect.

The second lie, contained in the charge, is, that I
endorsed the vote as he states it. It would have
been a lie if he had said I endorsed the vote Mr.
Lincoln really did give. Mr. Lincoln needs no endorsement ; his character in this community for
talents, integrity and patriotism, needs no endorsement from me or any one else. What I did say in
regard to Mr. Lincoln, was, that much as the democrats here abused his speech on the commence-
ment of the war, it was very strange that none of
them had undertaken to answer the argument of it.

It is also said in the same article, "That Logan

The Democrats tried to force Logan to
defend Lincoln's record on the Mexican
War. *(Library of Congress)*

Mr. Lincoln's Speech.

We give, on our first page, the speech of Mr.
Lincoln, in the House of Representatives, on the
14th, from the Congressional Globe. Since it was
printed, we have received a copy of the speech, as
reported by Mr. Lincoln himself. The speech is
an able one, and was listened to by the House with
marked attention.

The Register has denounced this speech in all
the set styles with which the editor is familiar.—
Will he do the member the justice to publish his
speech ?—Or does he fear to have it go to his readers ?

Despite editor Albert Bledsoe's later criticism
of Lincoln for his stand on the Mexican War,
in 1848 Bledsoe's paper only said kind things
about Lincoln's performance in office.
(Library of Congress)

Small wonder many Whigs left Logan for war hero Harris. He and Harris stumped the district beginning in April and on August 6 the voters made their choice. By a narrow margin of only 106 votes, Democrat Harris was elected to Congress. He got 7,201 votes, Logan 7,095, and the Liberty party candidate 166. The Liberty party held the balance of power in the election. It is reasonable to assume that most of its strength came from former Whigs. Without the Liberty candidate Logan would have won. The congressional district often described as the one sure Whig stronghold had fallen to the Democrats.

Did this vote imply a repudiation of Lincoln's record in Congress? Lincoln's law partner, William H. Herndon, later said yes. In a letter to Jesse Weik on February 11, 1887—thirty-eight years after the fact—Herndon said, "When Lincoln returned home from Congress in 1849, he was a politically dead and buried man; he wanted to run for Congress again, but it was no use to try." Herndon said that Lincoln himself on one occasion confessed that in Congress he had committed political suicide.

And in his *Life of Lincoln,* published two years later in 1889, Herndon reviewed Lincoln's career in Congress with these words:

> They [the "spot" resolutions] and the speech which followed on the 12th day of January in support of them not only sealed Lincoln's doom as a Congressman, but, in my opinion, lost the district to the Whigs in 1848 when Judge Logan had succeeded at last in obtaining the nomination.

Herndon can hardly be described as an unprejudiced witness, however. When he set down his "political suicide" theory and pinned on Lincoln the blame of Logan's defeat, Herndon sought to establish his own credentials as a trusted lifelong adviser to the martyred President. He had strongly and persistently opposed Lincoln's antiwar positions in Congress. It therefore suited his own purposes to assert that Lincoln got into trouble by failing to take his advice. It was a self-serving analysis.

Who else blamed Logan's defeat on Lincoln? The Illinois *State Register,* the principal Democratic party organ, voiced that sentiment but it too could hardly be considered an unprejudiced witness. Without exception it found fault with Whig politicians. Caleb Birchall wrote in a private letter to a friend that Lincoln's record brought Logan down. However, it should be noted that earlier Lincoln had refused to recommend Birchall for the postmastership of Springfield. Stephen A. Douglas alluded to the issue during the 1858 debates. He took Lincoln to task for his antiwar stand and maintained that he voted contrary to the wishes of his constituents. On such occasion, Douglas would have had a natural impulse to make the least favorable construction of Lincoln's record.

Albert Taylor Bledsoe, former editorial writer for the Illinois *Journal* in Springfield, is the only other contemporary who voiced the belief that Lincoln's war views hurt him. He did so in 1873, while editor of the *Southern Review,* a magazine espousing the sentiments of the Deep South. In an article on Lincoln, Bledsoe said that Lincoln in 1848 had reached "such low repute among his neighbors, and with his former political friends, that he could not have been elected a constable or a justice of the peace." Bledsoe had been a friend of Lincoln in the 1840s but his sentiments changed drastically over the years. He had served as Assistant Secretary of War in the Confederacy and by the 1870s had become one of Lincoln's most severe critics. He called Lincoln "the low, ignorant and vulgar, rail splitter of Illinois."

In any event, the opinion of Herndon, Birchall, Douglas, Bledsoe, and the Illinois *State Register* constitute the sum total of all evidence that Lincoln hurt himself, Logan, and the Whig cause because of his record in Congress.

The evidence to the contrary is substantial. Logan himself never blamed Lincoln. In fact, the two remained intimate friends. Logan never rose to higher office than a seat in the state legislature. In 1855 he campaigned as a candidate for the Illinois Supreme Court but, as Lincoln described the result, he came away from the contest "worse beaten than any other man since elections were invented."

Not a single Whig newspaper put the blame on Lincoln. In fact, Lincoln returned home from Washington a figure of national prominence. In Congress he had kept his own district political fences well mended. He had kept the home folks well supplied with copies of speeches delivered under his congressional frank. His "press" in Illinois, as well as nationally, had been substantial. He had matured as a debater, an organizer, and vote getter. The fact that he drew criticism from Democratic newspapers outside Illinois stands as evidence of his national standing.

Nor did Logan's defeat have any apparent adverse effect on Lincoln's standing within the Whig party. He remained the leading Whig of the entire state, as well as one of national prominence. He continued to be sought after as a Whig speaker in his home district. Shortly after Logan's defeat, he received a strong vote of confidence from his fellow Whigs when they made him an assistant elector, an appointive party position reserved for Whigs able to campaign effectively for the national party ticket. If Whigs had blamed Lincoln for Logan's defeat, they surely would not have given him this responsibility.

Even Herndon himself provides evidence contradicting his "political suicide" view. Though he blamed Lincoln for the loss of the district in 1848, he offered this appraisal of Logan the candidate:

> He [Logan] had some fondness for politics, and made one race for Congress, but he lacked the elements of a successful politician.

On another occasion, Herndon described Logan as "a failure, and a fizzle. Here was a cold, avaricious, and little mean man as the people saw him."

Herndon's uncomplimentary opinion of Logan was widely shared. In a letter to William Schouler on August 28, 1848, Lincoln himself stated:

> I would rather not be put upon explaining how Logan was defeated in my district. . . . A good many Whigs, without good cause, as I think were

215

unwilling to go for Logan, and some of them so wrote me before the election. . . . Harris was a major of the war. . . . These two facts and their effects, I presume tell the whole story. That there is any political change against us in the District I cannot believe.

Lincoln had summed the situation up accurately. Logan was a poor candidate. Harris, a good candidate, took full advantage of the "war spirit" that had swept the country—a spirit that brought votes to him as a war hero and produced unprecedented organizational work by the Democratic party in the 7th District. The Beardstown *Gazette*, searching for a reason for Logan's defeat, said the campaign work of the Democrats had been "not even remotely anticipated by the Whigs."

The vote in the presidential contest in November of the same year lends credence to Lincoln's judgment. The 7th District gave Whig candidate Zachary Taylor a handsome majority of more than 1,500 votes out of approximately 15,000 cast. Taylor received the same margin as Lincoln had received two years before. Lincoln had been closely identified in the district, as well as elsewhere, with Taylor's candidacy. It would have been difficult to find a single voter in the district who did not know of Lincoln's hard campaigning for the Whig presidential candidate. Lincoln's antiwar record appeared prominently and not always favorably as he stumped for Taylor. A Democratic newspaper called him a "second Benedict Arnold."

Harris's letters to Charles Lanphier and contemporary newspaper accounts make clear that the Democrats deliberately exploited Lincoln's antiwar stand as an issue. Predictably, not all newspaper accounts or campaign participants gave Lincoln's record dispassionate appraisal.

Yet, despite all this, Taylor won in Lincoln's district by a wide margin.

Despite Logan's handicaps, he came close. He lost to Harris by only 106 votes. Had Lincoln instead of Logan been the candidate for Congress, he would have had some natural advantage as the incumbent. A seasoned campaigner with a wide acquaintance and support, Lincoln would have been more than a match for Harris. The record leaves no real doubt: had Lincoln been running for reelection he would have won.

Lincoln came home from Congress politically strong, and he remained that way. He remained prominent in speculation as a candidate for Congress for two years after Logan's defeat. In fact, he exerted a prominent influence in all elections in the congressional district through the campaign of 1854.

The contention that Lincoln's antiwar record led to "political suicide" is a myth. Most historians largely recognized it as such for sixty-five years after Lincoln's death and ignored Herndon's evaluation. The lengthy biography written by Lincoln's secretaries, John Hay and John G. Nicolay, concluded that Lincoln's congressional term had done him "no damage." They accepted as sincere and principled Lincoln's antiwar views. So did almost all other biographers of Lincoln—all, that is, until a curious resurrection of Herndon's "political suicide" myth occurred in 1928.

(Library of Congress)

In that year Senator Albert Beveridge's widely acclaimed biography of Lincoln's life to 1858 first appeared. Beveridge picked up and dignified the Herndon myth. He did so against the advice of historians Charles Beard and Samuel Eliot Morison. Beveridge's book had been so impressively researched in other respects that it carried the Herndon myth to an unwarranted eminence from which, unfortunately, it has never fallen.

Beveridge's attachment to the Herndon myth is understandable. As a popular U.S. Senator, Beveridge had attempted to revive the "manifest destiny" spirit. He declaimed on the "divine mission of America." He had no use for war critics. Even though he had personal reservations about the United States entry into World War I, he voiced no public dissent. He believed that everyone had a duty to support the government during wartime. In Beveridge's eyes, Lincoln's opposition to the Mexican War displayed an egregious lack of patriotism and principles. In his opinion, Lincoln had erred gravely and must, therefore, have paid a proper price for the error. Beveridge seized enthusiastically on Herndon's myth. He cited the Herndon statements and accounts in Democratic newspapers to prove that Lincoln's antiwar views caused the Whigs to lose the 7th Congressional District. Although all solid historical evidence was to the contrary, Beveridge concluded that Lincoln "knew his fortunes were ended forever." Beveridge's faulty and unscholarly interpretation has been accepted by later generations of biographers, including Donald Riddle, author of *Congressman Abraham Lincoln*, the only previous major work devoted to Lincoln's congressional experience. Thanks largely to Beveridge, Herndon's mythology is still accepted as fact in almost all writings about Lincoln's congressional service. The Herndon myth fits preconceptions widely held about Lincoln. It helps to create the image of the post-Congress Lincoln arising, phoenixlike, from the ashes of an unprincipled and partisan past—suddenly struck and transformed by the politics of morality. Biographers are not immune to such preconceptions and imagery. And certainly Herndon's false appraisal of

Albert Beveridge—*picked up and dignified the Herndon myth. (Library of Congress)*

Lincoln's congressional career helped them accept myth as fact.

In fact, Lincoln remained a viable candidate and considered, then rejected, running for Congress in 1850. On January 12 Congressman Harris asked Lanphier, "Who will the Whigs have for the next canvass? Baker told me a day or two ago that Yates would be—Dr. Newell of N.J. told me that Lincoln had told him he should be." Both Yates and Lincoln, as well as William Brown, sought the Whig nomination. Harris hoped to divide Lincoln and Yates: "You say Lincoln is pushing after Congress," he said. "[G]et him in a quarrel with Yates."

On June 5, in the interest of party unity, Lincoln decided to ease speculation about his own candidacy. He wrote to the editor of the Illinois *Journal:*

> An article in the Tazewell Mirror in which my name is prominently used, makes me fear that my position, with reference to the next Congressional election is misunderstood, and that such misunderstanding may work injury to the cause of our friends. I therefore take occasion to say that I neither seek, expect, or desire a nomination for a seat in the next Congress; that I prefer my name should not be brought forward in that connection; and that I would now preemptorily forbid the use of it, could I feel entirely at liberty to do so. I will add, that in my opinion, the Whigs of the district have several other men, any one of whom they *can* elect, and that too quite as *easily* as they could elect me. I therefore shall be obliged, if any such as may entertain a preference for me, will, at once turn their attention to making a choice from others. Let a Convention be held at a suitable time, and in good feeling, make a nomination; and I venture the prediction we will show the District once more *right side up.*

The letter, however, did not prevent others from pushing Lincoln for the nomination. The convention would not be held until August, and Thomas Harris continued to try to measure the respective strengths of Lincoln and Yates: "Letters from the upper end of the District say that Lincoln is much stronger there than Yates—My own opinion is, that Lincoln is *not* as strong a man in the District as Yates. . . . Dick [Yates] can most likely [carry] Morgan and Scott—which Lincoln could not do—in Sangamon I should judge they would be about of equal strength." Lincoln had obviously retained support or Harris would not have bothered to weigh the relative strength of Lincoln and Yates.

At the convention Lincoln had some followers, but he refused to become an active candidate, and the nomination went to Yates. After the convention Harris made this somewhat revised estimate of Yate's strength:

> Yates will be stronger in Morgan & Scott (possibly in Cass) than Lincoln—but in Tazewell & the upper counties he will not be as strong. But strong or weak we must beat him. We must start off for the purpose and must accomplish it.

In the same letter Harris tended to confirm Lincoln's opinion regarding the Democratic victory of 1848: "I believe the Whig Party proper is not as strong in the district as in 1848, but Logan raised no enthusiasm and no sympathy in it. Dick [Yates] will do it." And indeed, Dick did it. When the election returns came in November, Yates had been elected to Congress by the substantial margin of 954 votes and the Whig party once again controlled the 7th Congressional District.

With Congress foreclosed, where could Lincoln go to satisfy his ambitions? A return to the state legislature would seem to be a step backward. The Whig party had been unable to carry Illinois, so candidacy for Governor or other statewide administrative office would seem to be futile.

Lincoln took his time in reviewing the prospects. In Springfield the law office overlooking the State House and the house at 8th and Jackson were places for reflection. Besides, Mary needed him. On February 1, 1850, little Eddy died of diphtheria, and his mother succumbed to deep anguish. The humor and self-control that had marked her behavior during the stress and turmoil of the 30th Congress gave way to fearfulness, self-indulgence, and sudden outbursts. These were sometimes directed at her husband or Bobby, and sometimes overheard by neighbors.

Within a month of Eddy's death she was again pregnant. Willie was born December 17.

Lincoln's law office—
a place for reflection.
(James Myers)

14

"What to do and how to do it"

IS PARTY HAD FAILED to win a statewide election in Illinois, and Abraham Lincoln gave only passing thought in 1850 to becoming a Whig candidate for the United States Senate.

He had rejected the idea of running for Governor or other statewide administrative office. But in some ways a race for the Senate was different. Senators were chosen by the state legislature, not by direct popular vote. Lincoln knew many of the legislators well. His acquaintance and respect cut across party lines. He himself had served in the legislature four terms and this service had earned him special standing with some of his former colleagues. Since returning from Congress he had kept up his contacts. He did lobbying work when the legislature was in session. His law office faced the State House from across the street. Although these factors were all to the good, Lincoln finally concluded they were insufficient to overcome the minority position of the Whig party in the legislature.

He could not reasonably count on enough Democratic legislators to break party ranks to help him gain election just out of friendship or past favors. And no issue had reached sufficient intensity to pave the way for a Whig to capture a statewide seat by splitting enough Democratic votes.

He decided he would have to bide his time until some great issue arose that could divide the ranks of the Democratic legislators and rally some of them to support him. He had been patient as a candidate for the House in Washington. He could be patient for the Senate.

Actually the issue already existed in 1850. It was slavery, the same basic controversy that had been smoldering for years, now and then erupting into flames that crackled across the continent.

When the Congress convened with Richard Yates representing the 7th District, the issue of slavery had become paramount but wise legislative leadership had kept it from bursting into a holocaust. Both the House and the Senate possessed men of great influence and sagacity. They hammered out a compromise that promised an end to the bitter struggle over slavery. Known as the Compromise of 1850, the measure provided that California be admitted as a free state; the slave trade be abolished in the District of Columbia; governments be established without reference to slavery in the territory gained from the Mexican War; a more stringent fugitive slave law be enacted; the United States assume the debts of Texas; the western boundary of Texas be drawn to exclude

Death of Zachary Taylor. *(Kiplinger Washington Collection)*

Franklin Pierce—the Kansas-Nebraska bill he signed raised the potential for unlimited expansion of slavery. *(Library of Congress)*

New Mexico; and the Congress make a formal declaration that it had no right to interfere with the interstate slave trade. The principal architect of the compromise had been Henry Clay, Lincoln's idol. As a result, agitation over slavery subsided and seemed to be drawing to an end. There were moments during this interlude when Lincoln's political activities seemed to be headed the same way. Whig fortunes were waning.

The year of the compromise Zachary Taylor, for whose election Lincoln had worked so hard, died. Lincoln was asked to deliver a eulogy to Taylor in Chicago on July 25, and in his remarks he praised Taylor's military accomplishments and his fidelity to the nation. Interestingly, he did not touch on General Taylor's political views.

During the autumn, Lincoln supported Richard Yates's nomination to Congress and his vote helped to elect him.

The months passed. Occasionally patronage matters came up. Lincoln tended to his law practice. He lobbied in the state legislature. In a letter to William Martin on February 19, 1851, Lincoln noted, "The legislature having got out of the way, I at last find time to attend to the business you left with me."

Still he waited for the right political opportunity. It did not come in the 1852 campaign, however, and while Lincoln responded to a speech of Stephen A. Douglas in August, Whig prospects were depressingly bleak. He spoke in Peoria in September, and lauded Whig presidential candidate Winfield Scott but to no avail. When the returns were tabulated in November, Democrat Franklin Pierce had been elected President.

By 1854 Lincoln had become discouraged by the lack of opportunity to run for office again. He recorded in an autobiography that at the time thoughts of politics had largely left his mind. But, on May 30, 1854, President Pierce signed into law the Kansas-Nebraska Act and Lincoln had the compelling issue he had long sought. Section 14 of this bill repudiated the Missouri Compromise and raised the potential for unlimited expansion of slavery. The act, introduced by Stephen A. Douglas, provided that the residents of the Kansas and Nebraska territories would decide whether or not slavery was to be established through Douglas's cherished principle of "popular sovereignty." This established a doctrine of congressional noninterference regarding slavery in the territories. The country reacted immediately. The South gloated at the opportunity to expand slavery. The North felt outraged, not only by the possible extension of slavery, but by the repudiation of the Missouri Compromise, which many people viewed as sacrosanct. For Lincoln, who had always stoutly opposed the extension of slavery, it came as a clarion call to action. Like a careful lawyer preparing a brief, Lincoln refrained from speaking on the bill publicly until he had completely marshaled his arguments. Not until August 26, 1854, did he speak out. Then he delivered a blistering speech denouncing the act in Winchester. In a letter to the Illinois *Journal,* one hearer reported:

> The Hon. A. Lincoln . . . who was present, was loudly called for to address the meeting. He responded to the call ably and eloquently, doing complete justice to his reputation as a clear, forcible and convincing public speaker. His subject was the one which is uppermost in the minds of the people—the Nebraska-Kansas bill; and the ingenious, logical, and at the same time fair and candid manner, in which he exhibited the great wrong and injustice of the repeal of the Missouri Compromise, and the extension of slavery into free territory, deserves and has received the warmest commendation of every friend of freedom who listened to him. His was a masterly effort—said to be equal to any upon the same subject in Congress,—was replete with unanswerable arguments, which must and will effectually *tell* at the coming election.

Several other speeches followed shortly. On August 28 he spoke in Carrollton and on September 2 in Jacksonville.

On September 4 he once more entered the political arena as a candidate. On that date the Illinois *Journal* announced Lincoln's candidacy for Representative in the next session of the Illinois general assembly. This seemed, in some respects, a step backward for Lincoln. For years he had rejected any serious thought of running again for the legislature. He had already served four terms in that body and since that service had achieved higher elective office. Now he had reconsidered. Lincoln later stated, and there is no reason to disbelieve him, that he ran mainly because he believed his candidacy would help Richard Yates's reelection to Congress. In addition, it gave him a chance to make his convictions against the Kansas-Nebraska bill better known. He perceived the party cleavage emerging from the divisive issue. Politicians were no longer judged as either Democrats or Whigs, but as Nebraska men or anti-Nebraska men. In that cleavage lay a chance for Lincoln to secure a seat in the United States Senate.

As a candidate, Lincoln continued to speak out against the Kansas-Nebraska bill and the theory of popular sovereignty that Stephen A. Douglas used to defend the bill. In Springfield, Bloomington, Chicago, Quincy, and Peoria, Lincoln addressed crowds, rising occasionally to fervor and eloquence. At Peoria on October 16, 1854, he declared:

> This . . . zeal for the spread of slavery, I can not but hate. I hate it because of the monstrous injustice of slavery itself. I hate it because it deprives our republican example of its just influence in the world—enables the enemies of free institutions, with plausibility, to taunt us as hypocrites—causes the real friends of freedom to doubt our sincerity, and especially because it forces so many really good men amongst ourselves into an open war with the very fundamental principles of civil liberty.

This speech has often been cited as a milestone in Lincoln's movement toward the politics of morality. On close examination the speech reveals no fundamental change from his earlier views on the extension of slavery. His style had grown more eloquent, to be sure, but the only element added to his principles since his term as a Congressman was an ardent espousal of colonization as a long-term solution to the racial problems that plagued the nation, and this element did not clash with the principles he had formulated and embraced on Capitol Hill.

When the 1854 elections ended, Lincoln was both exultant and disappointed—disappointed because Whigs Richard Yates and his old friend Archibald Williams had both lost congressional races, and exultant for three reasons: he had won his own election to the state legislature; the incoming legislature was markedly anti-Nebraska; and finally, the way had opened for him to campaign for the U.S. Senate.

In fact, no sooner had he won election to the state legislature than he became an active Senate candidate. Just three days after the election, on November 10, Lincoln wrote to Charles Hoyt of Dewitt County:

> You used to express a good deal of partiality for me; and if you are still so, now is the time. Some friends here are really for me for the U.S. Senate; and I should be very grateful if you could make a mark for me among your members.

He sent similar letters to Jacob Harding, Thomas J. Henderson, Hugh Lemaster, Herbert Fay, and Joseph Gillespie (who had once jumped out a window with Lincoln to avoid making a quorum when both served in the Illinois House of

Representatives). The wide majority of anti-Nebraska legislators gave him, he felt, a good chance to win the Senate seat. The legislature would make the decision, and he was one of the state's most prominent anti-Nebraska spokesmen.

Under the Illinois Constitution, however, a member of the legislature could not run for an office to be filled by a vote of that body. To clear the way, Lincoln declined to accept the seat to which he had just been elected. Then, with the technical problem solved, Lincoln threw all his energy into winning votes.

On February 8, 1855, the legislature met to elect a Senator. On the first ballot, Lincoln received 44 votes; James Shields (who had once challenged Lincoln to a duel) received 41 Democratic votes, and Lyman Trumbull, an anti-Nebraska Democrat and a former colleague of Lincoln's in the state legislature, received 5 votes. That put Lincoln within a few votes of election, but when the day was over, Trumbull had won. The best explanation for this turnaround can be found in Lincoln's letter to Elihu B. Washburne of February 9, 1855:

> The agony is over at last; and the result you doubtless know. I write this only to give you some particulars to explain what might appear difficult of understanding. I began with 44 votes, Shields 41, and Trumbull 5—yet Trumbull was elected. In fact 47 different members voted for me—getting three new ones on the second ballot, and losing four old ones. How come my 47 to yield to T's 5? It was Govr. Matteson's work. He has been secretly a candidate ever since (before even) the fall election. All the members round about the canal were anti-Nebraska; but were, nevertheless nearly all Democrats, and old personal friends of his. His plan was to privately impress them with the belief that he was as good Anti-Nebraska as any one else—at least could be secured to be so by instruction, which could be easily passed. In this way he got from four to six of that sort of men to really prefer his election to that of any other man—all "sub rose" of course. One notable instance of this sort was with Mr. Strunk of Kankakee. At the beginning of the session he came a volunteer to tell me he was for me and would walk a hundred miles to elect me; but lo, it was not long before he leaked it out that he was going for me the first few ballots & then for Govr. Matteson.
>
> The Nebraska men, of course, were not for Matteson; but when they found they could elect no avowed Nebraska man they tardily determined, to let him get whomever of our men he could by whatever means he could and ask him no questions. In the mean time Osgood, Don. Morrison & Trapp of St. Clair had openly gone over from us. With the United Nebraska force, and their recruits, open and covert, it gave Matteson more than enough to elect him. We saw into it plainly ten days ago; but with every possible effort, could not head it off. All that remained of the Anti-Nebraska force, excepting Judd, Cook, Palmer, Baker & Allen of Madison & two or three of the secret Matteson men, would go into caucus, & I could get the nomination of that caucus. But the three senators & one of the two representatives above named "could never vote for a whig" and this incensed some twenty whigs to "think" they would never vote for the man of the five.

So we stood, and so we went into the fight yesterday; the Nebraska men very confident of the election of Matteson, though denying that he was a candidate; and we very much believing also, that they would elect him. But they wanted to make a show of good faith to Shields by voting for him a few times, and our secret Matteson men also wanted to make a show of good faith by voting with us a few times. So we led off. On the seventh ballot, I think, the signal was given to the Neb. men, to turn on Matteson which they acted on to a man, with one exception; my old friend Strunk going with them giving him 44 votes. Next ballot the remaining Neb. man, & one pretended Anti went on to him, giving him 46. The next still another giving him 47, wanting only three of an election. In the mean time, our friends with a view of detaining our expected bolters had been turning from me to Trumbull till he had risen to 35 & I had been reduced to 15. These would never desert me except by my direction; but I became satisfied that if we could prevent Matteson's election one or two ballots more, we could not possibly do so a single ballot after my friends should begin to return to me from Trumbull. So I determined to strike at once; and accordingly advised my remaining friends to go for him, which they did & elected him on the 10th ballot.

Such is the way the thing was done. . . . I regret my defeat moderately, but I am not nervous about it. . . . His [Matteson's] defeat now gives me more pleasure than my own gives me pain.

The anti-Nebraska groundswell that propelled Lincoln's unsuccessful quest of the Illinois senatorial seat also affected profoundly the national political picture. The strong antislavery elements in the North and Midwest had taken the form of splinter parties, among them the Liberty and Free-Soil parties. These elements now began to coalesce with disaffected Democrats and Whigs of marked antislavery views, and a new political movement—the Republican party—began to emerge.

The new party found strong support in Midwestern states—Michigan, Wisconsin, Ohio, and Indiana. Most Illinoisans opposed the Kansas-Nebraska Act, but antislavery Illinoisans moved slowly toward Republicanism.

So did Lincoln. An early organizing meeting of Republicans was held in Springfield in 1854, and Lincoln did not attend. Nevertheless, his name was placed on a letterhead as a member of the State Republican Central Committee. When Lincoln found out, he quickly acted to repudiate those trying to co-opt him. In a letter to Ichabod Codding, a noted abolition and temperance lecturer who was one of the most prominent leaders in the new Republican party in Illinois, Lincoln noted:

I have been perplexed some to understand why my name was placed on that committee. I was not consulted on the subject; nor was I apprized of the appointment, until I discovered it by accident two or three weeks afterwards. I suppose my opposition to the principle of slavery is as strong as that of any member of the Republican party; but I had also supposed that the *extent* to which I feel authorized to carry that opposition, practically, was not at all satisfactory to that party. The leading men who organized that party, were present, on the 4th of Oct. at the discussion between Douglas and myself at Springfield, and had full opportunity to not misunderstand my position.

Lincoln was not yet willing to embrace the abolitionist doctrines espoused by most Republicans; nor was he willing just then to forsake the Whig party, which had been his home for more than twenty years.

Another early leader of the new party in Illinois was Owen Lovejoy of Princeton, brother of Elijah Lovejoy, the abolitionist editor killed by a mob in Alton, Illinois, in 1837. In his campaign for the Senate, Lincoln had impressed Lovejoy with the force of his anti-Nebraska views. On August 7, 1855, Lovejoy wrote to Lincoln, apparently trying to convert him to Republicanism. In response, Lincoln wrote:

> Not even you are more anxious to prevent the extension of slavery than I; and yet the political atmosphere is such, just now, that I fear to do anything, lest I do wrong. Know Nothingism has not yet entirely tumbled to pieces— nay, it is even a little encouraged by the late elections in Tennessee, Kentucky & Alabama. Until we can get the elements of this organization, there is not sufficient materials to successfully combat the Nebraska democracy with. We can not get them so long as they cling to a hope of success under their own organization. . . . Of their principles, I think little better than I do of those of the slavery extensionists. Indeed I do not perceive how any one professing to be sensitive to the wrongs of the Negroes, can join in a league to degrade a class of white men.
>
> I have no objections to "fuse" with any body provided I can fuse on ground which I think is right; and I believe the opponents of slavery extension could do this, if it were not for this K.N.ism.

Lincoln had no objections to a fusion party, but wanted to preserve his integrity. From that time on Lincoln began to move in the direction of Republicanism.

In February 1856, several antislavery newspaper editors held a convention in Decatur. According to historian Don Fehrenbacher, "This Decatur editorial convention marks the launching of the state Republican Party, and Lincoln significantly was the one prominent political leader who attended it." At this point Lincoln embraced Republicanism. Traditionally, the Bloomington convention, a meeting of state anti-Nebraska men that occurred three months later in May, has been cited as the turning point in Lincoln's partisan affiliation. Whatever date is used, in 1856 Lincoln committed himself to a new party. By June his ties to Republicanism had become so strong that he was one of ten nominated by the Republican national convention in Philadelphia for the Vice-Presidency. On the first ballot Lincoln received 110 votes. The nomination eventually went to the better known William L. Dayton of Ohio, a former Whig Congressman whose ties with the antislavery branch of the party were longstanding.

New-York Daily Tribune.
FRIDAY, JUNE 20, 1856.

Governor Seward's Speech.

THE PEOPLES' CONVENTION.

From Our Own Reporters.

WM. L. DAYTON FOR VICE-PRESIDENT.

LAST DAY.

PHILADELPHIA, Thursday, June 19—10 A. M.

The Convention reassembled—the President, Col. LANE of Indiana, in the Chair. The proceedings were opened by a prayer by the Rev. Mr. LEVY.

Mr. LEIGH of New-Jersey offered the following resolution:

Resolved, That a National Convention of young men in favor of free speech, free soil, free Kansas and Fremont for President, be held during the month of September, in the City of New-York, under the call of the National Republican Convention.

Mr. WHELPLEY of New-Jersey said, that he arose to nominate a man for candidate for the Vice-Presidency who in the House of Representatives steadfastly opposed the passage of the Compromise measures in 1850, and was stricken down for that act and for the advocacy of the very principles which we advocate here [Cheers]. He referred to WILLIAM L. DAYTON of New-Jersey [Loud cheers].

Mr. FISHER of Penn. said he took the liberty to nominate a man whose name would be a tower of strength in Pennsylvania—David Wilmot of Penn. [Loud cheers].

Mr. ALLISON of Penn. presented the resolutions which had been adopted by the Republican State Convention. Mr. Allison said he had been requested to nominate as a candidate for the Vice-Presidency Abraham Lincoln of Ill [Cheers]. He knew him to be the prince of good fellows, and an old-line Whig [Cheers].

Col. W. B. ARCHER of Ill. said he was acquainted with Mr. Lincoln, and had known him over thirty years. He was a native of Kentucky, and had always

The Convention then went into an informal ballot for Vice-President, with the following result:

	Wilmot.	Lincoln.	Dayton.	Ford.	C. M. Clay.	Sumner.	J. Collamer.	Giddings.	W. F. Johnston.	Banks.	Pennington.	Wilson.	King.	Carey.	Pomeroy.
Me.		1	20	1	1										
N. H.		8	7												
Vt.							15								
Mass.	2	7	21					2	2						
R. I.		2	8		1				1						
Conn.			1						17						
N. Y.	1	3	15	6	30	1			24	1	1	9			
N. J.			21												
Penn.	31	11	28		2							4		3	
Del.			9												
Md.			6												
Va.	3														
Ky.	5														
Ohio.	1	2	65			1									
Ind.		26	13												
Ill.		33													
Mich.		1	18												
Iowa.			7		1					4					
Wis.			15												
Cal.		12													
Kan.							1								8
Minn.			3												
D. C.			3												
Total	43	110	259	7	35	4	15	2	2	46	1	5	9	3	8

At the Republican nominating convention in 1856 Lincoln proved to be so popular that he received 110 votes for his nomination as Vice-President. *(Library of Congress)*

THE LATE HON. OWEN LOVEJOY.—PHOTOGRAPHED BY WILLIAMSON, BROOKLYN.—[SEE PAGE 591.]

Owen Lovejoy—an intimate friend and political adviser. *(Library of Congress)*

Roger B. Taney—*Taney's decision outraged . . . [even] moderate antislavery men. (Library of Congress)*

Following the convention, Lincoln campaigned arduously for candidate John C. Frémont, the famed "Pathfinder of the West," who undoubtedly hoped to trade the military reputation his explorations had garnered him for political power, not unlike Zachary Taylor eight years before. Lincoln's personal choice for the presidential nomination had been John McLean, a Supreme Court Justice whose centrist views were more in accord with his own. Later, he estimated that he delivered as many as fifty speeches on behalf of the Republican party. He limited campaigning to Illinois, however, with the exception of a single speech in Kalamazoo, Michigan. Not only did he campaign for Frémont, but he set the stage for the Illinois senatorial contest in 1858. By the end of the campaign he had become the leading and best known Republican in the state of Illinois. And national events were inexorably pushing sectional tensions to the breaking point.

In 1857 U.S. Supreme Court Chief Justice Roger B. Taney declared that Negroes "had no rights which the white man was bound to respect." The occasion for this statement was the infamous Dred Scott decision. Scott, a slave who had been taken by his master to a free state for a considerable period of time, had sued for his freedom. Taney's decision outraged abolitionists and moderate antislavery men.

In June that same year a convention met at Lecompton, Kansas, to draft a constitution under which the territory would apply for statehood. Proslavery factions dominated the convention, and they included a provision in the constitution that would permit slavery in Kansas. President Buchanan urged acceptance of the Lecompton constitution, but Senator Stephen A. Douglas, who was chairman of the Senate Committee on Territories, opposed it. A bitter struggle followed between Douglas and Buchanan. Buchanan turned support of the Lecompton constitution into a measure testing party loyalty. That politics makes strange bedfellows is apparent in the fight between Douglas and Buchanan. To some, Douglas emerged as an opponent to the extension of slavery, and because of this perception many Republicans, including Horace Greeley, urged his reelection to the Senate. Not Lincoln. He correctly perceived Douglas's position as unchanged, but momentarily the point was difficult to make. Eventually he successfully noted that Douglas did not oppose the extension of slavery but instead sought only to protect his cherished notion of popular sovereignty.

The senatorial race of 1858 loomed large on Lincoln's personal horizon, and in that race he and the Republican party introduced several innovative techniques. Until 1913, when the 17th Amendment took effect, United States Senators were chosen by state legislatures. Most candidates for the office, like Lincoln in 1854, courted the legislators more than the people. In addition, party conventions scrupulously avoided endorsing candidates for the Senate lest they seem to be infringing upon a legislative prerogative.

The Senate race in 1858 was different. When the Republican state

Dred Scott—*"had no rights which the white man was bound to respect." (Library of Congress)*

convention met on June 16, 1858, it designated Lincoln as its choice for the Senate seat occupied by Douglas. The convention did not want to usurp the legislative prerogative and the endorsement of Lincoln was not intended to be a nomination. Rather it was meant to voice strong disapproval of Greeley and other non-Illinois Republicans who supported Democrat Douglas. These interlopers were put on notice that Illinois Republicanism was none of their business. It nevertheless settled the question of candidacy and had the effect of a nomination. Lincoln was the Republican choice and could be assured of election if Republicans won control of the legislature. After the "nomination" Lincoln, unlike in 1854, took his campaign directly to the people.

He opened his campaign in Springfield the evening of his nomination. Speaking in Representative Hall, he said:

> If we could first know *where* we are, and *whither* we are tending, we could better judge *what* to do, and *how* to do it. . . . 'A house divided against itself cannot stand.'
> I believe this government cannot endure, permanently half *slave* and half *free*.

The speech received an interpretation Lincoln did not intend, and it certainly provided Stephen A. Douglas with campaign material. He continually charged that Lincoln wished to abolish slavery and advocated the political and social equality of the races.

Lincoln, however, was a careful and conscious stylist. In the course of the campaign he succeeded in defending himself adequately. He insisted that his controversial "house divided" statement was more a look ahead than a recommendation. In that speech Lincoln had not suddenly become an abolitionist. His objective remained that of restricting the extension of slavery. Except for the District of Columbia, he did not propose abolition where slavery existed. Nevertheless, he forecast that slavery would eventually disappear.

The campaign proceeded for two months with Douglas and Lincoln responding to each other in separate speeches. This led to suggestions of joint debates between the two men. Lincoln wrote to Douglas on July 24, 1858, asking if he would be agreeable to a "joint canvass." Douglas replied that he had already made a number of commitments, but that he would be willing to have one joint discussion with Lincoln in a prominent place in each congressional district, except the two in which each had already spoken. With this agreement, the Lincoln-Douglas debates were born.

The Illinois senatorial campaign attracted far more nationwide attention than had any other state election in the nation's history.

The reason may be found in the prominence of Douglas and the controversy and confusion over his position in opposition to the Lecompton constitution. Many observers felt that the future of the Democratic party nationally was at stake in the Illinois race. Republicans, some of whom saw Douglas as a prospective and valuable convert, also watched the race with heightened interest.

Lincoln's views were illuminated in the reflected limelight of Douglas's reputation. He emerged from the campaign as a respected and prominent national Republican figure. So high was the interest in the contest that two Illinois newspapers printed the complete texts of the debates between Lincoln and Douglas. This made Lincoln's arguments far more accessible nationally than any amount of nationwide stump speaking could have accomplished.

There were seven debates in all. They were held in Ottawa, Freeport, Jonesboro, Charleston, Galesburg, Quincy, and Alton between August 21 and October 15. Many historians contend that the debate at Freeport marked a turning point in the future nationally of both the Republican and Democratic parties. In that debate Lincoln answered seven questions that Douglas had posed in the previous debate and asked four questions of his own.

For his second question Lincoln queried: "Can the people of a United States territory, in any lawful way, against the wish of any citizen of the United States, exclude slavery from its limits prior to the formation of a State Constitution?"

Douglas responded by asserting that slavery could not exist anywhere without the support of "local police regulations." By reasserting the doctrine of popular sovereignty, Douglas took a position widely popular in Illinois but one that made slaveholding states uneasy. He had already jeopardized his standing there by opposing the Lecompton constitution. Some historians contend that by the "Freeport Doctrine" Douglas gained the Senate but lost the Presidency. If so, Lincoln lost the Senate but won the White House. But while that proved to be the effect of the Freeport debate, there is little evidence that Lincoln even then looked toward the Presidency. Only one thing was sure: Senator Douglas won. When the legislature met, the young Republican party had failed to win enough seats to elect a Senator.

Lincoln had become accustomed to defeat; for the second time he had lost a Senate bid. Paradoxically, however, his defeat thrust him into a larger political arena, a national one. He had held his own against the leading Democratic

Even "Honest old Abe" was pictured as talking out of both sides of his mouth in his campaign for the Senate and for the Presidency. *(Library of Congress)*

He emerged from the campaign as a respected and prominent national Republican figure. *(James R. Mellon II)*

As a result of the debates with Douglas, Lincoln lost the Senate but won the White House. *(Library of Congress)*

contender for the next presidential nomination. Republicans throughout the country were looking with curiosity at this tall Illinoisan of whom they knew so little. Once again events helped him.

John Brown's ill-fated expedition against the federal arsenal at Harper's Ferry roused both applause and outrage. Public reaction to Brown's raid damaged the two leading prospects for the Republican presidential nomination, William H. Seward and Salmon P. Chase. They had long been identified with the more ardent antislavery factions, and the violence of Brown's raid and the emotional reaction to it linked their position in the public mind with extremism and lawlessness. Lincoln, a man of greater moderation on the slavery issue, became more and more appealing.

In speeches in Cooper Union, New York, and throughout New England, Lincoln was the voice of moderation. His adamant stand against extension of slavery coupled with his equally adamant stand against federal interference with slavery where it existed placed him near the broad center of public sentiment.

As the Republican national convention of 1860 approached, pro-Lincoln sentiment grew. Traditional political wisdom gave William H. Seward the edge when delegates began to arrive at the Chicago Convention hall called the Wigwam. Then David Davis, Lincoln's shrewd manager, took charge. A telegram from Lincoln demanding that Davis make no promises on his behalf went ignored. Davis and his lieutenants promised a Cabinet post here, a judgeship there, and so it went. Their adept grasp of political reality and tough resourcefulness greased the wheels of the Lincoln bandwagon.

Attracted by the political pragmatism of Davis and the moderation of Lincoln's views, the delegates steadily moved to support Illinois's "lone star." On the third ballot Lincoln became the Republican nominee for President. A rooftop cannon boomed the news to the throng gathered outside.

The message came clattering by telegraph to Springfield and to the anxious candidate sitting in a hickory chair in the office of the *Sangamo Journal.* With a smile on his face, he stood up and announced, "Well, there's a little lady down on Eighth Street who'll want to hear the news."

A divided Democratic party nominated two candidates—the northern wing put forward Stephen A. Douglas of Illinois. The South rallied behind John C. Breckinridge of Kentucky. A hastily formed party, the Constitutional Union party, vainly struggled to defuse the incendiary slavery issue by running on a simple plank of love of country. Its candidates were John Bell and Edward Everett, who later achieved fame by preceding Lincoln at Gettysburg, and eschewed his own two-hour lecture in favor of Lincoln's three-minute address. The split in the Democratic party, plus the new splinter party, sealed its doom and election day saw Lincoln emerge victorious. Once more compromise had proven its election-day value.

The Wigwam in Chicago. *(Library of Congress)*

A banner proudly displaying the Republican nominees for President and Vice-President. *(Library of Congress)*

David Davis—*greased the wheels of the Lincoln bandwagon. (Library of Congress)*

The chair Lincoln was sitting in when he learned of his nomination for the Presidency. *(Illinois* State Journal Register)

George Ashmun's letter to Abraham Lincoln, officially informing him of his nomination by the Republican party in 1860. *(Library of Congress)*

John C. Breckinridge—James Buchanan's Vice-President. He was the southern Democrat's candidate for President in 1860, and destined to become Secretary of War in the Confederacy. *(Kiplinger Washington Collection)*

Candidate John Bell ran on a simple plank of love of country. *(Library of Congress)*

Baseball was popular even in 1860. In this cartoon Lincoln used a huge split rail for a bat and hit a "home run" to win the election. *(Library of Congress)*

15

"Important principle may and must be inflexible."

THE MONTHS THAT PASSED between Lincoln's election in November and his inauguration in March were filled with feverish activity. The threat of disunion became a reality when South Carolina enacted an ordinance of secession in December 1860. President James Buchanan—the "understrapper" of Lincoln's congressional term—hoped desperately to end his term before the conflict mushroomed into war. And southerners within Buchanan's cabinet—including Vice-President John C. Breckinridge—were taking steps to have the Army and Navy dispersed to far-flung outposts and to have as many weapons as possible moved to southern arsenals.

Under such inauspicious circumstances, on March 4, 1861, Abraham Lincoln walked onto the hastily constructed wooden stand on the Capitol steps to take his oath of office. Derricks and scaffolding thrust out from the unfinished new dome of the Capitol, now vastly larger and more impressive than when he served there as Congressman.

He was introduced by his friend and sometime political competitor, Edward D. Baker. On the roofs of the building, and peering from upper windows, Army sharpshooters watched for rumored secessionist assassins. With such an ominous beginning, Lincoln uttered his first words as President.

His first inaugural address mixed firmness and conciliation. Reiterating his vow to leave slavery alone in the South, he thrust the responsibility for the looming fratricidal war on the nation that had elected him. "In your hands, my fellow countrymen, and not mine, rests the momentous issue of Civil War."

The war shortly erupted.

For four years the Civil War overshadowed everything. Huge masses of troops were organized and thrown into battle. The names of Bull Run, Shiloh, Antietam, Fredericksburg, Vicksburg, Gettysburg, Cold Harbor, and Appomattox became familiar headlines, while the long casualty lists sowed tears and sorrow. President Lincoln, as commander in chief, took a vigorous and active role in the prosecution of the war. He shared the glory and the blame of the Union Army's successes and failures.

Understandably, the public and historians have paid most attention to the war. It claimed more American lives than all our other wars combined at a time when our population was only a fraction of what it is today. Overlooked, however, are important and vast accomplishments in less bloody areas. Throughout the tumultuous war years, on both civil and military fronts, Lincoln

The Capitol Lincoln returned to in 1861 was greatly expanded from the building he knew as a Congressman, including new Senate and House wings and the beginning of the dome that is now famous worldwide. *(Library of Congress)*

VIEW ON PENNSYLVANIA AVENUE, WASHINGTON, MONDAY MARCH 4TH, 1861—MR. LINCOLN, ACCOMPANIED BY PRESIDENT BUCHANAN ON HIS WAY TO THE CAPITOL TO BE INAUGURATED.—FROM A SKETCH BY OUR SPECIAL ARTIST

On the roofs of the building . . . Army sharpshooters watched. (Kiplinger Washington Collection)

leaned heavily on the valuable experiences that had been his during the 30th Congress.

As he selected the members of his Cabinet, he hewed to the patronage lessons he had bitterly learned following Zachary Taylor's election. Promises had been made at the Chicago convention, and while they were in violation of Lincoln's own instructions to his campaign manager, David Davis, Lincoln kept those promises rather than risk disharmony within his own party. He would deal fairly with those who had a right to expect his consideration and patronage, even as he had been disappointed in his own quest for patronage from the Taylor administration.

William H. Seward became Secretary of State, and Simon Cameron took over the post as Secretary of War. Salmon P. Chase of Ohio became Secretary of the Treasury, Gideon Welles of Connecticut headed the Navy Department, and Edward Bates of Missouri became Attorney General. Nor did Lincoln forget his congressional colleagues of a dozen years past. Caleb B. Smith of Indiana was put in charge of the Interior Department, and, in an effort to make the South a part of his administration, his former Georgia colleague Alexander Stephens was reportedly offered a Cabinet position. Stephens declined, however, and Lincoln instead named Montgomery Blair of Maryland as Postmaster General.

Lincoln's selections reflected not only geographical diversity but every ideological hue the Republican party represented. Seward and Chase had been abolitionists of long standing; Bates and Smith were old-line Whigs, and Montgomery Blair stood as a staunch unionist.

The formation of a Cabinet complete, a far more formidable challenge now loomed. On April 12, 1861, Confederate States' artillery under the direction of General P. G. T. Beauregard fired on Fort Sumter to begin the Civil War. Lincoln had to prepare the Union for the coming battles that now were unavoidable. Ironically, Congress was not in session when the war broke out, and Lincoln initially federalized the 75,000 members of the state militias, invoking a 1795 statute of questionable legality. Southern states did not heed the President's call, and Lincoln asked for volunteers for the regular Army, a marked break with past tradition requiring congressional action before there could be any increase in the size of the Army. In fact, it had been requests for increases in the strength of the Army during the Mexican War that caused Whigs like Lincoln to stand in opposition to President James K. Polk. The new President's action not only seemed to fly in the face of everything he had said as Congressman about presidential war-making powers, but it also seemed to skirt the very laws and Constitution he had sworn to uphold both as Congressman and now as President. No doubt he recalled with a certain sense of irony some of his own statements about President Polk's conduct of the Mexican War.

In fact, acutely aware that his actions came perilously close to exercising authority that he had strenuously fought against in 1848, Lincoln went to great lengths to make clear the difference between defending against a foreign attack

Col. Edward D. Baker

Lincoln was introduced by his friend Colonel E. D. Baker, who only a few months later would fall at the Battle of Ball's Bluff, causing a deep personal loss to the President. *(Library of Congress)*

n these rare and hitherto-unpublished photographs by Montgomery C. Meigs, the crowd is shown assembling in front of the Capitol to witness Lincoln's first inauguration. *Library of Congress)*

The White House when Lincoln came to Washington as President. *(Library of Congress)*

and the southern insurrection. The existence of an internal rebellion, he maintained, conferred upon the President greater power in order to preserve the Union. No declaration of war, and hence no prior approval by Congress, was required, for no foreign power was involved. Congress, in a special session called by Lincoln, agreed, and on August 6, 1861, ratified his unusual action. There was no dissension in Congress from southern Congressmen; virtually all had resigned when their states seceded.

The special session of Congress received Lincoln's first message and immediately confronted an additional abuse of the war power by Lincoln. Shortly after the firing on Fort Sumter, on April 27, President Lincoln wrote the Commanding General of the U.S. Army:

> If at any point on or in the vicinity of any military line which is now or which shall be used between the city of Philadelphia and the city of Washington you find resistance which renders it necessary to suspend the writ of *habeas corpus* for the public safety, you personally, or through the officer in command at the point where resistance occurs, are authorized to suspend that writ.

A few weeks after Lincoln authorized the suspension of the writ, a Baltimore secessionist named Merryman was preemptorily picked up and thrown into jail by Union troops for raising and training men for the Confederacy. On the same day Merryman's attorney hastened to Washington to challenge Lincoln's right to suspend the writ. Scurrying back to Baltimore with the attorney went Chief Justice Roger Taney. Taney, sitting in his capacity as a circuit judge in Baltimore, declared that the President had no right to suspend the writ of habeas corpus. The provision for the suspension of the writ, he asserted, appeared in the Article of the Constitution dealing with the powers of Congress, and therefore only Congress could authorize suspension of the writ.

Lincoln was not cowed. On July 2, 1861, he expanded the area in which the writ could be suspended to include as far north as New York City. When others raised questions about the propriety of his action, Lincoln responded in his message to the special session of Congress that:

> the Constitution itself is silent as to which or who is to exercise this power [to suspend the writ]; and as the provision was plainly made for a dangerous emergency, it can not be believed the framers of the [Constitution] intended that in every case the danger should run its course until Congress could be called together, the very assembling of which might be prevented, as was intended in this case, by the rebellion.

Over the years, thousands of civilians were clapped into military prisons. "Copperheads," northern men with southern sentiments, seemed to abound. If they became too vociferous in their criticism of Lincoln and his efforts to preserve the Union, into prison they went, without charges being filed against them, without a trial, and without prospect for release.

Lincoln with the first Cabinet he appointed. *(Library of Congress)*

Jefferson Davis, President of the Provisional Government of the Confederate States of America, had served in the same Congress with Lincoln. *(Library of Congress)*

Lincoln federalized the state militias, which, when they finally arrived in Washington, calmed an anxious President fearful that the city would be overrun by secessionists. *(Library of Congress)*

Northern boasts that the southern insurrection would be quelled in less than ninety days died quickly when the Confederacy scored a resounding success at the first battle of Bull Run on July 21, 1861. Because of the rout, Lincoln fired aging General Winfield Scott and went in search of a new leader. *(Library of Congress)*

After Bull Run, Lincoln turned over control of the Army of the Potomac to dashing and popular George B. McClellan. *(Library of Congress)*

Lincoln also occasionally acquiesced in the closing of newspapers whose sentiments did not suit him, including one New York City paper. His measures were, perhaps, extralegal and even unconstitutional as some critics charged, but, as he pointed out, without them there might have been no Constitution to protect.

Despite the objections raised against suspending the writ, Lincoln did not ask Congress for authority to continue the suspension at that time and Congress took no action.

Years before, Congressman Lincoln had warned his colleagues against Presidents who acted without legislative sanction to trample the rights of the people. He warned that Congress must keep a close rein on the war powers lest the country be embroiled in conflict, violence, and loss of life through abuse of presidential authority.

As a Congressman in 1848 he had warned:

> The provision of the Constitution giving the war making power to Congress, was dictated, as I understand it, by the following reasons: Kings had always been involving and impoverishing their people in wars, pretending generally, if not always, that the good of the people was the object. This our Convention understood to be the most oppressive of all Kingly oppressions, and they resolved to so frame the Constitution that no one man would hold the power of bringing this oppression upon us. But your view destroys the whole matter, and places our President where kings have always stood.

Now, just thirteen years later, he acted like the kings he abhorred. He suspended the writ of habeas corpus, subjected civilians to indefinite detention, and closed newspapers that opposed his administration.

Did President Lincoln remember the injunctions he had voiced with such vehemence? Did he agonize as he put these injunctions aside? Of course. Every President I have known has had to change his position on vital questions once he assumed the duties of chief executive. The view from the President's desk is far different than from a seat in the House of Representatives.

Franklin Roosevelt won election in 1932 on a platform of fiscal conservatism, and reelection in 1940 with promises to keep our nation out of war. He changed his view dramatically on both issues. Lyndon Johnson also won election in 1964 with promises to keep our nation out of war. Circumstances and perspectives can change radically and swiftly. Certainly, circumstances changed enormously for the nation between Lincoln's service in Congress and his presidential years.

When Congressman Lincoln challenged the constitutionality of U.S. entry into the Mexican War, our nation was not threatened in any serious way. Military forces of Mexico were thousands of miles from the U.S. seat of government. They constituted, at worst, a nuisance along the border of a distant territory.

The extraordinary measures Lincoln sanctioned during his Presidency were taken because of the extremity of the situation. The lifeline of the nation was

Fear of the secessionists led Lincoln to suspend the writ of habeas corpus and turn Washington into the most heavily fortified city in the world—here Fort Albany, located across the Potomac River in Arlington, Virginia. *(Library of Congress)*

threatened, the capital itself under siege, the entire constitutional structure on the verge of collapse.

In this circumstance the man who years before had warned of the abuse of power by Presidents justified extreme measures repressing basic liberties with the same claim of "military necessity" that later impelled him to free several million slaves by executive order.

In 1861, faced with the greatest peril that had ever faced any President, he quickly took a series of steps that surely would have shocked him twelve years earlier. His devotion to the Constitution was no less. But his love of country and his responsibility to preserve the Union was now paramount. It was not until March 1863 that Congress decided to clarify the legal and constitutional issues involved and to grant Lincoln (specifically) the authority to suspend the writ that he had long been exercising. The result was the Habeas Corpus Indemnity-Removal law.

In addition to the vexing legal and constitutional issues that Lincoln faced in his first few months, there was the pressing problem of finding leadership for the armed forces. Along with the soldiers who were pouring into Washington, there also came a pack of politicians seeking command positions with the growing Army. Lincoln was importuned for commissions on all sides by politicians of virtually all stripes. Few of them had any military training, and fewer still had military experience—the Black Hawk or Mexican wars were in the distant past and had involved few Americans in combat. None of the West Pointers who

Lincoln appointed political allies and opponents to high ranks in the Army. John McClernand, a Democrat from Illinois, who served with Lincoln in the 30th Congress, received a post as General. *(Library of Congress)*

remained with the Union—and it seemed that all of the most promising had resigned to serve the Confederacy—had much experience either. Their education consisted for the most part of studying the accounts of the Napoleonic wars.

Politician-generals had been prominent since the early days of the American Revolution. In the new national crisis, there was no reservoir of potential military talent more readily available than those tested on the political battlefields. As a Congressman, Lincoln had chided politician Lewis Cass for pretending to be a war hero. As President he looked of necessity to politicians for military leadership. The commander in chief had to find those who could carry out military plans, a quantum jump from the work of the legislator.

An even more important function of these political appointees was their valuable role in healing factionalism and disunion and building support for the Republican administration's war. Any war causes some dissension internally among those who do not see the need. Some are pacifists, some disagree with the policy being pursued, some have ethnic ties that are jeopardized. But the Civil War brought yet a new horror—pitting friend against friend, relative against relative, and occasionally brother against brother. It is no wonder that Lincoln had to do everything in his power to keep the nation from literally coming apart at the seams. Political military appointments were one way to build cohesiveness. Thus, Democrats like John A. McClernand, Benjamin Butler, and Nathaniel P. Banks received commissions from Lincoln, not because of military brilliance (which they totally lacked) but because they would help

As the war droned on, Lincoln and his generals confronted the greatest challenge to the survival of individual liberty ever to face the United States. *(Library of Congress)*

unite the northern faction of their party behind the new President. Predictably, few were satisfied with these appointments. Republicans felt that he gave too many to Democrats, while the latter were always certain that it was the Republicans who were running the war. In walking this narrow middle ground, Lincoln often felt keenly disappointed in the performance of some of his military appointments. Once a brigadier general he had appointed was captured, along with some horses and mules. Expressing frustration at his inability to find competent military leadership, Lincoln remarked: "I don't care so much for brigadiers. I can *make* them. But horses and mules cost money."

Yet Lincoln did not always cave in to the politicians who came soliciting military appointments. Once the Pennsylvania delegation in Congress came to see him about a promotion for General Samuel P. Heintzelman, a native son. They told the President what a good man he was, and Lincoln readily agreed with their assessment. In fact, he said, Heintzelman is "a good egg" and therefore he will keep a little. He implored the Congressmen to "trust me," and with no more of a promise escorted them from his office. Such is the power of the Presidency over other politicians that the slightest word of encouragement will often be accepted as an affirmative and binding commitment. Lincoln knew this from his congressional years when he had vied for the attention of two Presidents and their administrations.

Regardless of how many unprecedented difficulties the war created, Lincoln still had to deal with a multitude of familiar issues given a new complexion by the erupting conflict.

Relations with Mexico were one such problem, as they had been when he was a Congressman. The Mexican War was past history, of course, and now the Mexicans feared aggression from France's Napoleon III. On January 19, 1861, just before leaving Springfield for Washington to assume office, President-elect Lincoln met with Matias Romero, the personal envoy of Mexico's President Benito Juarez. Romero wrote in his diary:

> Mr. Lincoln told me that during his administration he would try to do everything within his power in favor of the interests of Mexico; that he would in all instances do her justice; and that he would consider her as a friendly sister nation.

By December 1861, both Mexico and the United States were again at war, although this time not with each other. The Mexican leader knew that under the circumstances he could not look to the United States for salvation. Juarez wrote Romero in Washington:

> It is necessary to convince ourselves that the leaders of that Republic [the United States] must give every priority to reestablishing and consolidating their domestic peace and that they will not wish to distract their resources nor their attention to help other people, no matter how good their intentions may be toward us.

Yet Lincoln, besieged by all manner of problems at home, still found time to help the struggling Mexicans in the only way he could. Before the end of the year he sent a message to Congress requesting authority to make a substantial loan to his friends south of the border.

Foreign aid was no more popular then than today, and the Senate dawdled over the request. Finally, on January 24, 1862, Lincoln sent a strongly worded plea to Capitol Hill. He put before the Senate a report from the U.S. Minister in Mexico containing

> important information concerning the war which is waged against Mexico by the combined powers of Spain, France, and Great Britain . . . I have heretofore submitted to the Senate a request for its advice upon the question pending by treaty for making a loan to Mexico, which Mr. Corwin thinks will in any case be expedient. It seems to be my duty now to solicit an early action of the Senate upon the subject, to the end that I may cause such instructions to be given to Mr. Corwin as will enable him to act in the manner which, while it will most carefully guard the interests of our country, will at the same time be most beneficial to Mexico.

The warm attitude of President Lincoln toward the Mexicans over more than a decade undoubtedly helped keep a secure border on the southern flank of the United States and prevented other nations from recognizing the Confederacy or joining it in its struggle against the Union. In fact, so grateful were the Mexicans for Lincoln's support of their cause that a hundred years later, in a ceremony in Washington, Mexican Ambassador Antonio Carrillo Flores told a gathering of dignitaries:

> Thank you Mr. President [Lincoln], in the name of all Mexicans, of those who have already died, of the living, and of those who are not yet born, for your speeches in our defense, as a Member of the House of Representatives, when our countries were at war.

Without question, Lincoln's activities as a Congressman had an important influence on the attitude the Mexicans took toward the United States not only during his subsequent Presidency, but for a century thereafter.

On the domestic front, Lincoln was at long last able to realize his lifetime goal of fostering internal improvements. Scarcely a year after he took the oath of office he had succeeded in encouraging through Congress and signing into law measures that would develop the nation beyond anything then imagined. In rapid order during the spring and summer of 1862 Lincoln put his signature on three bills that rank among the greatest legislation in our history. These bills were to affect profoundly the development of the United States. They enhanced its role as a world power, gave hope to the homeless and destitute, brought physical unity to the nation from coast to coast, and provided the basis for a family-owned food production system that is the marvel of the world for efficiency and still provides the best hope for conquering famine worldwide.

The three bills were: the Railway Right-of-Way Act, which encouraged the rapid development of transcontinental railroads; the Homestead Act, which encouraged the settlement and agricultural development of wilderness and prairie regions; and the Morrill Act, better known as the Land-Grant College Act, which encouraged the development of a system of higher education for the masses of United States citizens, especially farmers. These bills were a natural outgrowth of Congressman Lincoln's commitment to internal improvements. In the 30th Congress his unceasing efforts had brought little advance. But as President he provided executive support for laws that accelerated migration to the West and Far West.

The transcontinental railroad act held out the hope for a vast improvement in commercial transportation over the system of canals, corduroy roads, and very limited railroad service located largely on the East Coast. Augmenting the transcontinental railroad act, the Homestead Act of 1862 provided rich land to anyone who would settle it and promised a booming growth in the production of agricultural commodities to be moved to market. As a candidate, Lincoln had insisted that both provisions be included in the 1860 platform of the Republican party, and he was delighted when he finally was able to sign them into law.

The one bill, however, that undoubtedly did the most to put our nation on solid economic footing was the Morrill Act. Under it, the United States became the first nation in history to provide higher education to the masses of its farmers. Farmers sent their children to universities by the millions and later updated their own education through an extension program directed by the same universities. More than any other single factor, the Morrill Act established the foundation for America's continued worldwide leadership in food production. One hundred thirteen years later it inspired a new law, the Famine Prevention Program—which Senator Hubert Humphrey and I led through Congress—under which the land grant universities are given the job of improving the systems for educating farmers in developing nations.

These great bills for the peaceable advancement of the United States moved to enactment during the agonizing days of military convulsion. At a time when the survival of the nation was more threatened by force of arms than at any time since its birth, the government found insight, wisdom, and energy to move forward programs that gave the nation new vitality and promise in pursuits that were purely peaceful.

Of all the nonwar problems he faced, of course, none required so much of his energy or had such a lasting impact as slavery. In the anxious months before his inauguration, he had, through Senator Lyman Trumbull, rejected a proposal by Senator John J. Crittenden to avert secession and war by extending the line of the Missouri Compromise—and thereby extending slavery—to the Pacific. His action should have been no surprise; he had rejected a similar proposal when it came up in the Congress in which he served. The time had come for the new President to scorn all ambiguity, and in his inaugural address he had spelled out exactly how he would act in this secession crisis. He told the South slavery could remain where it was, but it could not be extended. He stood firm on the principles he had staked out in his years in Congress.

Lincoln received constant criticism from the abolitionist press, antislavery Members of Congress and the public for his failure to take quick and decisive action to abolish slavery as soon as the war began.

In dealing with the controversy over slavery and seeking a middle ground that both extremes could accept, Lincoln's experience in the 30th Congress served him well. From the moment he took his seat in the House of Representatives, Lincoln made clear that he opposed the expansion of slavery into new territories. His repeated support for the Wilmot Proviso during the 30th Congress reflected this continued determination. He also acted on his belief that Congress had the power to abolish slavery in the District of Columbia. He drafted a bill to provide compensation to the owners of the slaves freed in the District and tried to convince his colleagues to support it.

In the years between Congress and the Presidency, his commitment to halt the expansion of slavery grew. Lincoln's reemergence in the political arena in 1854 grew out of the hotly debated Kansas-Nebraska Act, which heralded a resurgence in the growth of slavery. First as an Anti-Nebraskan and later as a stalwart Republican, Lincoln hit the hustings to denounce the act and the

Lincoln's predecessor as Republican candidate for President, John C. Fremont, threw a political bombshell when he issued his own order freeing the slaves. *(Library of Congress)*

growth of slavery. In 1858 he offered the following statement of his view of the Republican party's stand on slavery:

> The Republican Party . . . holds that . . . slavery is an unqualified evil. . . . Regarding it as an evil, they will not molest it in the states where it exists; they will not overlook the constitutional guards which our forefathers have placed around; they will do nothing which can give proper offence to those who hold slaves by legal sanction; but they will use every constitutional method to prevent the evil from becoming larger.

The last phrase was the key: the method adopted must be constitutional, and the goal was to prevent slavery from spreading. Despite the personal repugnance slavery held for Lincoln, the commonly held view in 1860, which he shared, was that the Constitution itself protected this inhuman institution. Indeed, had not Article II of the Constitution prohibited any interference with the slave trade in the early years of the Union? And did not the 10th Amendment reserve to the states powers not expressly given to the federal government by the Constitution? Even many abolitionists such as Samuel J. May acknowledged this constitutional protection, calling it a "sin framed by law."

Of course, Lincoln's insistence on upholding the constitutional protection of slavery at the beginning of the Civil War was motivated by more than strict adherence to legal dogma. Several border states, such as Kentucky and Maryland, kept close watch to make sure that he kept his promise not to interfere with slavery where it existed. Thus, when Generals John C. Frémont and David Hunter exceeded their authority and issued limited emancipation proclamations, Lincoln ordered them rescinded rather than endanger the then tenuous unionism of slaveholding border states. Indeed, Kentucky threatened to secede if Lincoln permitted Frémont's order to stand. Contending that states could not secede from the Union, Lincoln constantly reiterated his commitment not "to interfere with the institution of slavery where it exists."

Yet Lincoln also moved quickly to do everything within his constitutional power to eliminate and ease the pain of slavery. Within a few months of taking office, he sounded out several Delaware Congressmen on a proposed bill he had drafted to provide compensated emancipation in their state, with a provision for colonizing the freed blacks.

In his first message to Congress in December 1861, Lincoln sought congressional support for his plan of compensated emancipation. He hoped that states, encouraged by provision for federal compensation for the slaves freed, would abolish slavery. The slaves, he suggested, could then be sent to "a climate congenial to them." And on December 31, 1862, he signed a contract with Bernard Koch providing for a colony of free blacks in Haiti. Government funds were allocated, and Koch set off with some five hundred free blacks for Ilé a Vache, Haiti. To Lincoln's dismay, the colony failed and a year later a government ship had to go to Haiti to bring back the survivors of the ill-fated venture. Never, however, was colonization far from Lincoln's mind. From his days as a Congressman-elect when he heard Henry Clay propose colonization of blacks until long after the Emancipation Proclamation took effect, this means of dealing with the "peculiar institution" absorbed his attention. Repeatedly Lincoln urged Congress to take action facilitating compensated emancipation and colonization.

In the end, it was military necessity that prompted the government to take the first step toward freeing the slaves—and the first step was taken by Congress, not by Lincoln. If slaves were chattel, and useful in furthering the Confederate cause, then they were instruments of war just as much as cannon, and other weapons subject to seizure. General Benjamin F. Butler therefore concluded that the first escaped slaves to cross his lines were "contraband of war." Congress seized the straw and on August 6, 1861, enacted the First Confiscation Act, providing that owners of slaves engaged in military service forfeited their claim to them.

Congress thereby heeded John Quincy Adams's strident avowal that "during a war all laws governing the institution of slavery were swept aside." President Lincoln, of course, knew well his former colleague's dictum. While Congress prepared to strengthen its Confiscation Act, Lincoln scrawled the preliminary draft of a presidential proclamation freeing the slaves in the seceded states.

Military necessity required and justified it, he felt. And indeed it did. Slaves had been given work digging entrenchments for the Confederacy, throwing up earthworks, and in other military capacities short of fighting. This enabled the South to field more troops. The Union military situation was bleak after the first year of war. Federal troops dragged from defeat to defeat. By the spring of 1862 Lincoln wrote,

Things had gone on from bad to worse until I felt we had reached the end of our rope on the plan of operations we had been pursuing; that we had about played our last card, and must change our tactics or lose the game! Then I determined on the adoption of the emancipation policy; and without consultation with, or knowledge of the Cabinet, I prepared the original draft of the proclamation.

By early summer, Lincoln had discussed emancipation of the slaves with several of his cohorts. On May 28 he confidently predicted to antislavery Senator Charles Sumner that emancipation would be proclaimed in a short time. Hannibal Hamlin revealed that Lincoln went over the proclamation he had drafted with him in June.

Then, on July 17, 1862, Congress passed the Second Confiscation Act and set the stage for the President's proclamation. The act stated that the slaves of anyone who committed treason were free, and the slaves of everyone who supported the Rebellion were "forever free." Passage of the act provided Lincoln the political support and authorization he needed to issue his own proclamation. Back to his desk he went to put the finishing touches on his emancipation decree in light of Congress's new law. In less than a week, he had prepared a handwritten draft of the Proclamation in accordance with the Second Confiscation Act.

When he brought the draft to a Cabinet meeting, however, he found opinions deeply divided. The Cabinet feared that the proclamation would be viewed by the Confederacy and by foreign governments as a last desperate measure acknowledging the weakness of the Union's position. They urged Lincoln to withhold the proclamation until there was a Union military victory. Lincoln grudgingly went along with their advice.

The military victory soon came. In September 1862, the Confederate forces under Robert E. Lee marched into Maryland to bring the war home to the North and to gain leverage for acquiring recognition—and help—from foreign powers. Luck went with the Union, however, and on September 17, 1862, Union troops won a strategic victory over the Confederacy at the Battle of Antietam and sent them trekking back to the South.

Lincoln lost no time in seizing the chance to issue his Emancipation Proclamation. On September 22, 1862, he issued the Preliminary Emancipation Proclamation, to go into effect on January 1, 1863. The lapse between issuance and effective date provided time for southern states to consider, as Lincoln put it, "restoration of the constitutional relation between the United States, and each of the states."

Even this drastic war measure did not sacrifice Lincoln's pledge not to interfere with slavery where it already existed if only the slave states would restore the "constitutional relation" by ending their secession and the war. Yet Lincoln must have known how slim the chances of reconciliation were. Clearly, in the final analysis, he was willing to sacrifice a long-held view if the South remained intransigent.

The South believed the Emancipation Proclamation to be the work of a demonic mind, as expressed in this vitriolic cartoon by Adalbert Volck. *(Library of Congress)*

In September 1862, Confederate troops under Robert E. Lee tried to move the war into Union territory. General George McClellan, with a copy of Lee's secret battle orders, fought them to a standstill at Antietam and forced their retreat to the homegrounds of Virginia. *(Library of Congress)*

Why the complete turnabout, the repudiation of a principle Lincoln had voiced so consistently and vehemently over the years on this subject? Politicians often change positions in the light of experience and new conditions. I certainly have changed my positions on many questions, perhaps the most fundamental and visible being the Vietnam War—going from hawk to dove. A politician who is unwilling to reconsider his position in the light of new circumstances deserves oblivion. But changing a long-held position is never easy and usually painful. It is sure to elicit biting criticism. When a Congressman announces a change in position on a highly important issue, a colleague in the cloakroom is sure to say sarcastically, "He must have spent last night burning a lot of old speeches."

Lincoln changed dramatically on the nation's most persistent and burning issue, moving from one extreme to the other—from the position that the federal government could not constitutionally abolish slavery to the opposite pole. Did Lincoln have to spend the night before burning old speeches? Was it a painful experience? In doing so, did he throw principle to the wind and open himself to

Lincoln and McClellan at Antietam. *(Library of Congress)*

The price of freedom . . . dead before a church at Antietam. *(Library of Congress)*

contempt and scorn? Did he wrestle with his conscience, trying to rationalize the change? Probably the answer is a qualified yes to all these questions. But Lincoln had no difficulty explaining the decision. He was no longer just a legislator arguing the technicalities and niceties of constitutional law and legal process. Lincoln was now the chief magistrate of a nation under siege, in mortal danger. His primary responsibility was to conduct his authority as President and commander in chief in a way that would destroy at the earliest possible date the military forces threatening the life of the nation from within.

In a letter to A. G. Hodges, Lincoln explained with enlightening precision how he faced the Emancipation decision and settled it strictly in terms of military necessity:

> I am naturally anti-slavery. If slavery is not wrong, nothing is wrong. . . . I aver that, to this day, I have done no official act in mere deference to my abstract feeling and judgment on slavery. . . . I did understand, however, that my oath to preserve the Constitution to the best of my ability imposed upon me the duty of preserving, by every indispensable means, that government—that nation—of which that Constitution was the organic law. Was it possible to lose the nation and yet preserve the Constitution? . . . I could not feel that, to the best of my ability, I had even tried to preserve the Constitution, if, to save slavery or any minor matter, I should permit the wreck of government, country, and Constitution, all together.
>
> When, early in the war, General Frémont attempted military emancipation, I forbade it, because I did not think it an indispensable necessity. When, a little later, General Cameron, then Secretary of War, suggested the arming of the blacks, I objected, because I did not think it an indispensable necessity. When, still later, General Hunter attempted military emancipation, I again forbade it, because I did not yet think the indispensable necessity had come.
>
> When, in March and May and July, 1862, I made earnest and successive appeals to the border States to favor compensated emancipation, I believed the indispensable necessity for military emancipation and arming the blacks would come, unless averted by that measure. They declined the proposition, and I was, in my best judgment, driven to the alternative of either surrendering the Union, and with it the Constitution, or laying strong hand upon the colored element. I chose the latter.
>
> In choosing it, I hoped for greater gain than loss; but of this I was not entirely confident. More than a year of trial now shows no loss by it in our foreign relations, none in our home popular sentiment, none in our white military force,—no loss by it anyhow or anywhere. On the contrary, it shows a gain of quite one hundred and thirty thousand soldiers, seamen, and laborers. These are palpable facts, about which, as facts, there can be no cavilling. We have the men and we could not have had them without the measure.

The Emancipation Proclamation was an extraordinary war measure adopted, according to Lincoln, "out of military necessity." As commander in chief he decided the proclamation would help win the war and preserve the Union. It was as simple as that.

In practical terms, the Proclamation—affecting only slaves in seceded states—had little immediate effect. Yet as a symbol its impact was deep and profound. As historian John Hope Franklin noted, "Lincoln was compelled to forge a document of freedom for the slaves within the existing constitutional system and in a manner that would give even greater support to that constitutional system." The symbolism alone paved the way for the extensive use of Negro troops by the Union army, and as news of it spread among slaves there was a quantum leap in the number of runaways who straggled into Union quarters. Finally, once the South had rejected the olive branch, the Emancipation Proclamation established the groundwork for a constitutional amendment under which Lincoln would see slavery buried forever.

In fact, it was becoming increasingly clear to Lincoln that colonization was not the complete answer to the slavery question. With the Emancipation Proclamation as background he quietly encouraged Union generals who were beginning to organize civil governments in parts of the South to provide education to blacks. He wrote to General Nathaniel P. Banks, who was governing part of Louisiana, suggesting "some practical system by which the two races could gradually live themselves out of their old relation to each other, and both come out better prepared for the new."

He decided it was time to move directly on the slavery question. Now that victory seemed assured, he did not have to worry about what effect his actions might have on the border states that remained loyal to the North. On June 9, 1864, he gave his approval to inclusion in his party's platform of a declaration in favor of an amendment to the Constitution abolishing slavery. After his reelection, in a message to Congress he would urge them to pass the 13th Amendment. The amendment was the logical outgrowth of his personal antipathy toward slavery and the belief that the institution was protected by the Constitution. Yet it did not wholly satisfy the radical Republicans. Lincoln had to work closely with Senator Lyman Trumbull (whom he had known since the days both courted Mary) to assure that the radicals did not include in the amendment provisions calling for the extension of the franchise to freed blacks and an overweening generosity (the promise of forty acres and a mule was often suggested) that would only further alienate the already embittered South. Rarely has so legalistic a document as the Emancipation Proclamation had such a profound impact on our history. And the seminal ideas that Lincoln put into this document were first nurtured in the 30th Congress.

The 13th Amendment went out to the states just before Lincoln's Second Inaugural. A few weeks later, on April 9, 1865, Confederate General Robert E. Lee marked the end of the rebellion with his surrender to Ulysses S. Grant. The news sparked bonfires and celebrations in Washington. It also stirred a passion for revenge on the part of radicals in Congress, so much so that a new confrontation between them and the President seemed imminent.

But the confrontation never came. On April 14, 1865, while enjoying a play at Ford's Theater, Lincoln was fatally shot by a crazed assassin, John Wilkes Booth. Within a few weeks of the assassination, several conspirators were rounded up and thrown into prison to await trial by a military tribunal. In the War Department offices, Secretary Edwin M. Stanton worked feverishly at drafting charges against those in custody, as well as several Confederate government officials who remained free but were suspected of complicity in the

On November 19, 1863, jostling crowds hurried to the dedication of a cemetery on the Gettysburg battlefield, where they heard a brief—and most felt disappointing—address by the President. *(Library of Congress)*

Sherman's relentless march to the sea, which cut the South in two and assured Union victory, included the virtual destruction of Atlanta. *(Library of Congress)*

plot. One of those in the latter category was a member of Jefferson Davis's "Confederate Cabinet," Jacob Thompson—a former colleague of Lincoln's in the 30th Congress and also a fellow boarder at Mrs. Sprigg's!

In his service as President, Lincoln earned the characterization made years later by his greatest biographer, Carl Sandburg, that he was "both steel and velvet—hard as rock and soft as drifting fog." Conciliatory when he could be, Lincoln remained immovable on issues of fundamental importance. In his very last public address, delivered in Washington just three days before his assassination, he argued for conciliation and compromise in dealing with the

Lyman Trumbull, whom he had known since the days when they had both courted Mary, helped hold the Radicals in check. *(Library of Congress)*

Ulysses S. Grant—architect of union success and eventual victory. *(Library of Congress)*

South. Still, he warned, there was a limit: "Important principles may, and must, be inflexible."

He could not permit the South to leave the Union, but he had tried to let the South know that he would have acceded to reasonable requests and attempt to negotiate problems. Southern leaders had failed to accept his offer and their failure is both our tragedy and our heritage.

This remarkable mixture of velvet and steel, conciliation and inflexibility, brought Lincoln successfully through "the fiery trial," as he described the war years. A man committed throughout his public career to moderation—to the peaceful, evolutionary termination of slavery—ended slavery for four million blacks with the stroke of a pen in the name of military necessity and preserved the Union by serving as the victorious commander in chief of the most powerful armies until then ever assembled in the history of the world.

In preserving the Union he settled—hopefully for all time—the question of state's rights. He argued that no state by its own action could withdraw from the Union, and he backed his argument with more than four years of relentless, brutal military force. He knew the nation could not survive if pieces of it could pull away at will. He believed the Union to be indivisible, because structural cohesion was essential to the protection of the rights of individual citizens. If a state could succeed in separating itself from the Union, the rights of the citizens in that state as protected by the Constitution of the Union would be shattered. After all, the Union was a union of individual citizens, not just of states. Each citizen, whether he lived in the North or South, had rights protected by the United States Constitution, and the President had the duty under the Constitution to protect those rights, no matter from what source a threat might come. In short, the act of secession by a state government was an intolerable violation of the constitutional rights of people living within that state. An individual citizen could secede from the Union by renouncing citizenship and leaving, but a state could not.

The phrase "liberty and union, one and inseparable" that Daniel Webster, Lincoln's breakfast host of congressional days, used with force years earlier gained practical application in Lincoln's Presidency.

At stake in the Civil War was individual liberty, plain and simple. Not just the liberty of blacks. In contention as the armies maneuvered and fought was the basic liberty of every person. If secession was accomplished, the Union government would lose its capacity to maintain the free institutions that protected the rights of the citizens in the states that had left. And the successful removal of one part of the Union would leave open the possibility of the removal of other parts later on. The great edifice of individual liberty and free institutions would have been built on shifting sand.

Even before he took the presidential mantle, Lincoln said,

> It may be affirmed without extravagance that the free institutions we enjoy have developed the powers and improved the conditions of our whole people beyond any example in the world. . . . Most governments have been based, practically, on the denial of the equal rights of men. . . . Ours began by affirming these rights. We proposed to give all a chance; and we expected the weak to grow stronger, the ignorant wiser, and all better and happier together. We made the experiment, and the fruit is before us. . . . It was the Union that made our foreign and our domestic commerce. . . The effort for disunion produced the existing difficulty.

To Lincoln, individual liberty was the goal of the American Revolution as expressed in the Declaration of Independence. The Constitution established and exalted the free institutions through which individual liberty was to be attained. The government that executed and administered the terms of the Constitution

Lincoln's home in Springfield draped after the assassination. *(Library of Congress)*

was therefore essentially and indivisibly linked to the liberty of each citizen no matter where he might live. The individual citizen was supreme. He was the sovereign.

In reply to Douglas in Chicago, in 1858, Lincoln had made it clear that the sovereignty of the individual citizen was the very lifeblood of the Union. He said:

> Perhaps half our people are not descendents at all of these men [of the Revolution]; they are men who have come from Europe,—German, Irish, French and Scandinavian,—men that have come from Europe themselves, or whose ancestors have come hither and settled here, finding themselves our equals in all things.
>
> If they look back through this history, to trace their connection with those days by blood, they find they have none . . . but when they look through that old Declaration of Independence, they find that those old men say that "we hold these truths to be self-evident, that all men are created equal," and then they feel that that moral sentiment taught in that day evidences their relation to those men, that it is the father of all moral principle in them, and that they have a right to claim it as though they were blood of the blood, and flesh of the flesh, of the men who wrote that Declaration; and so they are. That is the electric cord in that Declaration that links the hearts of patriotic and liberty-loving men together; that will link these patriotic hearts as long as the love of freedom exists in the minds of men throughout the world.

Protection of individual liberty was the great constitutional principle at stake in the Civil War, and on that Lincoln remained inflexible.

Lincoln closed his letter of August 26, 1863, to his Springfield friend James C. Conkling with this eloquent reference to the same great principle:

> Thanks to all. For the great republic—for the principle it lives by, and keeps alive—for man's vast future, thanks to all. Peace does not appear so distant as it did. I hope it will come soon, and come to stay; and so come as to be worth the keeping in all future time.

Lincoln's understanding of this inflexible principle, and his commitment to it, were nurtured and refined in his congressional years. More than any other single influence, the Congress had provided him with both his introduction to national politics and the policies that would guide his conduct of the Presidency. For fifteen years, beginning with his first unsuccessful campaign for nomination to a House seat in 1843 and ending with his senatorial campaign of 1858, the Congress of the United States had dominated Lincoln's political life. Either as a candidate himself, or campaigning for another candidate, the marble pillars and great dome were the focus of his activities.

He spent only two years in Congress, yet they were formative years. He gained self-confidence. He worked daily with the prominent leaders of the nation. He watched them in action close up, noting their responses to varied pressures and circumstances. He engaged them in discussion and debate—pitted his own talents against theirs—and found that he could hold his own with the top politicians in Washington.

It was in Congress that Lincoln refined his skill in conciliation and compromise. He learned to temper his idealism with pragmatism, to reject unrealistic objectives and settle for steps that were within reach. The time and events that so profoundly shaped Lincoln, the issues with which he grappled for so long, seem far removed from the exigencies we face today. But the seeming difference is no more than superficial trapping. The fundamental issue that Lincoln perceived lay in the hideous hypocrisy that permitted a nation founded upon devotion to human freedom to perpetuate the most degrading deprivation of liberty ever devised—slavery.

It was Lincoln's recognition and fight for the fundamental principles embodied in the Declaration of Independence that have inspired succeeding generations, Congresses and Presidents to wage the battle to extend human rights instead of wavering in the face of popular opinion. To be sure, they have all fallen short of what hindsight alone tells us would have been the fulfillment of the ideals upon which our country was founded. Just as Lincoln himself is now found lacking, so will generations yet to be born find us lacking.

In my office on Capitol Hill I keep a reminder of the ugly past: an original bill of sale for five blacks. A Joseph Jeny of Louisiana bought the five for $380 on Christmas Eve, 1806. They were resold according to an endorsement on the back of the bill "for value received" to John McDanagh and Shepherd Brown on February 10, 1807—just two years and two days before the birth of the man who would later free all slaves in the states in rebellion.

That bill of sale stands as an eloquent symbol of how far we have come since Lincoln was refined and tested in the crucible of Congress—and a call to vigilance lest the liberty we enjoy be threatened anew. To Lincoln vigilance was more important than battlements and armies. He said, "Our defense is in the preservation of the spirit which prizes liberty as the heritage of all men, in all lands, everywhere. Destroy this spirit and you have planted the seeds of despotism around your own doors."

The yellowing bill of sale with its ink still vivid is a troubling relic of Lincoln's America. When the bill of sale was issued the brutal, inhuman traffic in slaves from Africa was still protected and guaranteed by our most basic shield of individual liberty, the Constitution of the United States. And the bill of sale may be a relic of Lincoln's own personal experience. Perhaps among the five were slaves Lincoln saw when his flatboat took him to New Orleans. They or their relatives may have been in a coffle marched in chains in front of the Capitol during the 30th Congress. Could Lincoln have seen one of them peeking over the fence around a slave pen on the mall? Could one have been the hapless waiter at Mrs. Sprigg's who was seized and hauled off while Lincoln and his messmates watched?

Their faces may have inspired Lincoln to write:

As I would not be a slave, so I would not be a master. . . . In giving freedom to the slave we assure freedom to the free, honorable alike in what we give and what we preserve.

"An eloquent symbol of how far we have come since Lincoln was refined and tested in the crucible of Congress." (Author's collection)

Bibliographic Essay

In preparing this book I relied on a wide variety of both primary and secondary sources. This bibliography includes only those volumes and primary sources that were essential. For example, there are hundreds of biographies of Lincoln, ranging from thin single volumes to a ten-volume treatment. Although I am familiar with many of these, William H. Herndon and Jess W. Weik's *Life of Lincoln* (New York: A. & C. Boni, 1936) and Albert J. Beveridge's *Abraham Lincoln* (Boston and New York: Houghton Mifflin, 1928) served pivotal purposes. A number of other biographies were consulted, but only to determine the extent to which other writers had adopted Herndon's and Beveridge's view of Lincoln's congressional career. Thus, this essay is limited in scope and intended to provide sources that interested readers will find worth consulting.

Chapter 1

Lincoln's early career is recounted in virtually every biography written. His years in New Salem are ably described in Benjamin P. Thomas's book, *Lincoln's New Salem* (Springfield, Illinois: Abraham Lincoln Association, 1934). His early political activities in the Illinois legislature are described in meticulous fashion in my colleague Paul Simon's excellent work, *Lincoln's Preparation for Greatness* (Norman: University of Oklahoma Press, 1965). Emmanuel Hertz's *The Hidden Lincoln* (New York: Blue Ribbon Books, 1940) provides recollections of Lincoln during these years from former fellow villagers of New Salem.

Chapter 2

By far the best account of Lincoln's determination to run for Congress and the campaign he conducted is Donald Riddle's *Lincoln Runs for Congress* (New Brunswick, New Jersey: Rutgers University Press, 1948). Supplementing Riddle are the John Hardin Papers in the Chicago Historical Society and newspaper coverage by the Illinois *State Journal* and the *Register* (respectively Whig and Democratic newspapers published in Springfield) and the *Illinois Gazette* (a Whig newspaper published in Lacon, Illinois).

Chapter 3

Within the last decade the shelf of literature on the antislavery movement has burgeoned tremendously. The most useful recent volumes are Richard H. Sewall's *Ballots for Freedom* (New York: Oxford University Press, 1976) and James B. Stewart's *Holy Warriors* (New York: Hill and Wang, 1976). Eric Foner's *Free Soil, Free Speech and Free Men* (New York: Oxford University Press, 1970) provides an engrossing account of the formation and development of the Republican party.

Chapter 4

Lincoln's activities during the interregnum between election and service in Congress are faithfully described in several biographies, notably Albert Beveridge's. William H. Townsend's *Lincoln in His Wife's Hometown* (Indianapolis: Bobbs-Merrill Company, 1929) provides an intimate glimpse of Lincoln's xington, Kentucky, just before he left for Washington. Particularly ˈe the chapters dealing with slavery, and an explicit description of ᴐn as Lincoln saw it there.

Chapters 5 and 6

ˈr of histories of Washington have been written, but most deal largely with its emergence as the federal capital. A recent exception is David L. Lewis's *District of Columbia: A Bicentennial History* (New York: W. W. Norton & Co., 1976). In my attempt to re-create the city as Lincoln knew it in 1847–1849, William Q. Force's *Guide to Washington* (Washington: W. Q. Force, 1845) was invaluable, and the letters of Maria Horsford from 1850 to 1852 provided intimate glimpses into the life of a Congressman in that era as well as the travails suffered by a Congressman's wife. The Horsford letters remain within the family, and I am deeply indebted to Mrs. Robert Ames Norton for providing transcripts of her great-grandmother's letters for my use.

Chapter 7

The *Congressional Globe and the House Journal* provide a generous glimpse of the issues that Lincoln and his colleagues faced during the 30th Congress. The New York *Tribune* provided one editor's estimate of the "promising" men of the Whig party in that Congress. Biographical information was culled from several sources, including the *Biographical Directory of the American Congress* (Washington: Government Printing Office, 1970) and biographies of several of the men discussed.

Chapter 8

Lincoln and the slavery issue has been discussed at length. Benjamin Quarles's *Lincoln and the Negro* (New York: Oxford University Press, 1962), George M. Sinkler's *Racial Attitudes of American Presidents* (Garden City, N.Y.: Doubleday & Co., Inc., 1971), and most biographies go into great detail. Lincoln's congressional period is given short shrift, however. The vitriolic and vituperative *Pearl* incident is rarely connected with Lincoln, but it must have had a profound impact on his thinking. Data on the *Pearl* derives from the Drayton, Sayres, and English papers in the Manuscript Division of the Library of Congress, the Horace Mann papers in the Massachusetts Historical Society, and the Joshua R. Giddings's papers at the Ohio Historical Society. In addition, Giddings's papers provided a useful glimpse of Lincoln's antislavery bill and a vehement abolitionist's practical political view of it. Information on slavery and the slave trade in the District of Columbia used in this and other chapters comes variously from Constance Green's *The Secret City* (Princeton, New Jersey: Princeton University Press, 1969), Walter C. Celephane's paper read to the Columbia Historical Society, March 6, 1899, *Records of the Columbia Historical Society*, Vol. 9, 1906 (Washington, D.C.) and William T. Laprade's essay on "The Domestic Slave Trade in the District of Columbia" in the *Journal of Negro History* Vol. II, January 1926 (Washington, D.C.).

Chapter 9

The Mexican War is scantily covered by historians. The opposition to it, on the other hand, has received more attention. Frederick Merk provides a succinct account in his essay in *Dissent in Three American Wars* (Cambridge, Massachusetts: Harvard University Press, 1970). An essay dealing solely with Lincoln, his dissent, and its repercussions in Illinois appeared in the *Journal of the Illinois State Historical Society*, Vol. 67, pp. 79–100, 1974 (Springfield, Illinois) by Gabor S. Boritt. Indeed, it was this outstanding piece of scholarship that led me to turn my deep interest in Lincoln's congressional career into a book.

Chapter 10

The Abraham Lincoln papers in the Library of Congress are the most useful source for reading the letters sent to Lincoln by constituents. His responses have been incorporated into Roy P. Basler's (ed.) *Collected Works of Abraham Lincoln*, eight volumes (New Brunswick, New Jersey: Rutgers University Press, 1953–1955 and a 1976 supplement). Information concerning Hezekiah Garber rests in the West Point files of the National Archives. The mileage scandal is reported in the New York *Tribune*, and congressional response can be seen in the *Congressional Globe* and the report of the Committee charged with investigating the mileage abuses.

Chapter 11

Lincoln's role in the 1848 campaign is best recorded in contemporaneous newspapers and in the letters in *The Collected Works of Abraham Lincoln*. Herbert Mitgang's *Abraham Lincoln: A Press Portrait* (Chicago: Quadrangle Books, 1971) reproduces several newspaper stories concerning Lincoln's speeches in the campaign.

Chapter 12

Once again the *Collected Works of Abraham Lincoln* contain many of the letters Lincoln wrote to secure the patronage post he was seeking. Additional letters were uncovered by a manuscript dealer just as this book was going to press, and have by now hopefully found their way into a public repository.

Chapter 13

Lincoln's activities during the period 1848 and 1860 are covered in most biographies. However, they accept without reservation Lincoln's statement that he virtually abandoned politics between 1849 and 1854, a view supported by Herndon and Beveridge. His political ambitions in 1850 are best described in the letters between Thomas L. Harris and Charles Lanphier. They remain in private hands, but a limited reproduction edition has been published under the title *Glory to God and the Sucker Democracy* (Springfield, Illinois: privately printed by Frye-Williamson Press, 1973). This sadly neglected compilation provides an unparalled view of Lincoln's standing in the 1850s and an opponent's surmise of his strength.

Chapter 14

Don H. Fehrenbacher's *Prelude to Greatness* (Stanford, California: Stanford University Press, 1962) fills in a detailed view of Lincoln's prepresidential political activities, and his campaigns for the Senate in 1854 and 1858. Lincoln's letter to Elihu Washburne is in the *Collected Works of Abraham Lincoln*.

Chapter 15

The reams of literature available on Lincoln and the Civil War make it difficult to select just a few that added to this chapter. James G. Randall and David Donald's biography of Lincoln have a focus that served me well. So too did David Potter and Don Fehrenbacher's *The Impending Crisis* (New York: Harper & Row, 1976) for the preinaugural activities. Kenneth P. Williams's *Lincoln Finds a General* (New York: The Macmillan Company, 1959) was also useful, as was J. G. Randall's *Lincoln, the President* (New York: Dodd, Mead & Company, 1945). The material on the importance of federalism, the distinction between individual liberty and state sovereignty, and the role these competing ideas have played in our nation's history is inspired by the writings of Clarence K. Streit, one of the most innovative and forward-looking political thinkers of this century.

General

No bibliography can cover all. Yet there are works that are always useful. Chief among them is Roy P. Basler's *The Collected Works of Abraham Lincoln*. The Lincoln Sesquicentennial Commission produced an admirable three-volume set, *Lincoln Day by Day* (Washington: Government Printing Office, 1971), that sketchily records all of Lincoln's proven activities.

Index

Page numbers in italics refer to illustrations.